MARK WAID • HORACIO DOMINGUES

INCORRUPTIBLE

VOLUME 2

ROSS RICHIE Chief Executive Officer • MATT GAGNON Editor-in-Chief • WES HARRIS VP-Publishing • LANCE KREITER VP-Licensing & Merchandising • PHIL BARBARO Director of Finance
BRYCE CARLSON Managing Editor • DAFNA PLEBAN Editor • SHANNON WATTERS Editor • ERIC HARBURN Assistant Editor • ADAM STAFFARONI Assistant Editor • CHRIS ROSA Assistant Editor
STEPHANIE GONZAGA Graphic Designer • EMILY MCGUINESS Marketing Coordinator • DEVIN FUNCHES Marketing & Sales Assistant • JASMINE AMIRI Operations Assistant

INCORRUPTIBLE Volume 2 — March 2012. Published by BOOM! Studios, a division of Boom Entertainment, Inc. Incorruptible is Copyright © 2012
Boom Entertainment, Inc. Originally published in single magazine form as INCORRUPTIBLE 5-8. Copyright © 2010 Boom Entertainment, Inc. All rights
reserved. BOOM! Studios™ and the BOOM! Studios logo are trademarks of Boom Entertainment, Inc., registered in various countries and categories.
All characters, events, and institutions depicted herein are fictional. Any similarity between any of the names, characters, persons, events, and/or
institutions in this publication to actual names, characters, and persons, whether living or dead, events, and/or institutions is unintended and purely
coincidental. BOOM! Studios does not read or accept unsolicited submissions of ideas, stories, or artwork.

A catalog record of this book is available from OCLC and from the BOOM! Studios website, www.boom-studios.com, on the Librarians Page.
BOOM! Studios, 6310 San Vicente Boulevard, Suite 107, Los Angeles, CA 90048-5457. Printed in Canada. Second Printing. ISBN: 978-1-60886-028-9

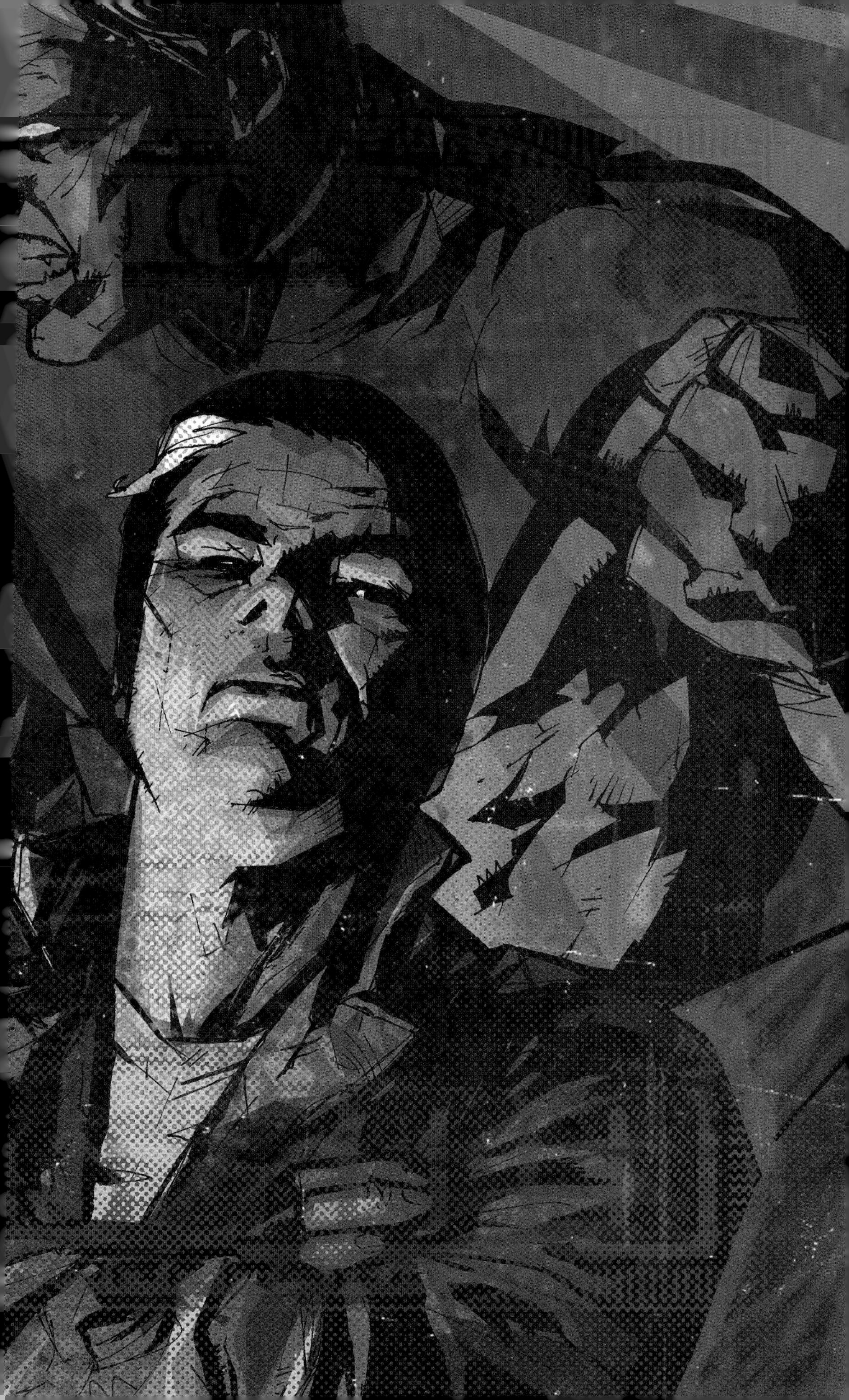

CREATED AND WRITTEN BY
MARK WAID

ARTIST:
HORACIO
DOMINGUES

INKS: JUAN CASTRO
COLORIST: ANDREW DALHOUSE
LETTERER: ED DUKESHIRE

EDITOR: MATT GAGNON
ASST. EDITOR: SHANNON WATTERS

COVER: DENNIS CALERO

DESIGN: BRIAN LATIMER

INCORR

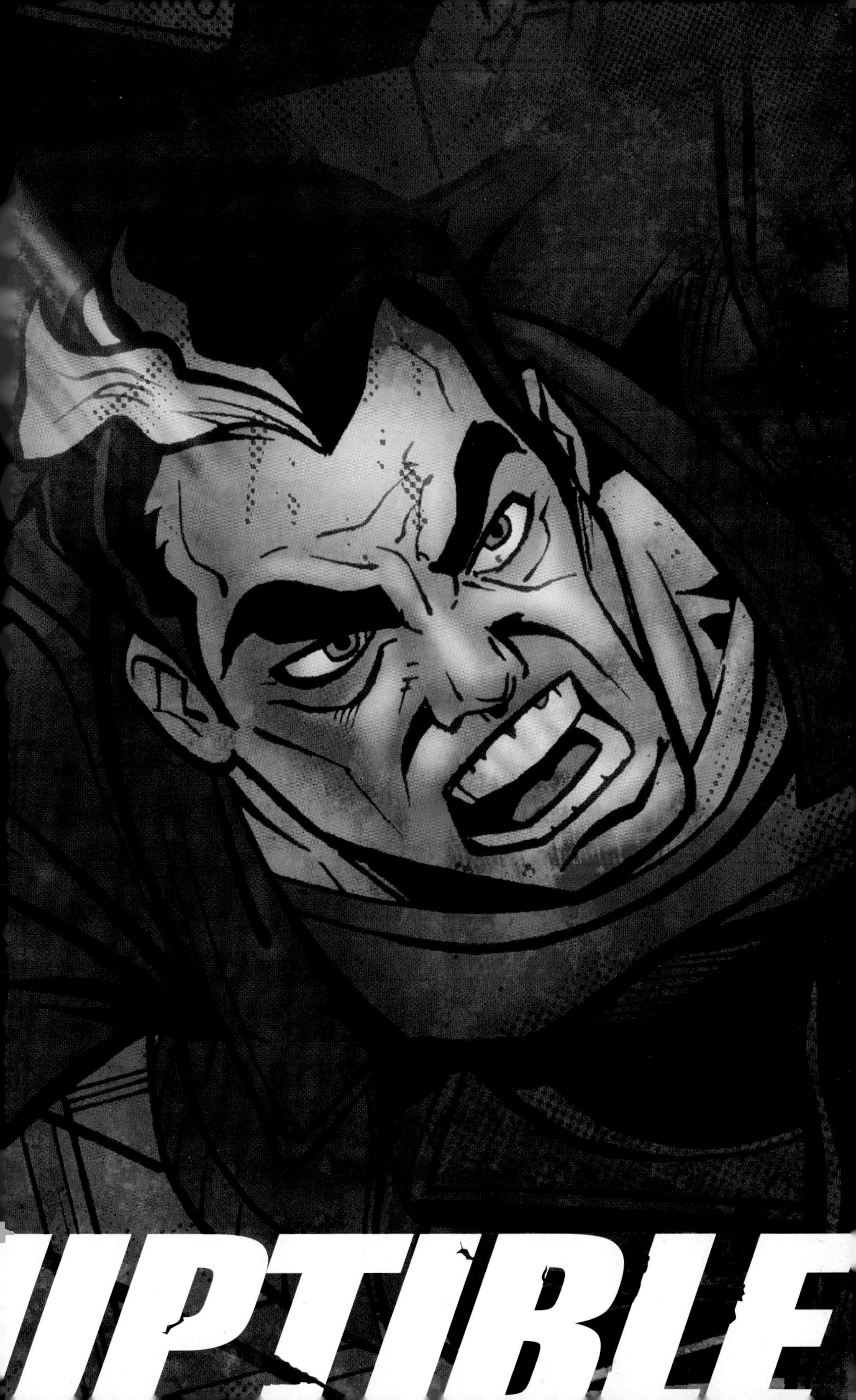
IPTIBLE

CHAPTER 5

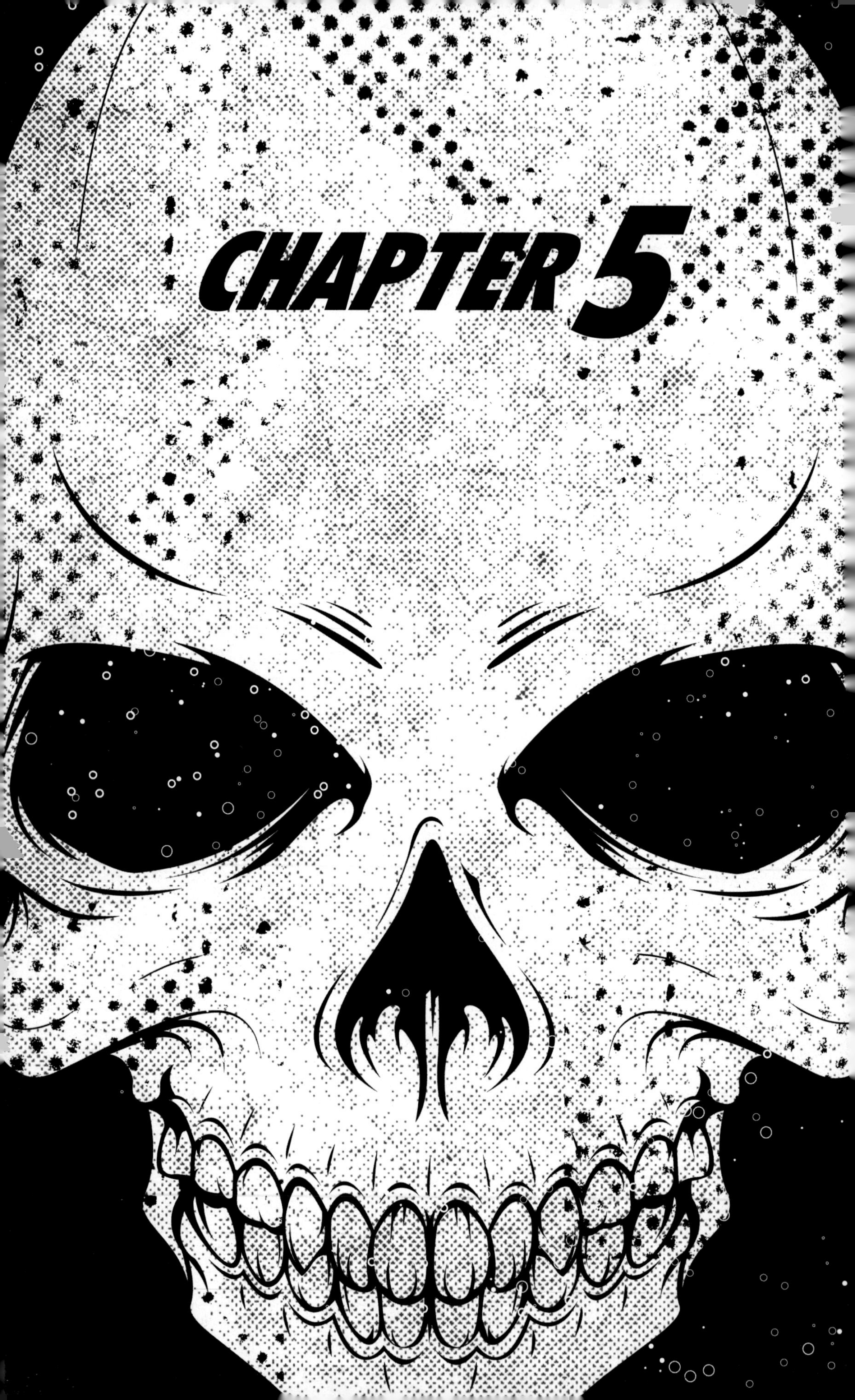

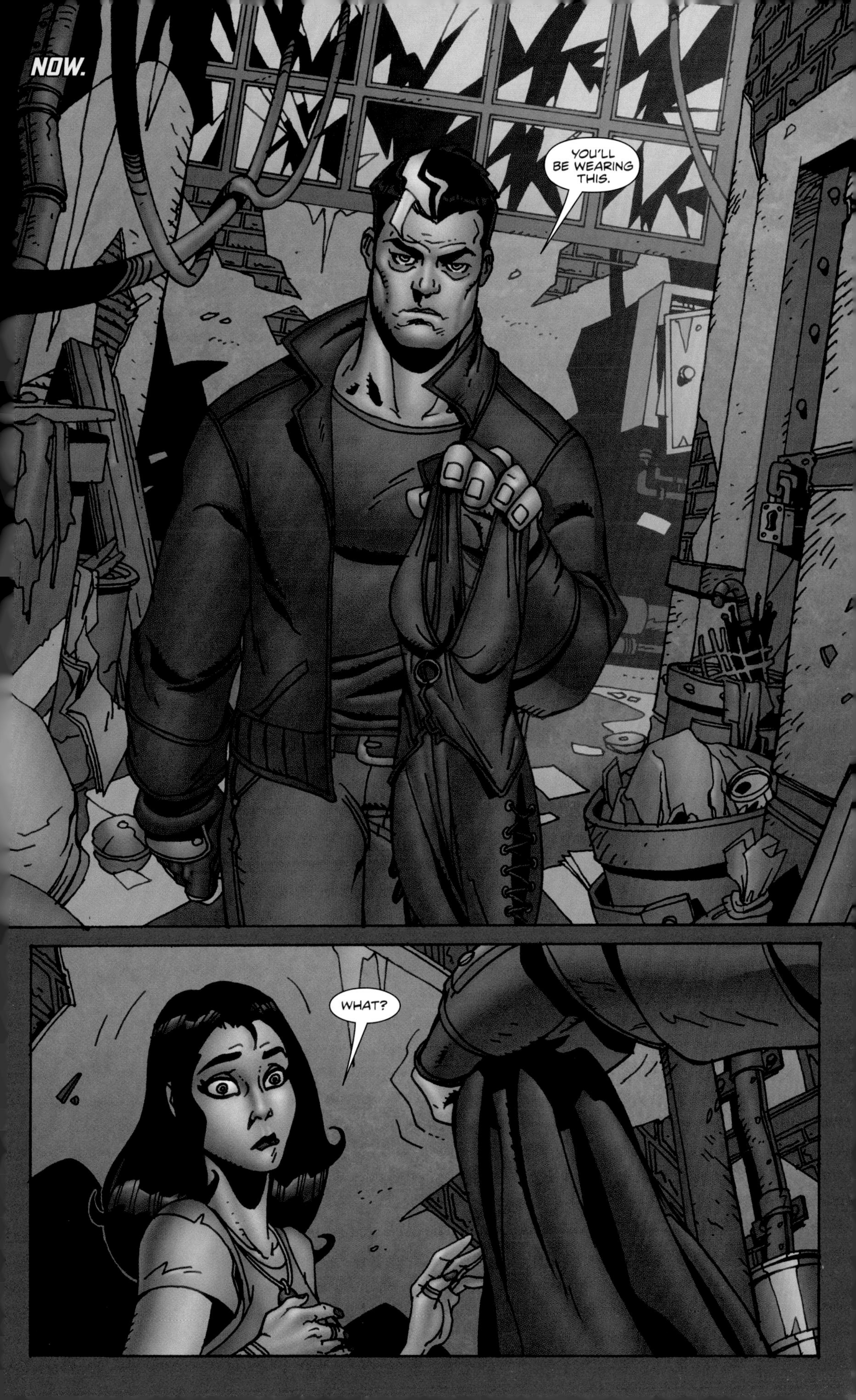
NOW.
YOU'LL BE WEARING THIS.
WHAT?

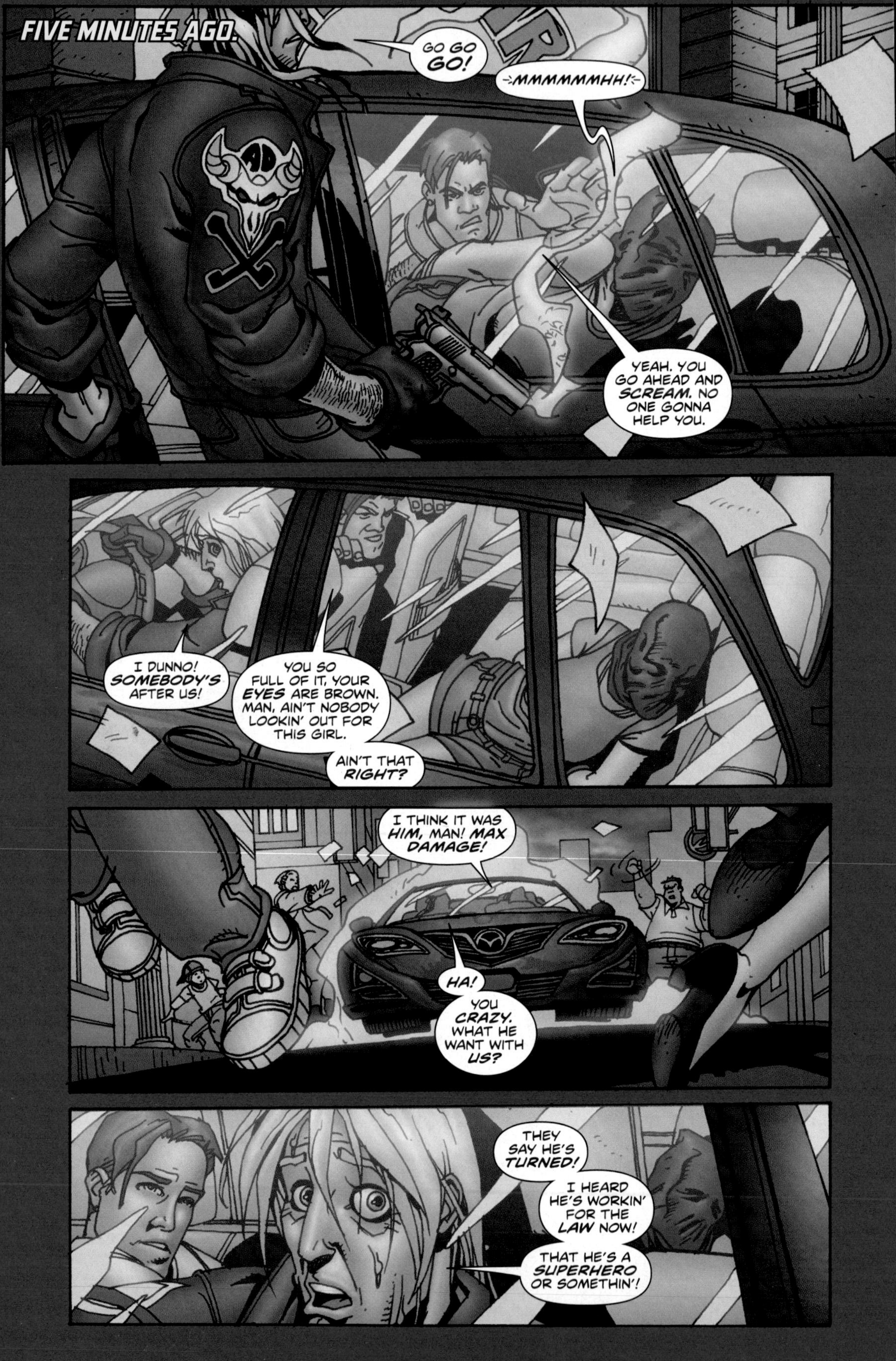
FIVE MINUTES AGO.
GO GO GO!
-MMMMMMHH!-
YEAH. YOU GO AHEAD AND SCREAM. NO ONE GONNA HELP YOU.
I DUNNO! SOMEBODY'S AFTER US!
YOU SO FULL OF IT, YOUR EYES ARE BROWN. MAN, AIN'T NOBODY LOOKIN' OUT FOR THIS GIRL.
AIN'T THAT RIGHT?
I THINK IT WAS HIM, MAN! MAX DAMAGE!
HA! YOU CRAZY. WHAT HE WANT WITH US?
THEY SAY HE'S TURNED!
I HEARD HE'S WORKIN' FOR THE LAW NOW!
THAT HE'S A SUPERHERO OR SOMETHIN'!

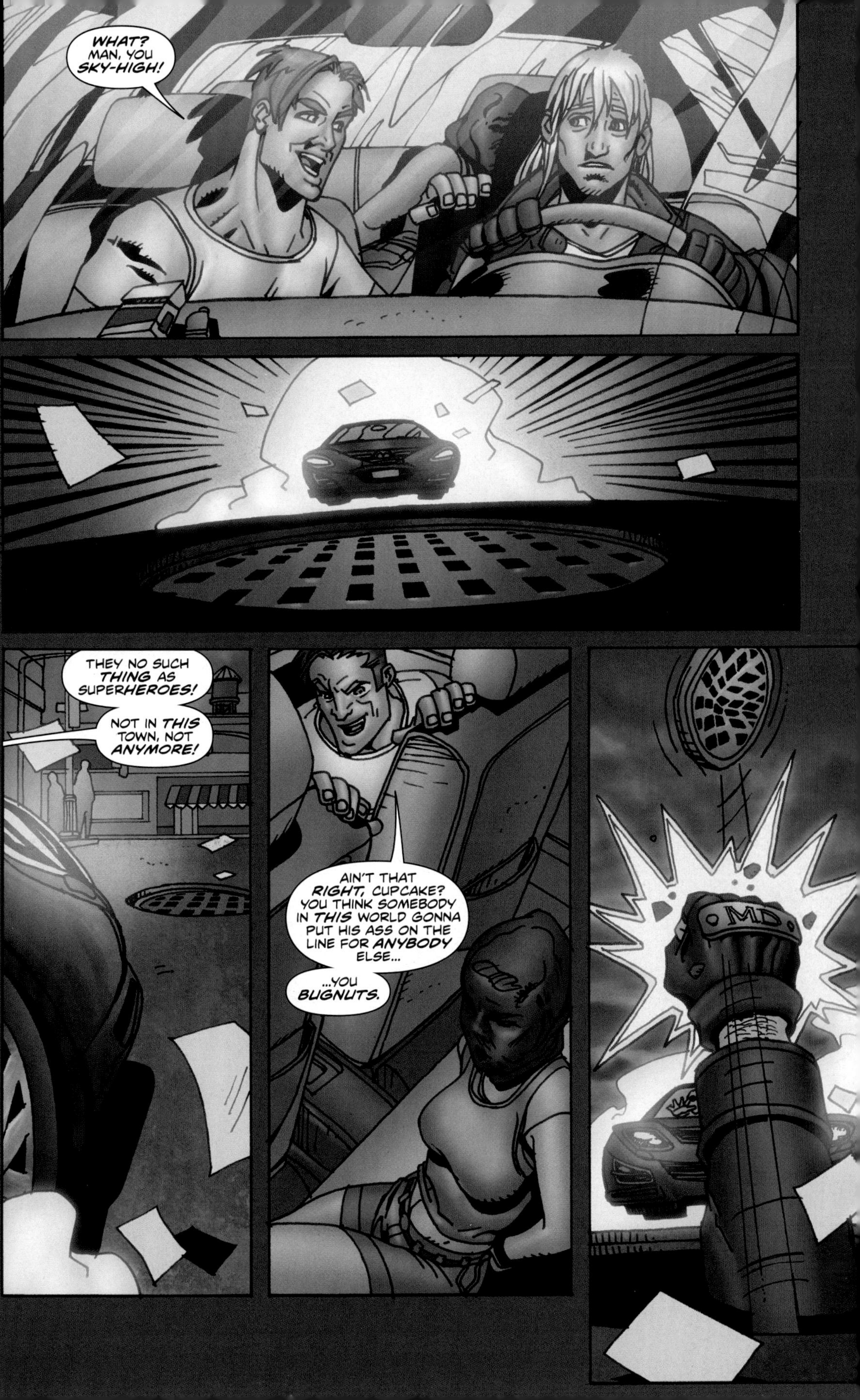
WHAT? MAN, YOU SKY-HIGH!
THEY NO SUCH THING AS SUPERHEROES!
NOT IN THIS TOWN, NOT ANYMORE!
AIN'T THAT RIGHT, CUPCAKE? YOU THINK SOMEBODY IN THIS WORLD GONNA PUT HIS ASS ON THE LINE FOR ANYBODY ELSE...
...YOU BUGNUTS.
MD

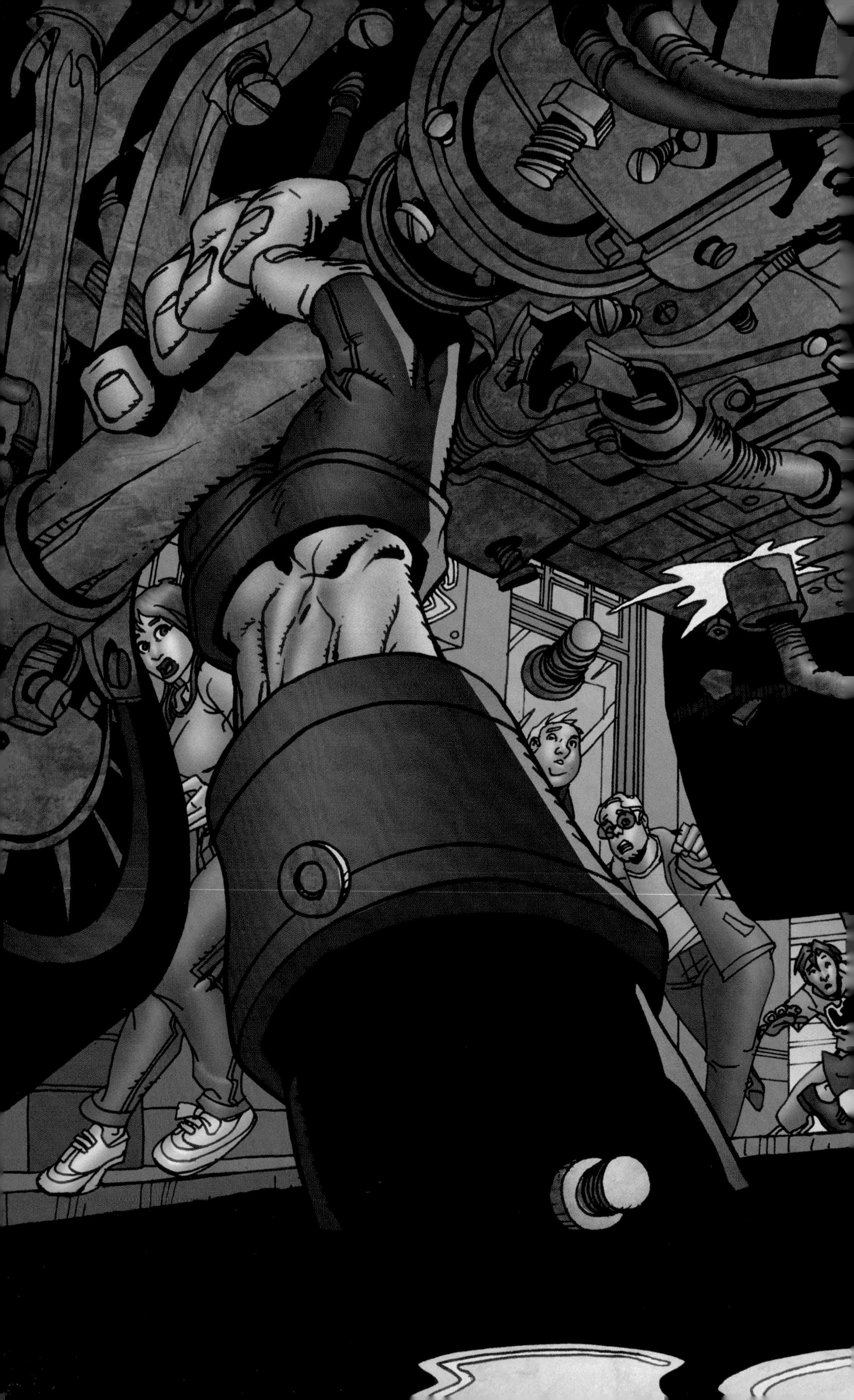

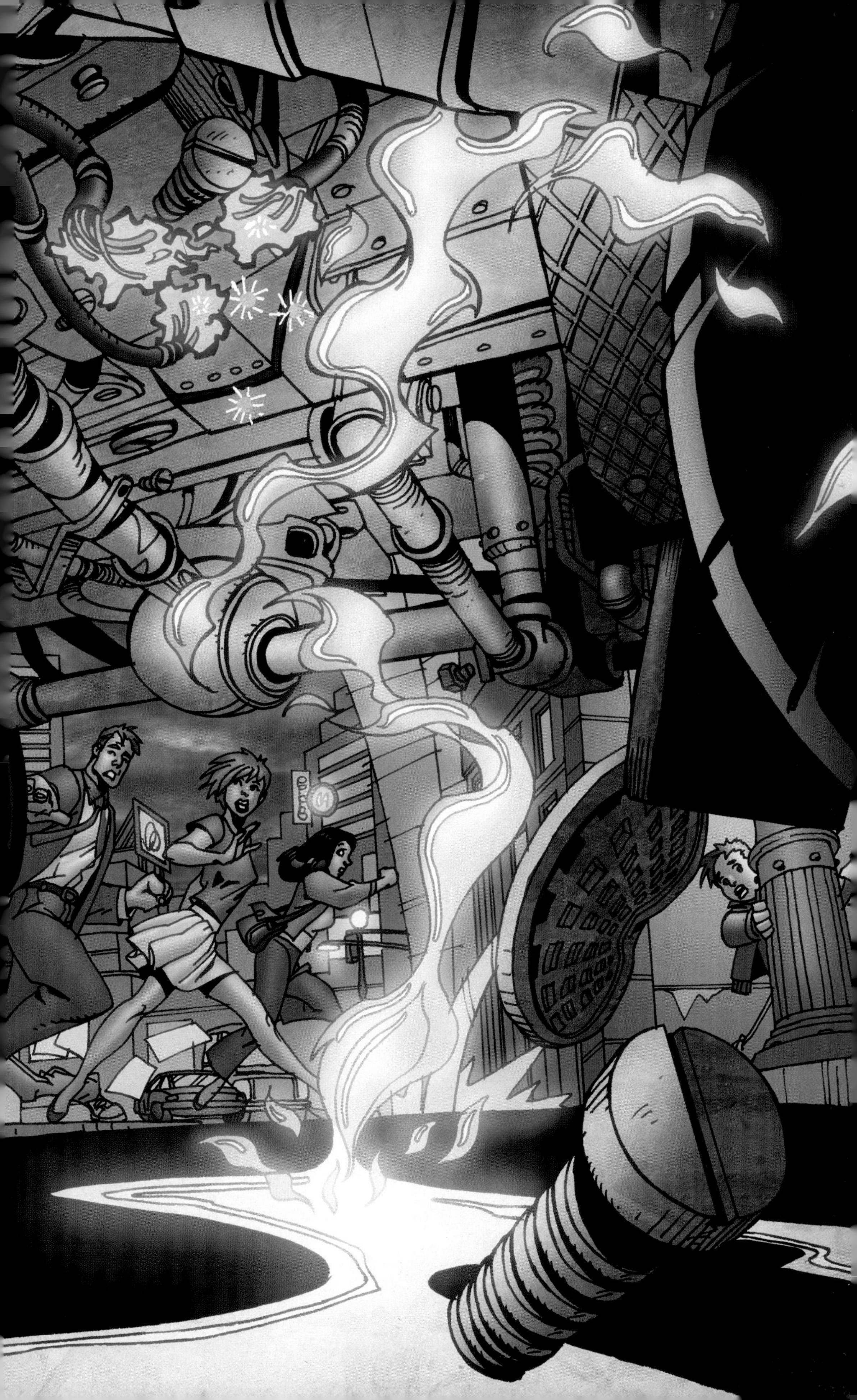

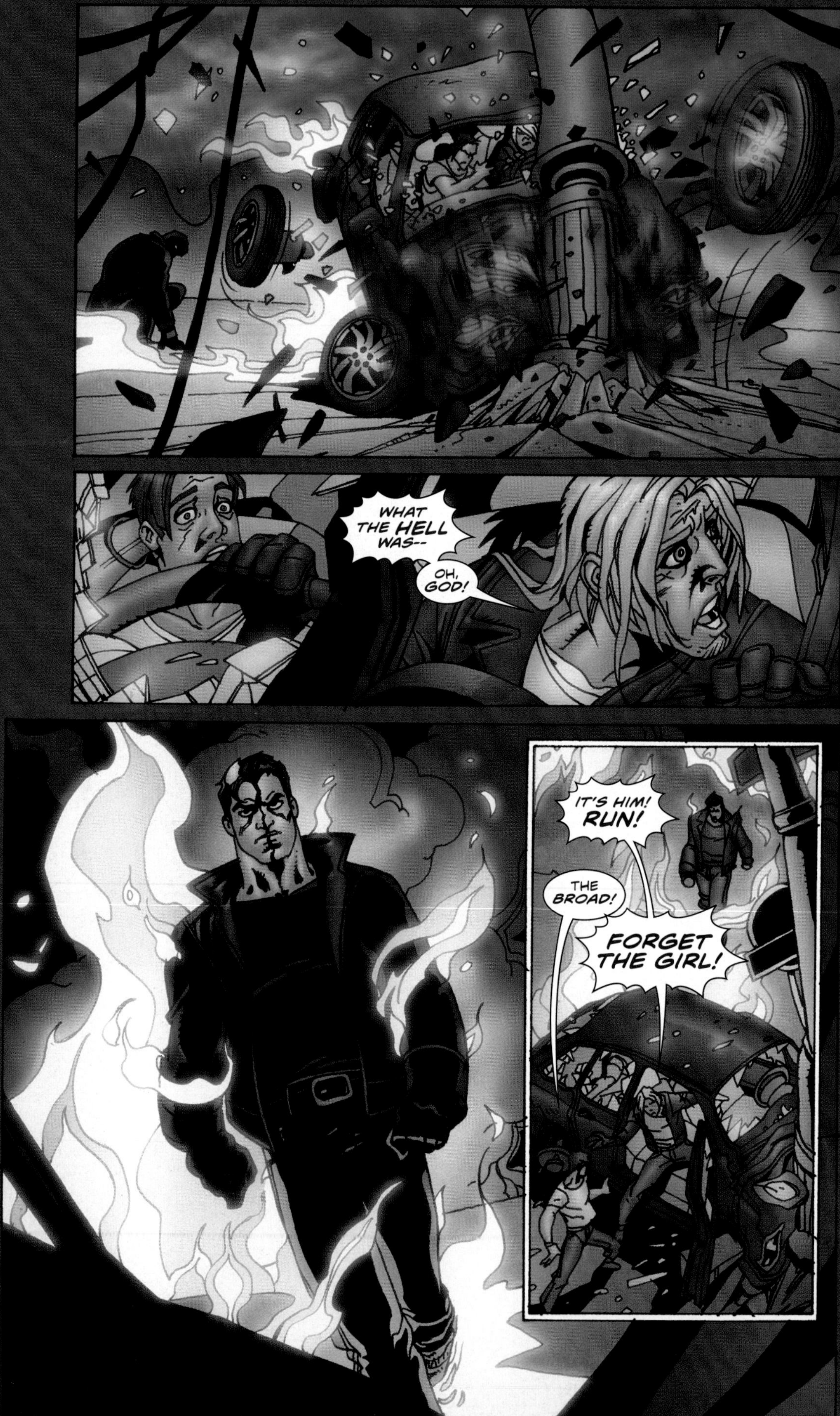
WHAT THE HELL WAS--
OH, GOD!
IT'S HIM! RUN!
THE BROAD!
FORGET THE GIRL!

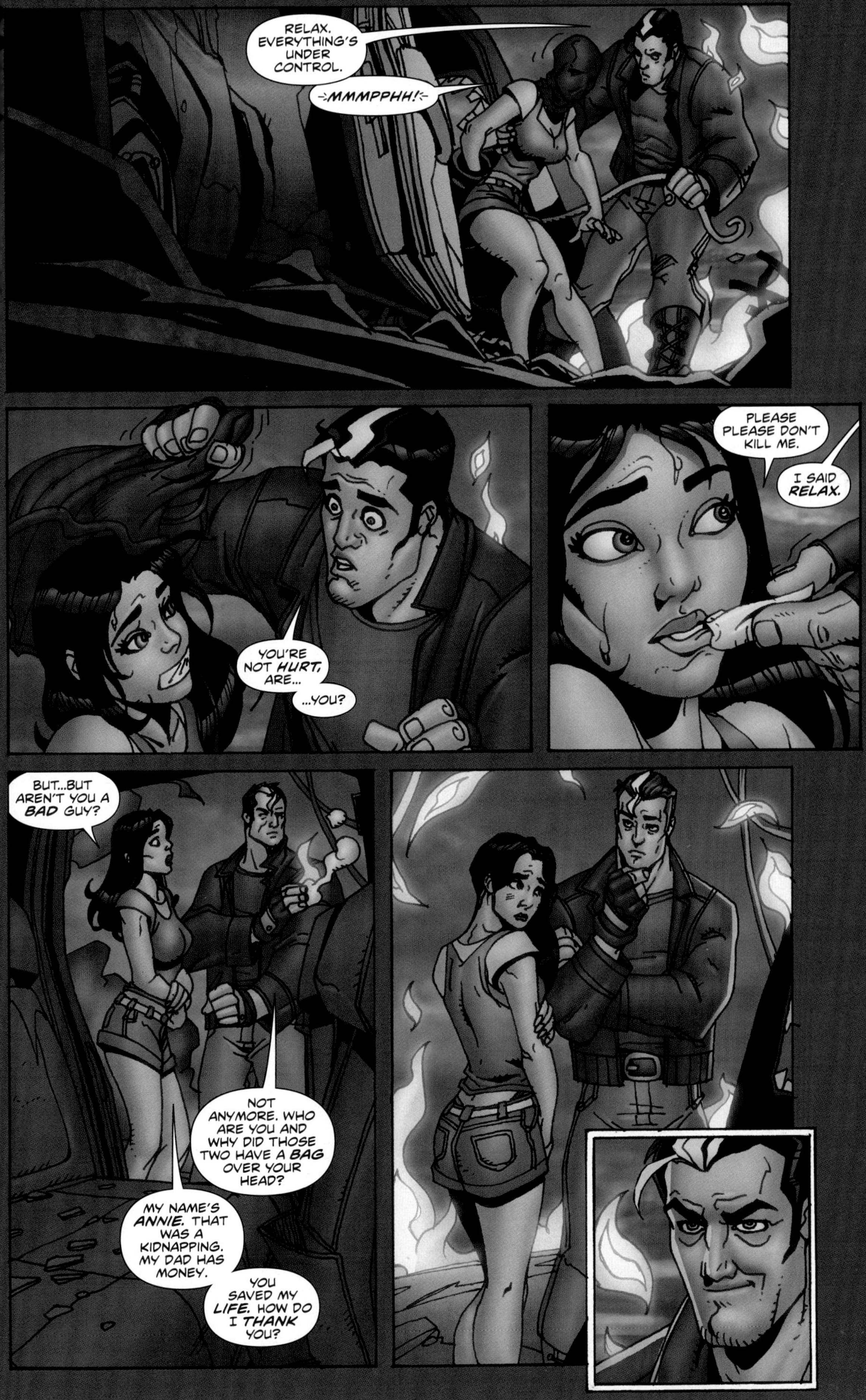

RELAX. EVERYTHING'S UNDER CONTROL.
-MMMPPHH!-
YOU'RE NOT HURT, ARE...
...YOU?
PLEASE PLEASE DON'T KILL ME.
I SAID RELAX.
BUT...BUT AREN'T YOU A BAD GUY?
NOT ANYMORE. WHO ARE YOU AND WHY DID THOSE TWO HAVE A BAG OVER YOUR HEAD?
MY NAME'S ANNIE. THAT WAS A KIDNAPPING. MY DAD HAS MONEY.
YOU SAVED MY LIFE. HOW DO I THANK YOU?

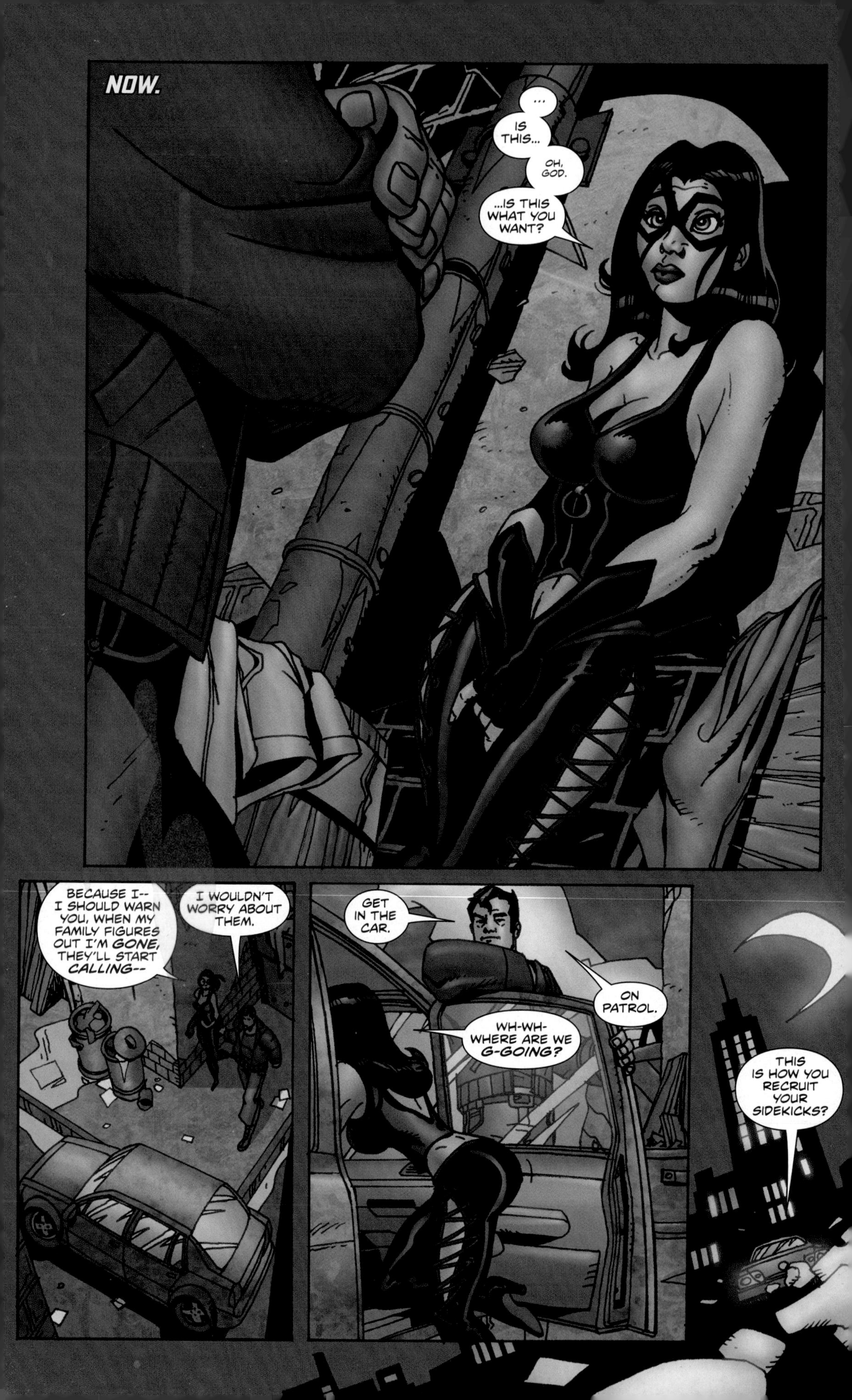
NOW.
...
IS THIS...
OH, GOD.
...IS THIS WHAT YOU WANT?
BECAUSE I-- I SHOULD WARN YOU, WHEN MY FAMILY FIGURES OUT I'M GONE, THEY'LL START CALLING--
I WOULDN'T WORRY ABOUT THEM.
GET IN THE CAR.
WH-WH-WHERE ARE WE G-GOING?
ON PATROL.
THIS IS HOW YOU RECRUIT YOUR SIDEKICKS?

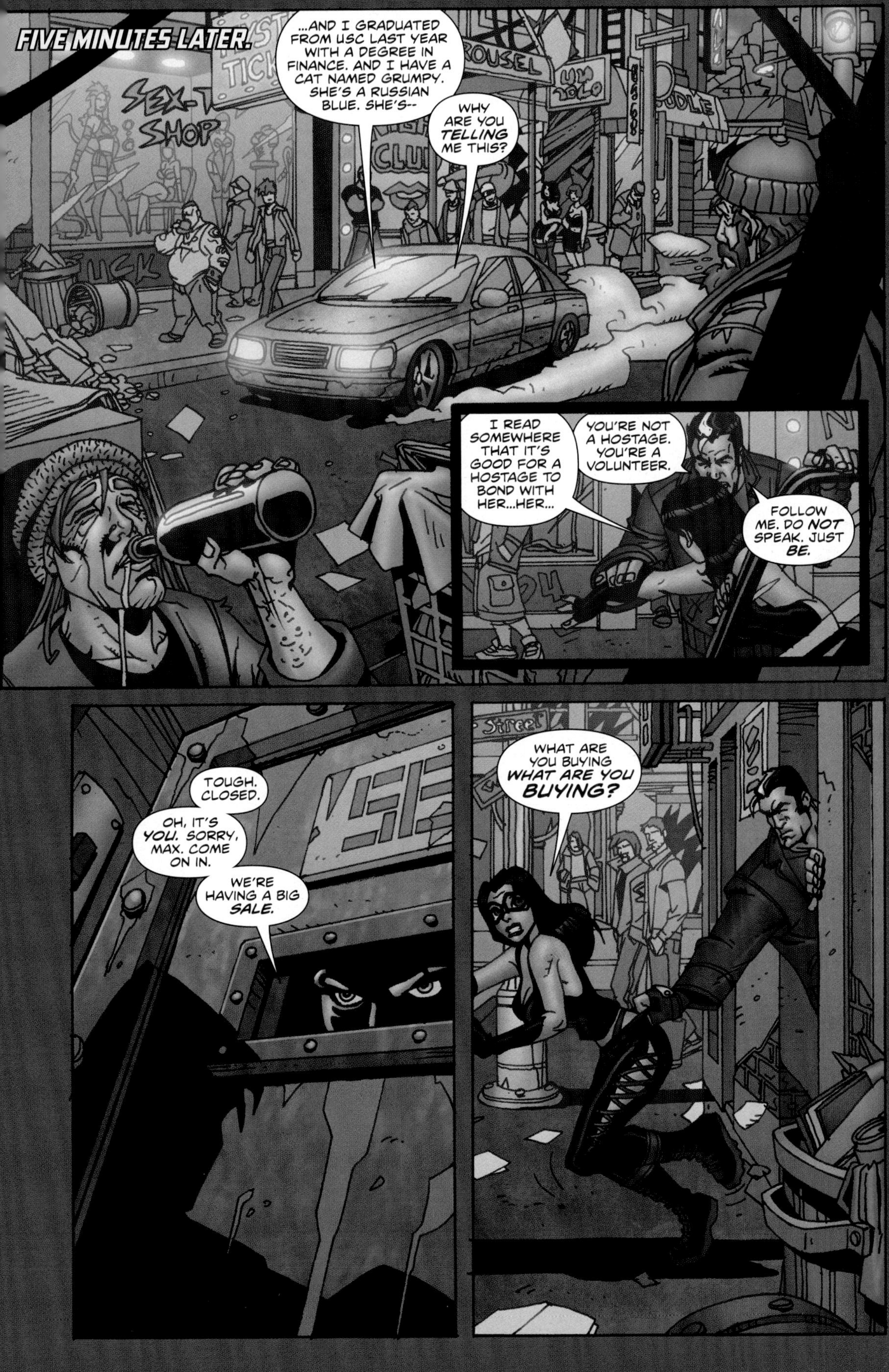
FIVE MINUTES LATER.
...AND I GRADUATED FROM USC LAST YEAR WITH A DEGREE IN FINANCE. AND I HAVE A CAT NAMED GRUMPY. SHE'S A RUSSIAN BLUE. SHE'S--
WHY ARE YOU TELLING ME THIS?
I READ SOMEWHERE THAT IT'S GOOD FOR A HOSTAGE TO BOND WITH HER...HER...
YOU'RE NOT A HOSTAGE. YOU'RE A VOLUNTEER.
FOLLOW ME. DO NOT SPEAK. JUST BE.
TOUGH. CLOSED.
OH, IT'S YOU. SORRY, MAX. COME ON IN.
WE'RE HAVING A BIG SALE.
WHAT ARE YOU BUYING WHAT ARE YOU BUYING?

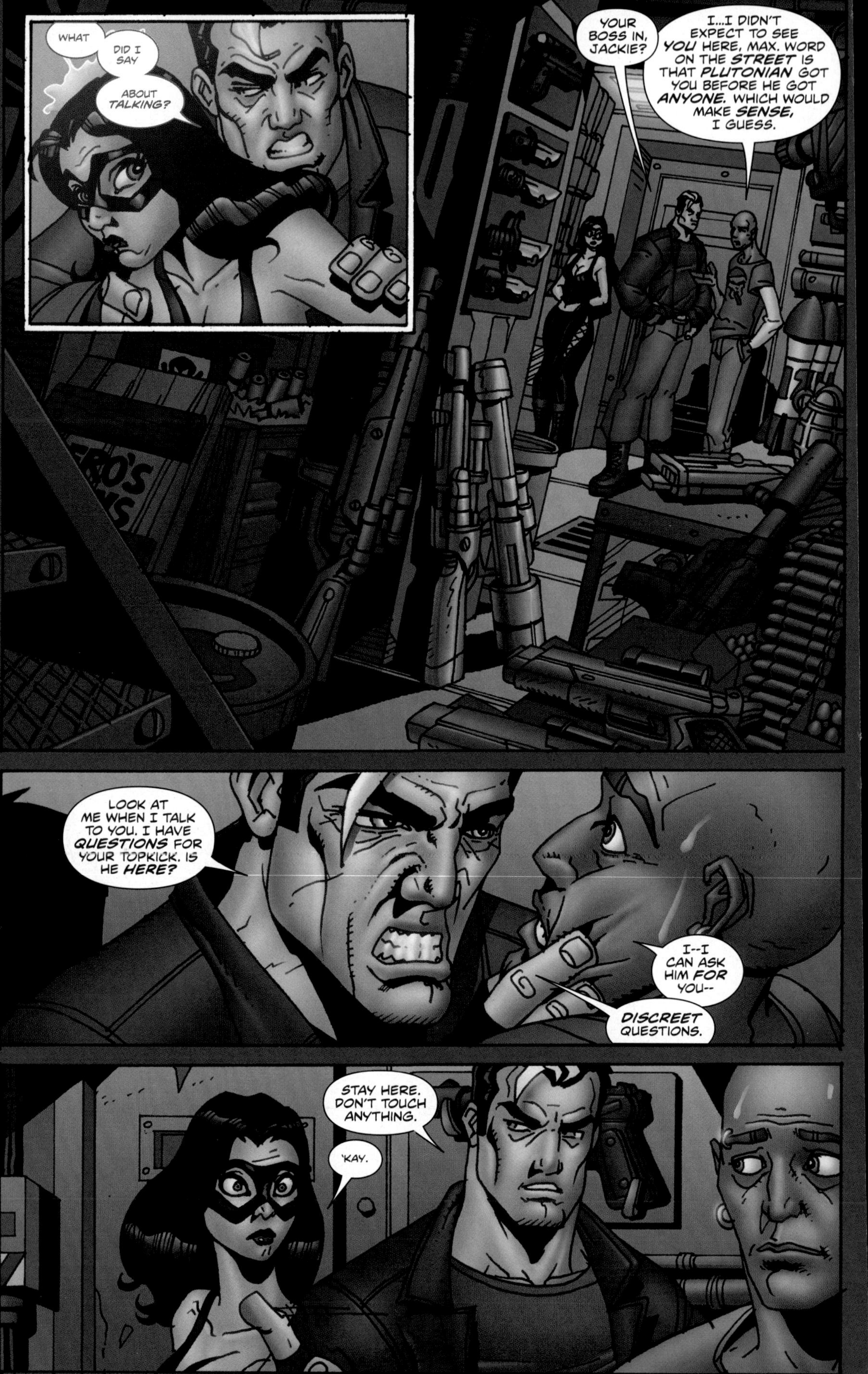
WHAT
DID I SAY
ABOUT TALKING?
YOUR BOSS IN, JACKIE?
I...I DIDN'T EXPECT TO SEE YOU HERE, MAX. WORD ON THE STREET IS THAT PLUTONIAN GOT YOU BEFORE HE GOT ANYONE. WHICH WOULD MAKE SENSE, I GUESS.
LOOK AT ME WHEN I TALK TO YOU. I HAVE QUESTIONS FOR YOUR TOPKICK. IS HE HERE?
I--I CAN ASK HIM FOR YOU--
DISCREET QUESTIONS.
STAY HERE. DON'T TOUCH ANYTHING.
'KAY.

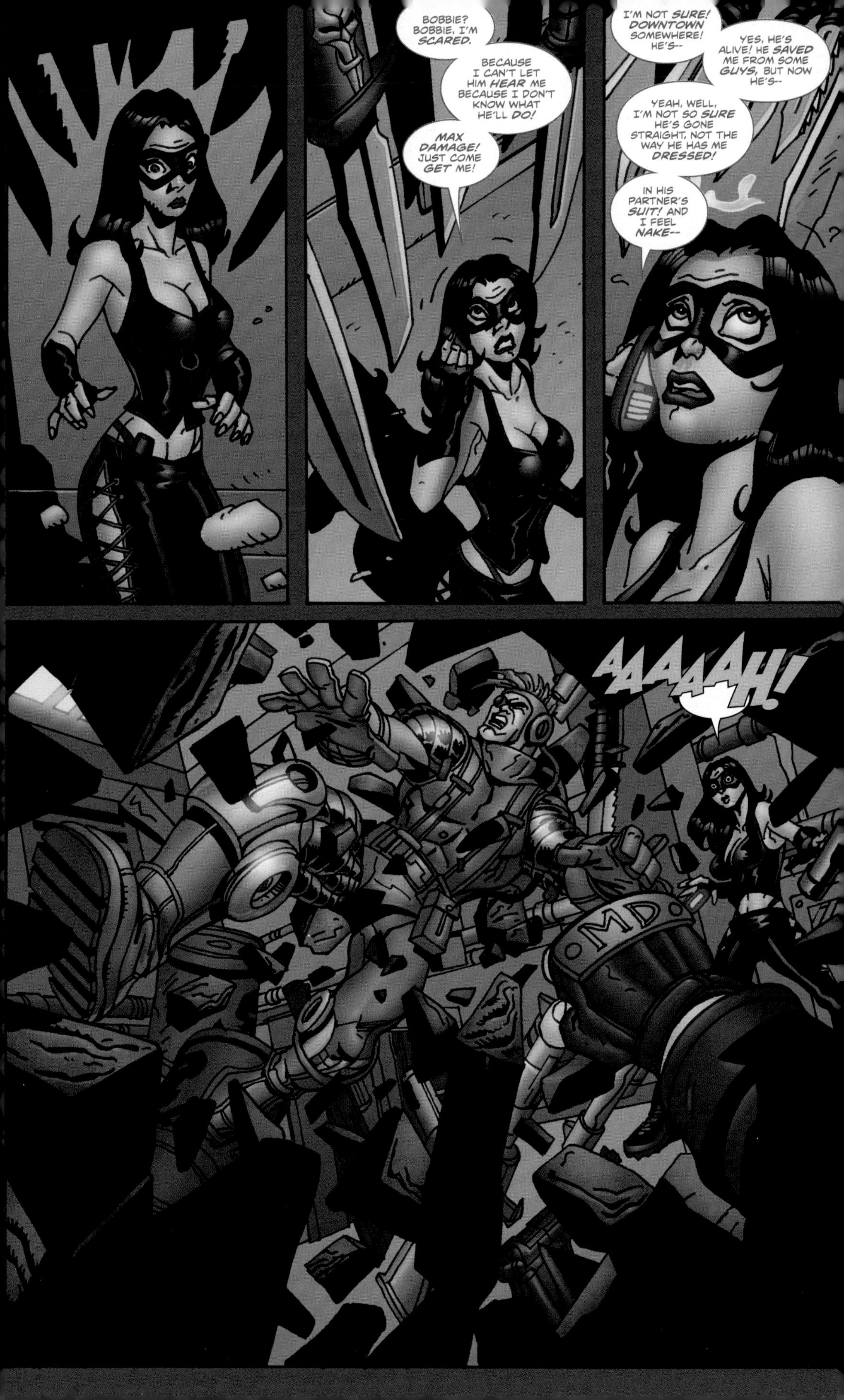
BOBBIE? BOBBIE, I'M SCARED.
BECAUSE I CAN'T LET HIM HEAR ME BECAUSE I DON'T KNOW WHAT HE'LL DO!
MAX DAMAGE! JUST COME GET ME!
I'M NOT SURE! DOWNTOWN SOMEWHERE! HE'S--
YES, HE'S ALIVE! HE SAVED ME FROM SOME GUYS, BUT NOW HE'S--
YEAH, WELL, I'M NOT SO SURE HE'S GONE STRAIGHT, NOT THE WAY HE HAS ME DRESSED!
IN HIS PARTNER'S SUIT! AND I FEEL NAKE--
AAAAAH!
MD

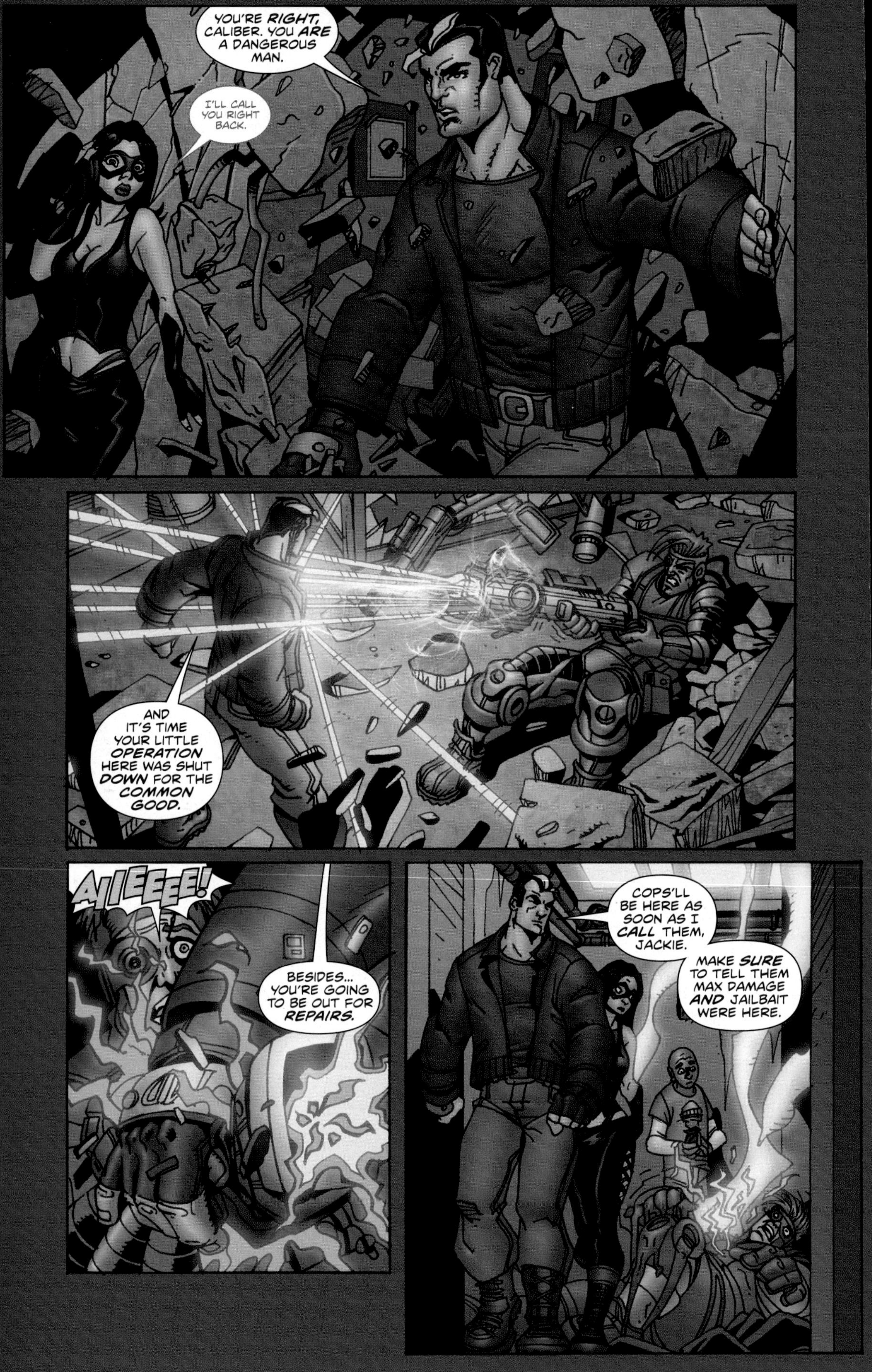
YOU'RE RIGHT, CALIBER. YOU ARE A DANGEROUS MAN.
I'LL CALL YOU RIGHT BACK.
AND IT'S TIME YOUR LITTLE OPERATION HERE WAS SHUT DOWN FOR THE COMMON GOOD.
AIIEEEE!
BESIDES... YOU'RE GOING TO BE OUT FOR REPAIRS.
COPS'LL BE HERE AS SOON AS I CALL THEM, JACKIE.
MAKE SURE TO TELL THEM MAX DAMAGE AND JAILBAIT WERE HERE.

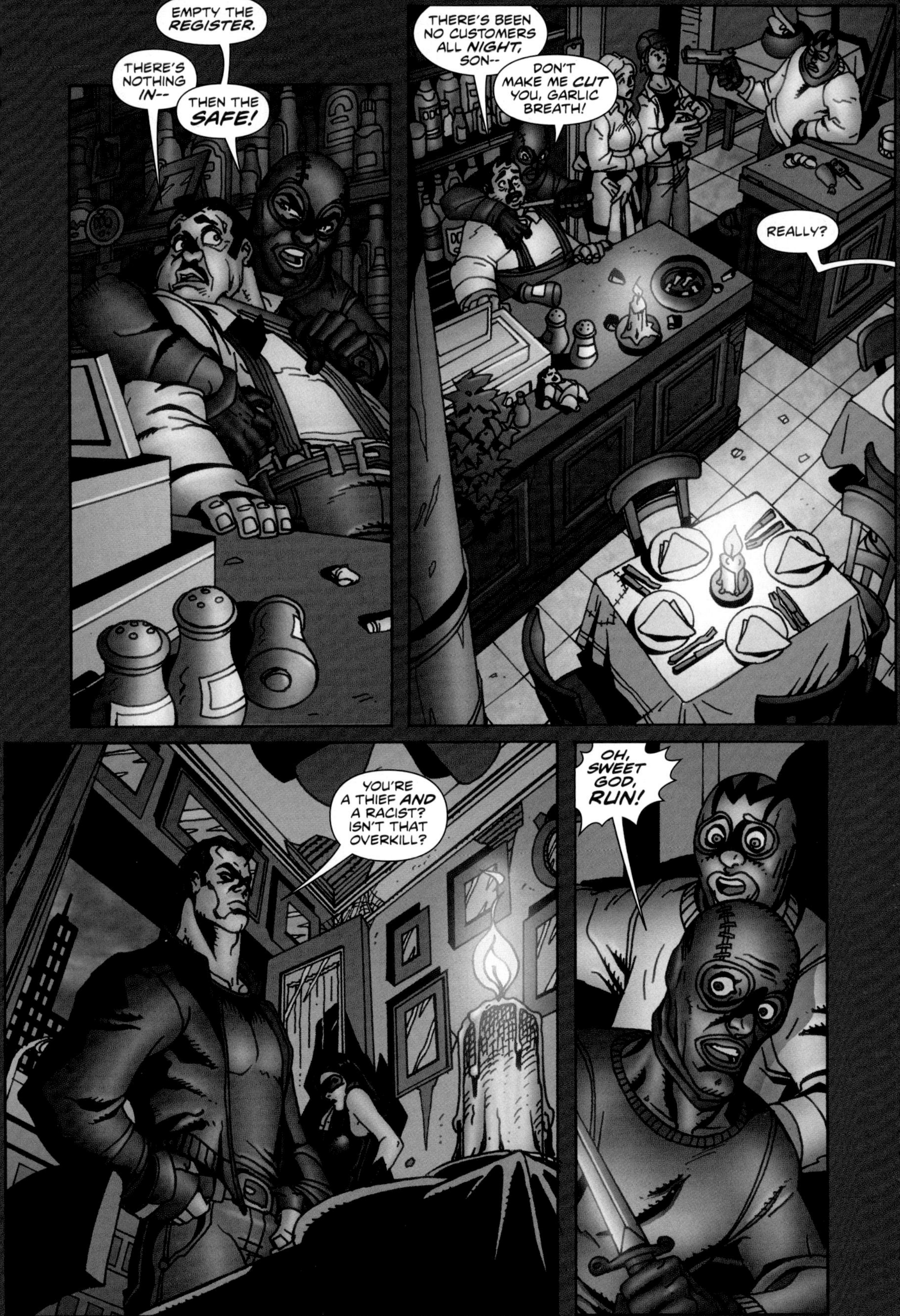
EMPTY THE REGISTER.
THERE'S NOTHING IN--
THEN THE SAFE!
THERE'S BEEN NO CUSTOMERS ALL NIGHT, SON--
DON'T MAKE ME CUT YOU, GARLIC BREATH!
REALLY?
YOU'RE A THIEF AND A RACIST? ISN'T THAT OVERKILL?
OH, SWEET GOD, RUN!

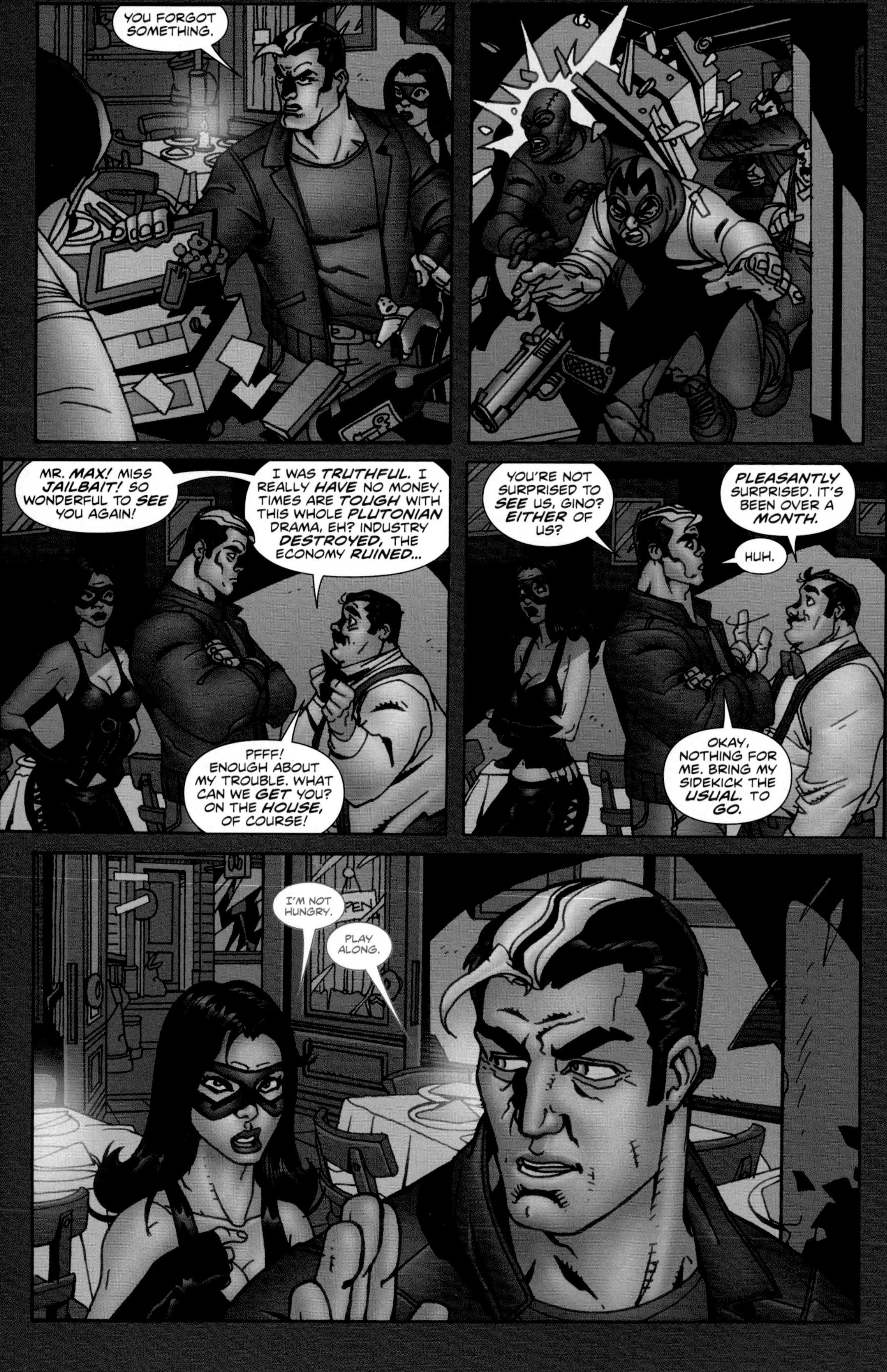
YOU FORGOT SOMETHING.
MR. MAX! MISS JAILBAIT! SO WONDERFUL TO SEE YOU AGAIN!
I WAS TRUTHFUL. I REALLY HAVE NO MONEY. TIMES ARE TOUGH WITH THIS WHOLE PLUTONIAN DRAMA, EH? INDUSTRY DESTROYED, THE ECONOMY RUINED...
PFFF! ENOUGH ABOUT MY TROUBLE. WHAT CAN WE GET YOU? ON THE HOUSE, OF COURSE!
YOU'RE NOT SURPRISED TO SEE US, GINO? EITHER OF US?
PLEASANTLY SURPRISED. IT'S BEEN OVER A MONTH.
HUH.
OKAY, NOTHING FOR ME. BRING MY SIDEKICK THE USUAL. TO GO.
I'M NOT HUNGRY.
PLAY ALONG.

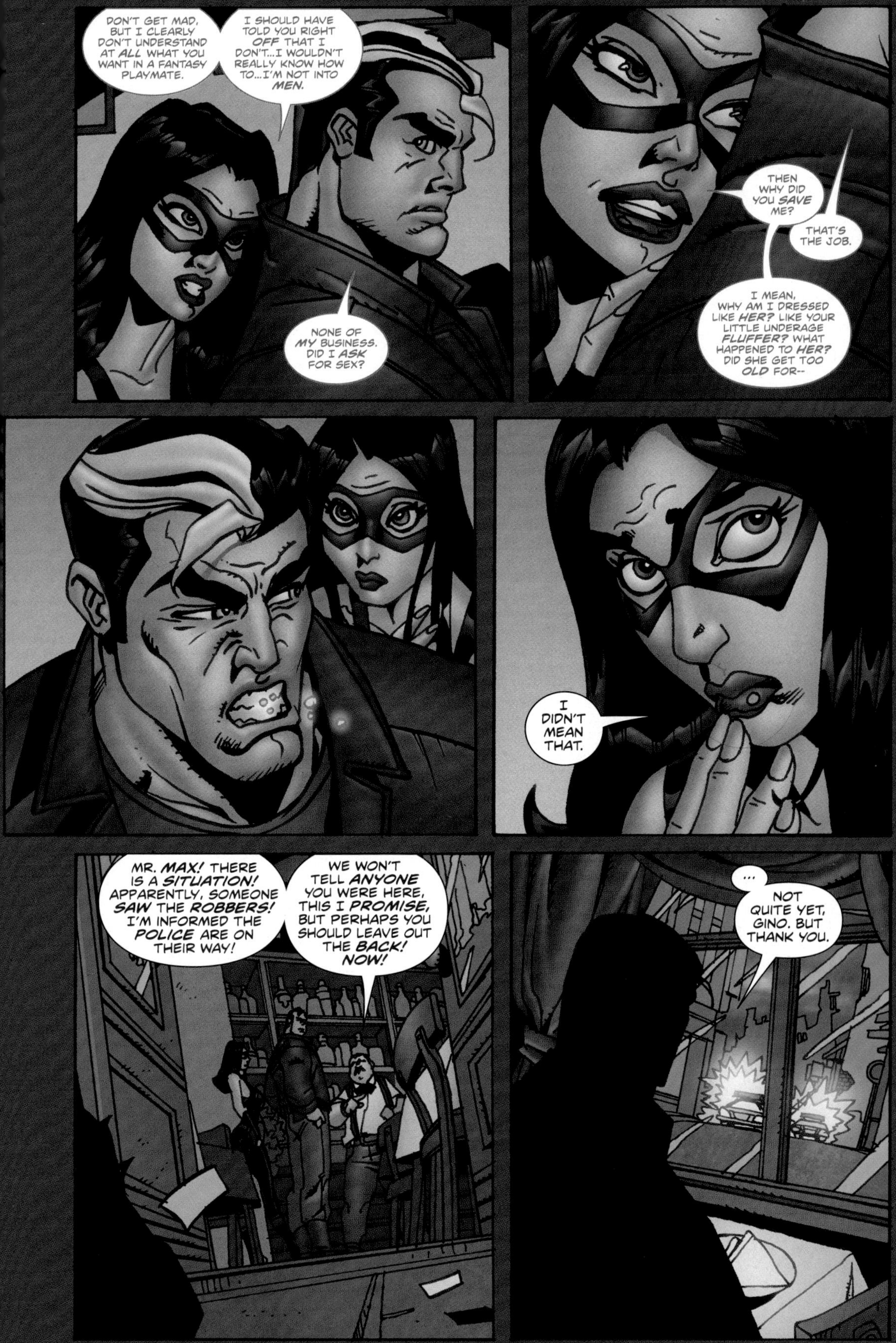
DON'T GET MAD, BUT I CLEARLY DON'T UNDERSTAND AT ALL WHAT YOU WANT IN A FANTASY PLAYMATE.
I SHOULD HAVE TOLD YOU RIGHT OFF THAT I DON'T...I WOULDN'T REALLY KNOW HOW TO...I'M NOT INTO MEN.
NONE OF MY BUSINESS. DID I ASK FOR SEX?
THEN WHY DID YOU SAVE ME?
THAT'S THE JOB.
I MEAN, WHY AM I DRESSED LIKE HER? LIKE YOUR LITTLE UNDERAGE FLUFFER? WHAT HAPPENED TO HER? DID SHE GET TOO OLD FOR--
I DIDN'T MEAN THAT.
MR. MAX! THERE IS A SITUATION! APPARENTLY, SOMEONE SAW THE ROBBERS! I'M INFORMED THE POLICE ARE ON THEIR WAY!
WE WON'T TELL ANYONE YOU WERE HERE, THIS I PROMISE, BUT PERHAPS YOU SHOULD LEAVE OUT THE BACK! NOW!
...
NOT QUITE YET, GINO. BUT THANK YOU.

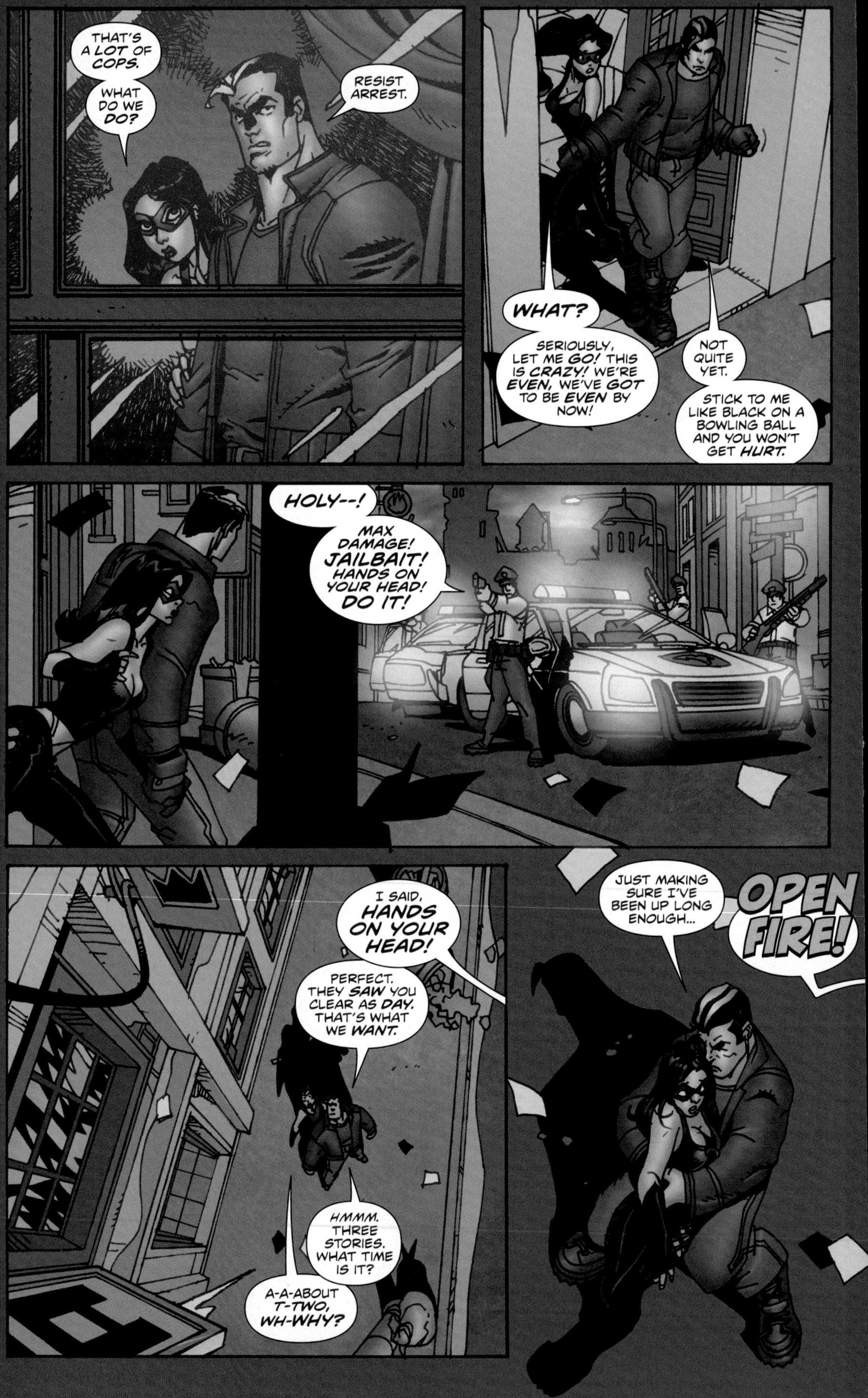
THAT'S A LOT OF COPS.
WHAT DO WE DO?
RESIST ARREST.
WHAT?
SERIOUSLY, LET ME GO! THIS IS CRAZY! WE'RE EVEN, WE'VE GOT TO BE EVEN BY NOW!
NOT QUITE YET.
STICK TO ME LIKE BLACK ON A BOWLING BALL AND YOU WON'T GET HURT.
HOLY--!
MAX DAMAGE! JAILBAIT! HANDS ON YOUR HEAD! DO IT!
I SAID, HANDS ON YOUR HEAD!
PERFECT. THEY SAW YOU CLEAR AS DAY. THAT'S WHAT WE WANT.
HMMM. THREE STORIES. WHAT TIME IS IT?
A-A-ABOUT T-TWO, WH-WHY?
JUST MAKING SURE I'VE BEEN UP LONG ENOUGH...
OPEN FIRE!

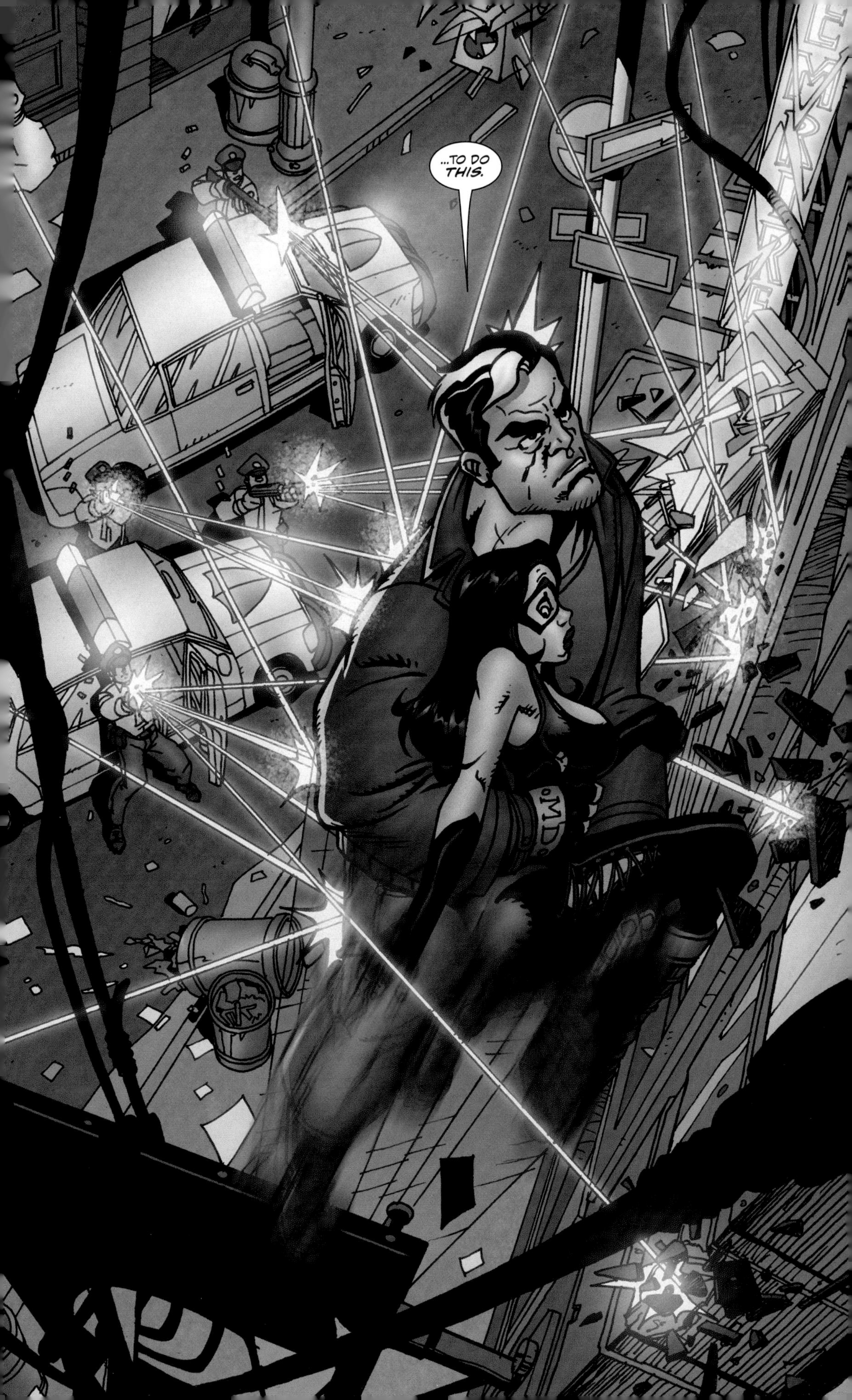
...TO DO THIS.

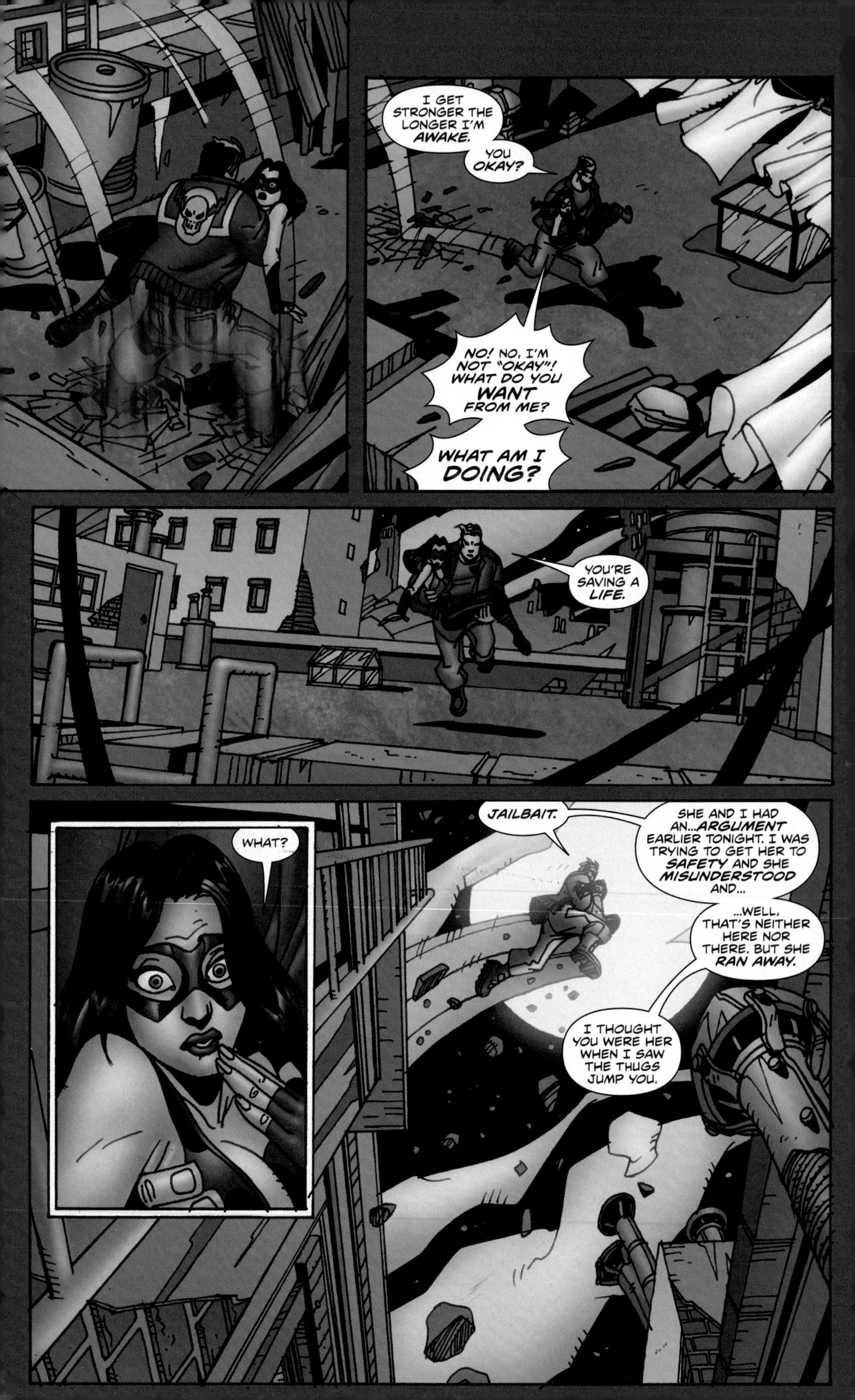
I GET STRONGER THE LONGER I'M AWAKE.
YOU OKAY?
NO! NO, I'M NOT "OKAY"! WHAT DO YOU WANT FROM ME?
WHAT AM I DOING?
YOU'RE SAVING A LIFE.
JAILBAIT.
WHAT?
SHE AND I HAD AN...ARGUMENT EARLIER TONIGHT. I WAS TRYING TO GET HER TO SAFETY AND SHE MISUNDERSTOOD AND...
...WELL, THAT'S NEITHER HERE NOR THERE. BUT SHE RAN AWAY.
I THOUGHT YOU WERE HER WHEN I SAW THE THUGS JUMP YOU.

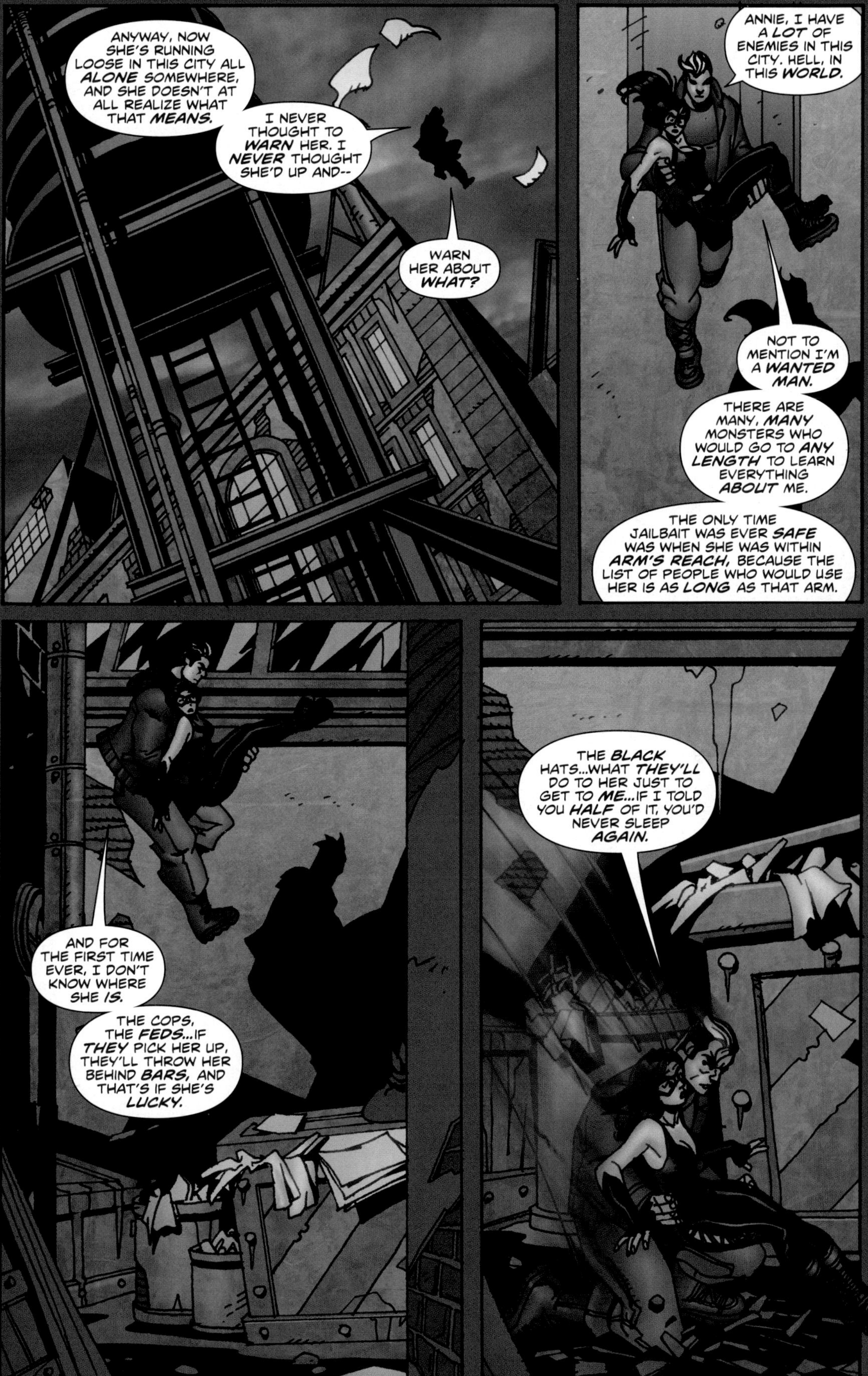
ANYWAY, NOW SHE'S RUNNING LOOSE IN THIS CITY ALL ALONE SOMEWHERE, AND SHE DOESN'T AT ALL REALIZE WHAT THAT MEANS.
I NEVER THOUGHT TO WARN HER. I NEVER THOUGHT SHE'D UP AND--
WARN HER ABOUT WHAT?
ANNIE, I HAVE A LOT OF ENEMIES IN THIS CITY. HELL, IN THIS WORLD.
NOT TO MENTION I'M A WANTED MAN.
THERE ARE MANY, MANY MONSTERS WHO WOULD GO TO ANY LENGTH TO LEARN EVERYTHING ABOUT ME.
THE ONLY TIME JAILBAIT WAS EVER SAFE WAS WHEN SHE WAS WITHIN ARM'S REACH, BECAUSE THE LIST OF PEOPLE WHO WOULD USE HER IS AS LONG AS THAT ARM.
AND FOR THE FIRST TIME EVER, I DON'T KNOW WHERE SHE IS.
THE COPS, THE FEDS...IF THEY PICK HER UP, THEY'LL THROW HER BEHIND BARS, AND THAT'S IF SHE'S LUCKY.
THE BLACK HATS...WHAT THEY'LL DO TO HER JUST TO GET TO ME...IF I TOLD YOU HALF OF IT, YOU'D NEVER SLEEP AGAIN.

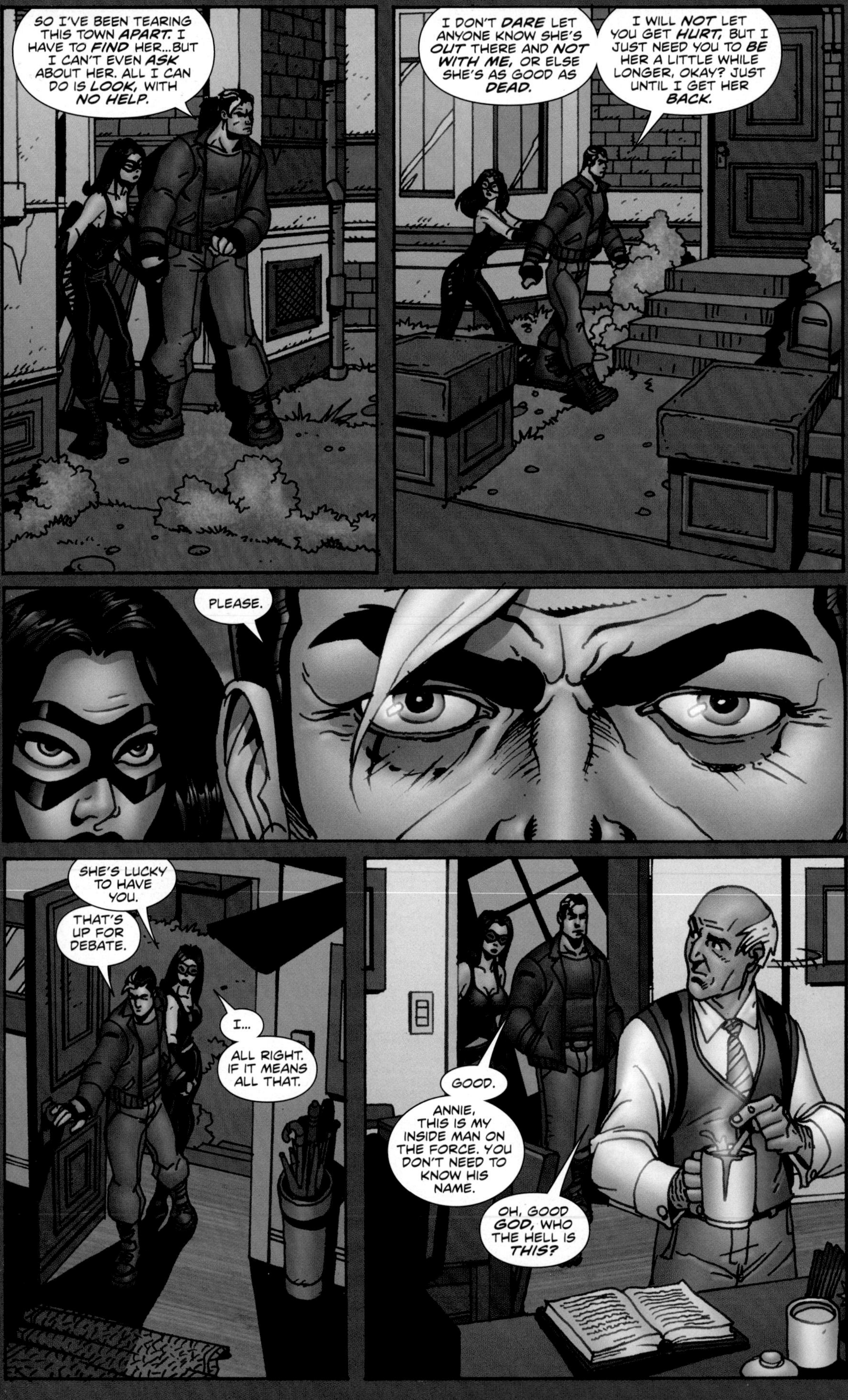
SO I'VE BEEN TEARING THIS TOWN APART. I HAVE TO FIND HER...BUT I CAN'T EVEN ASK ABOUT HER. ALL I CAN DO IS LOOK, WITH NO HELP.
I DON'T DARE LET ANYONE KNOW SHE'S OUT THERE AND NOT WITH ME, OR ELSE SHE'S AS GOOD AS DEAD.
I WILL NOT LET YOU GET HURT, BUT I JUST NEED YOU TO BE HER A LITTLE WHILE LONGER, OKAY? JUST UNTIL I GET HER BACK.
PLEASE.
SHE'S LUCKY TO HAVE YOU.
THAT'S UP FOR DEBATE.
I...
ALL RIGHT. IF IT MEANS ALL THAT.
GOOD.
ANNIE, THIS IS MY INSIDE MAN ON THE FORCE. YOU DON'T NEED TO KNOW HIS NAME.
OH, GOOD GOD, WHO THE HELL IS THIS?

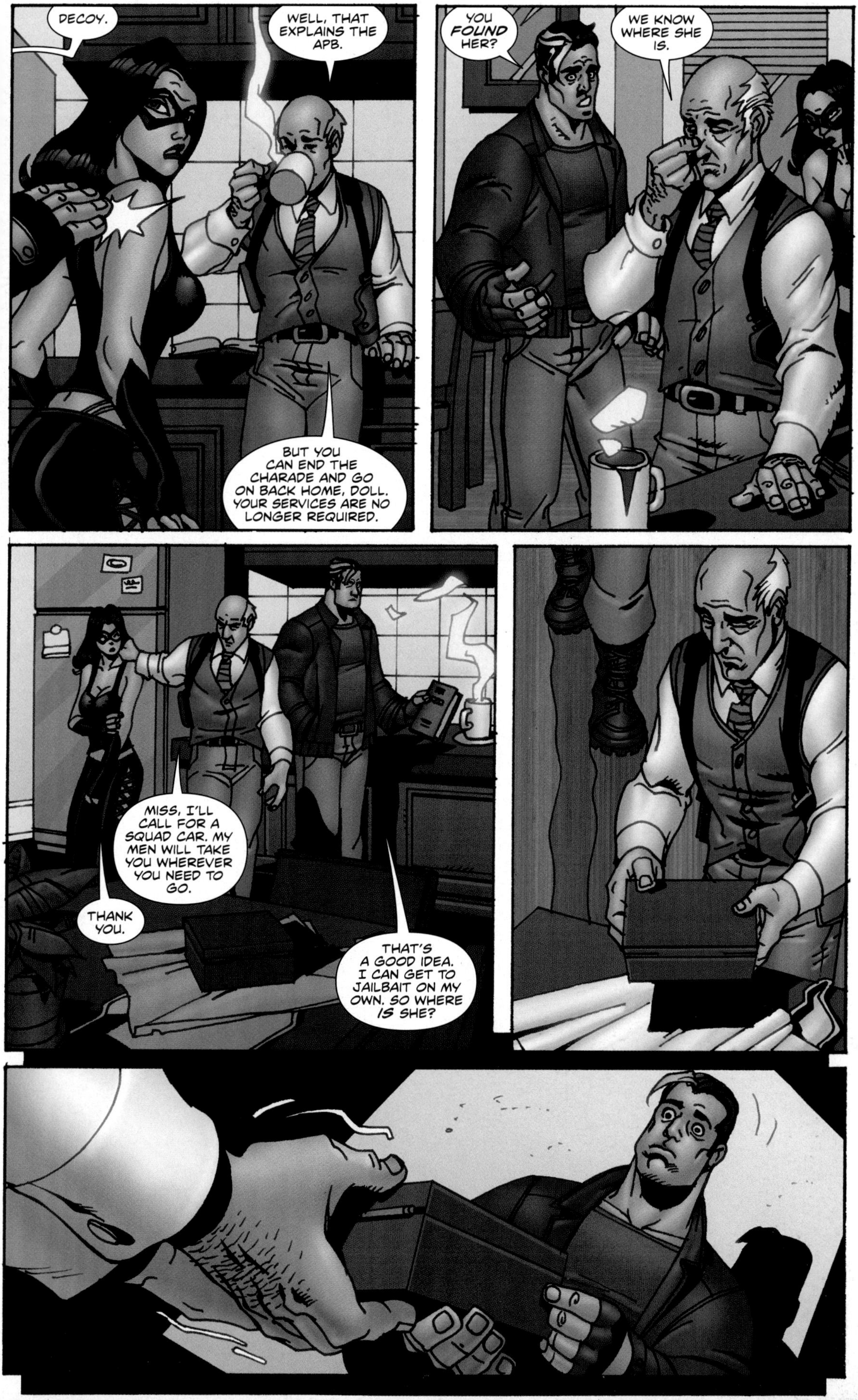
DECOY.
WELL, THAT EXPLAINS THE APB.
BUT YOU CAN END THE CHARADE AND GO ON BACK HOME, DOLL. YOUR SERVICES ARE NO LONGER REQUIRED.
YOU *FOUND* HER?
WE KNOW WHERE SHE IS.
MISS, I'LL CALL FOR A SQUAD CAR. MY MEN WILL TAKE YOU WHEREVER YOU NEED TO GO.
THANK YOU.
THAT'S A GOOD IDEA. I CAN GET TO JAILBAIT ON MY OWN. SO WHERE *IS* SHE?

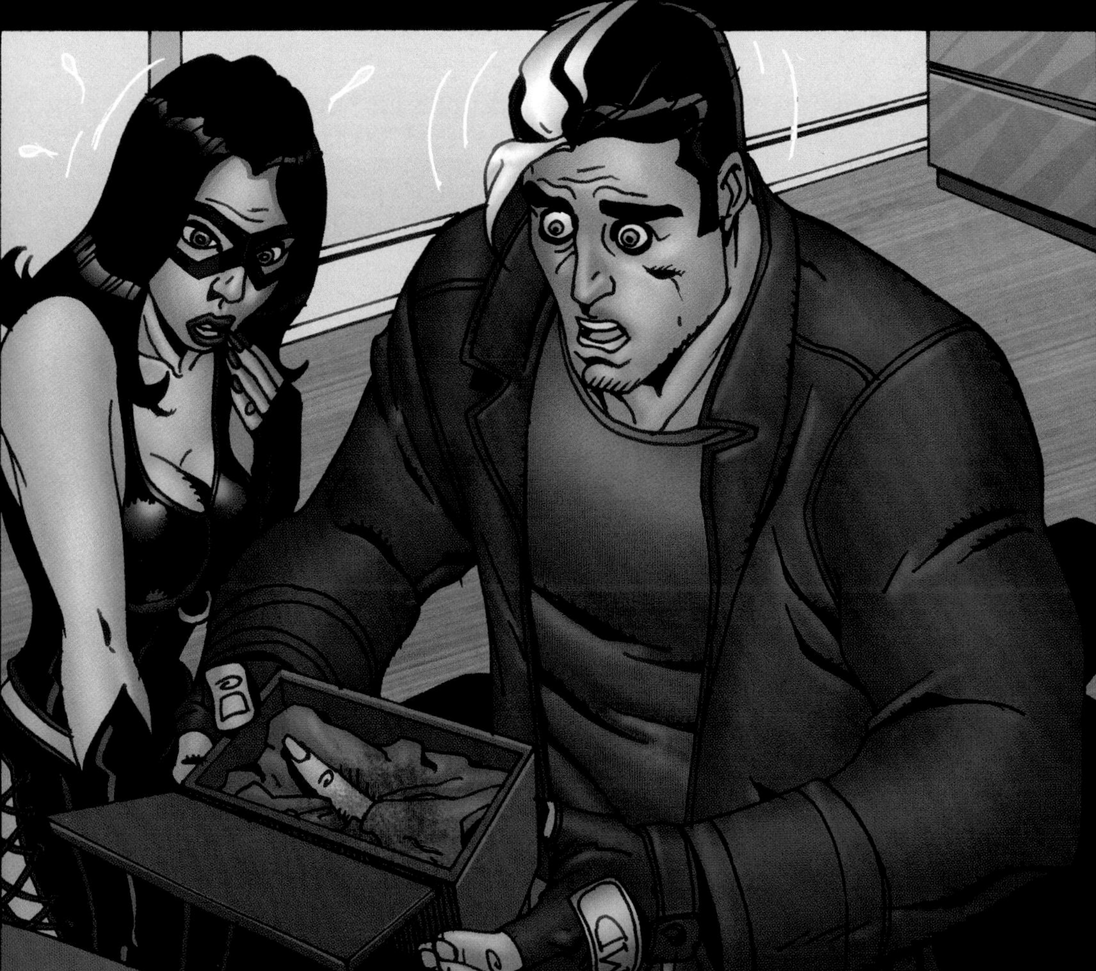

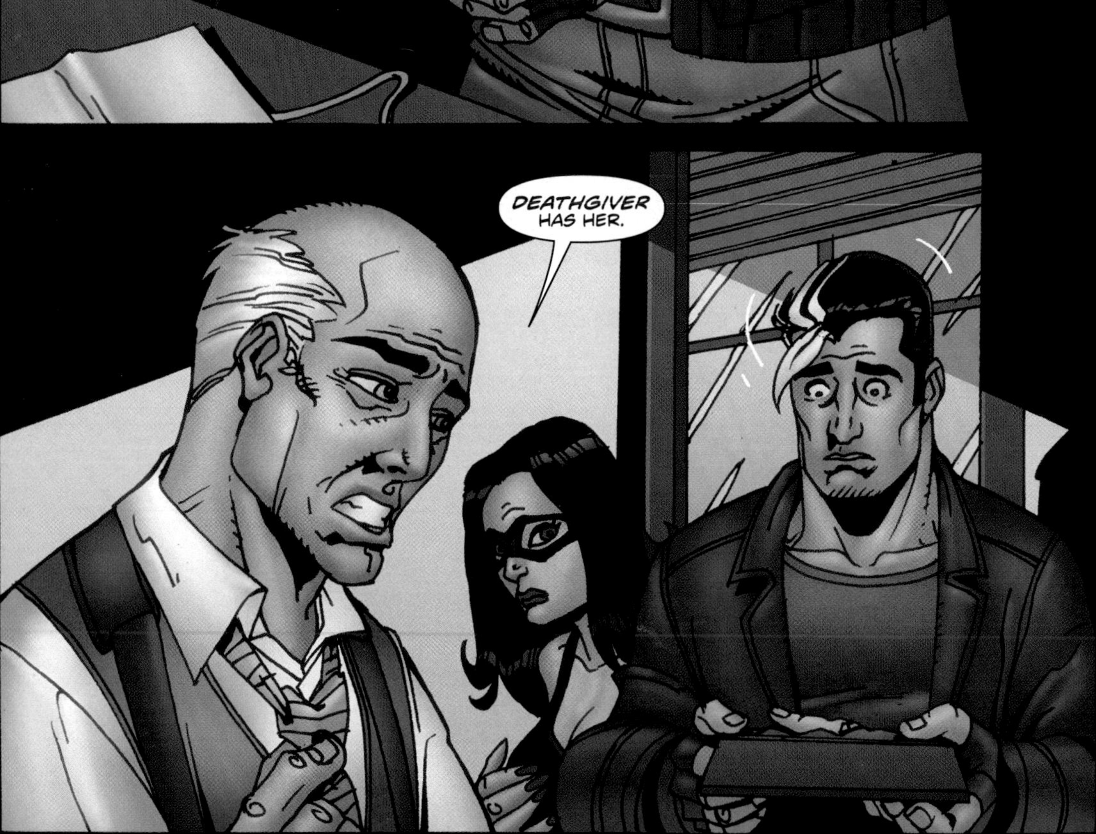
DEATHGIVER HAS HER.

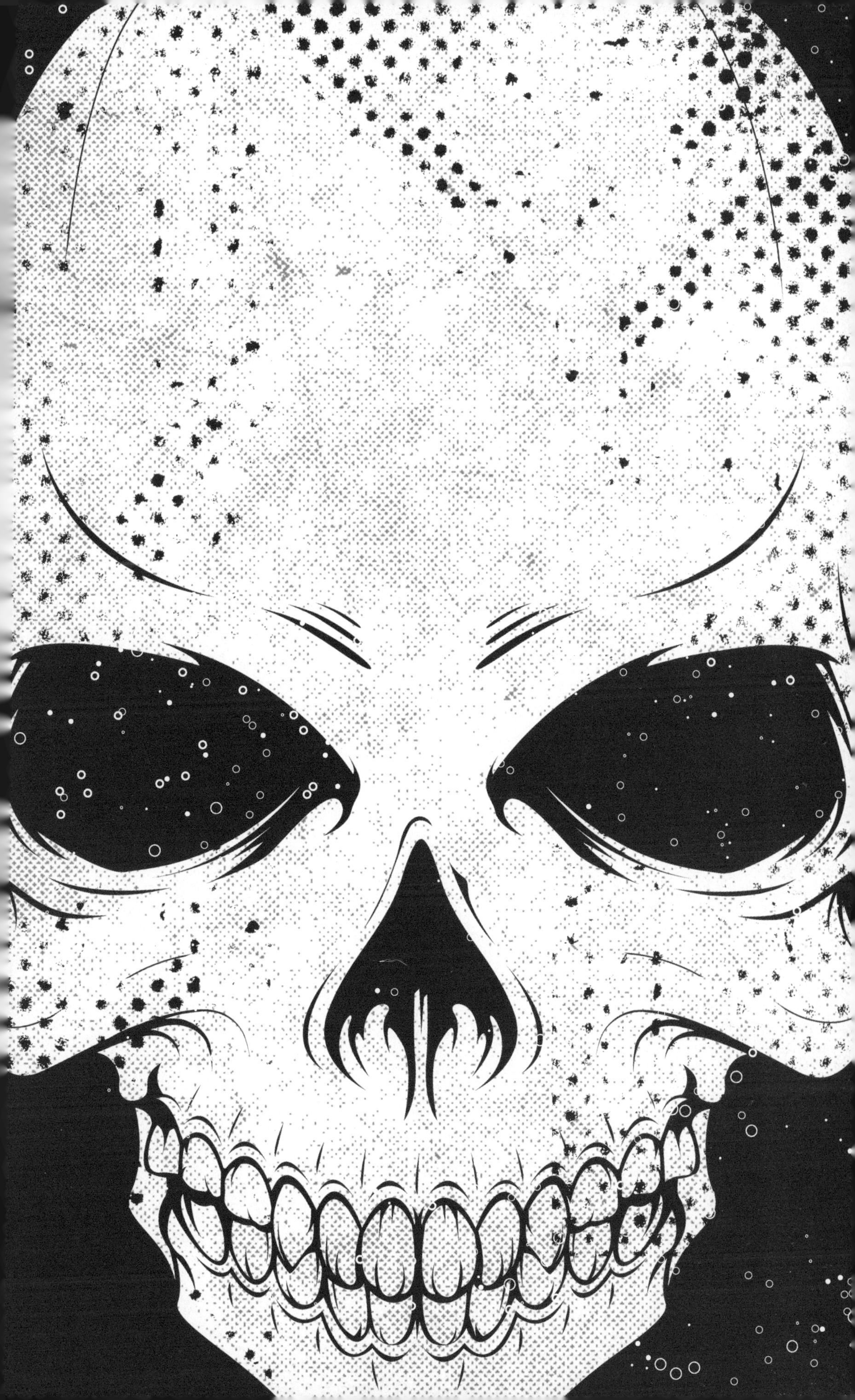

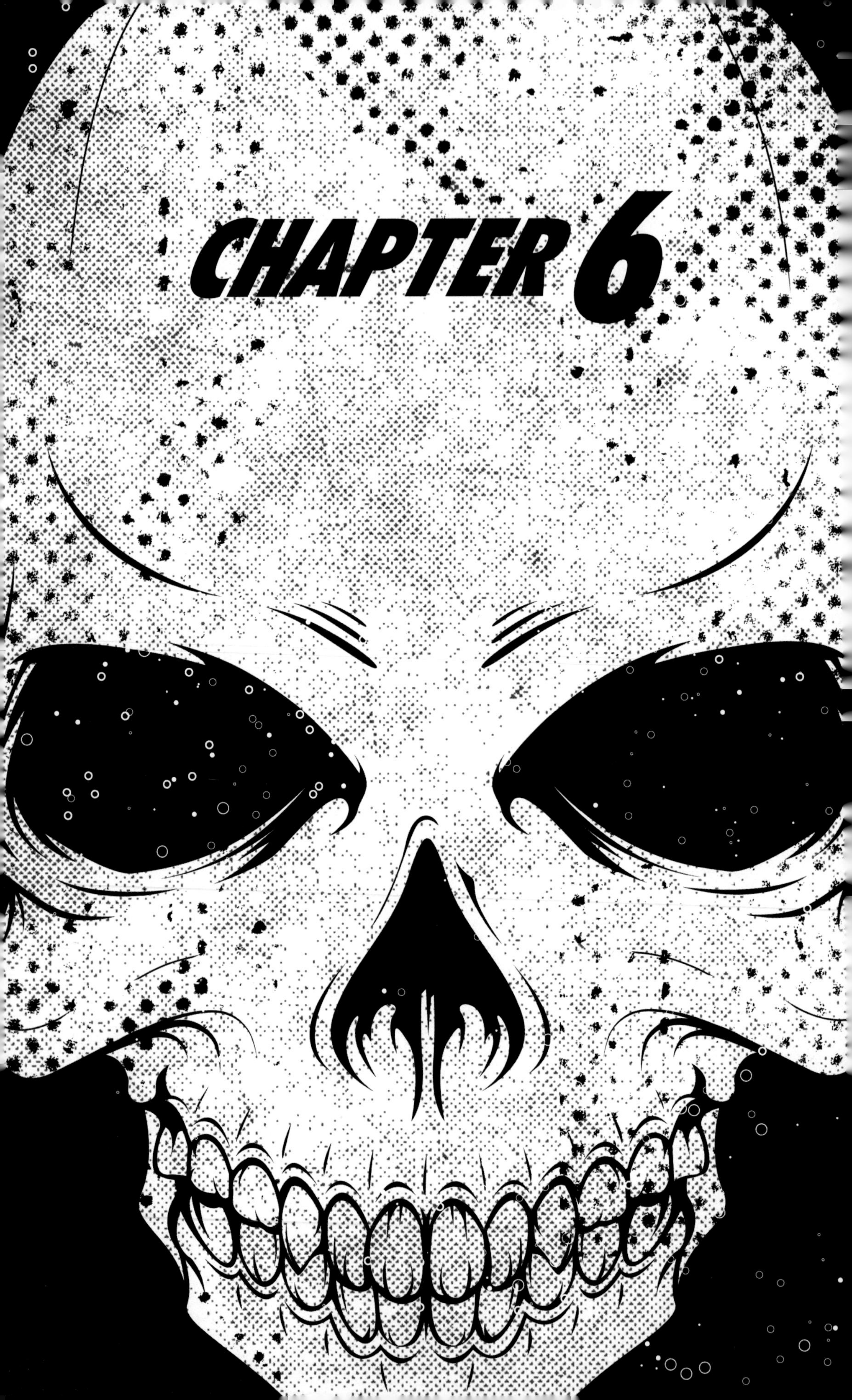
CHAPTER 6

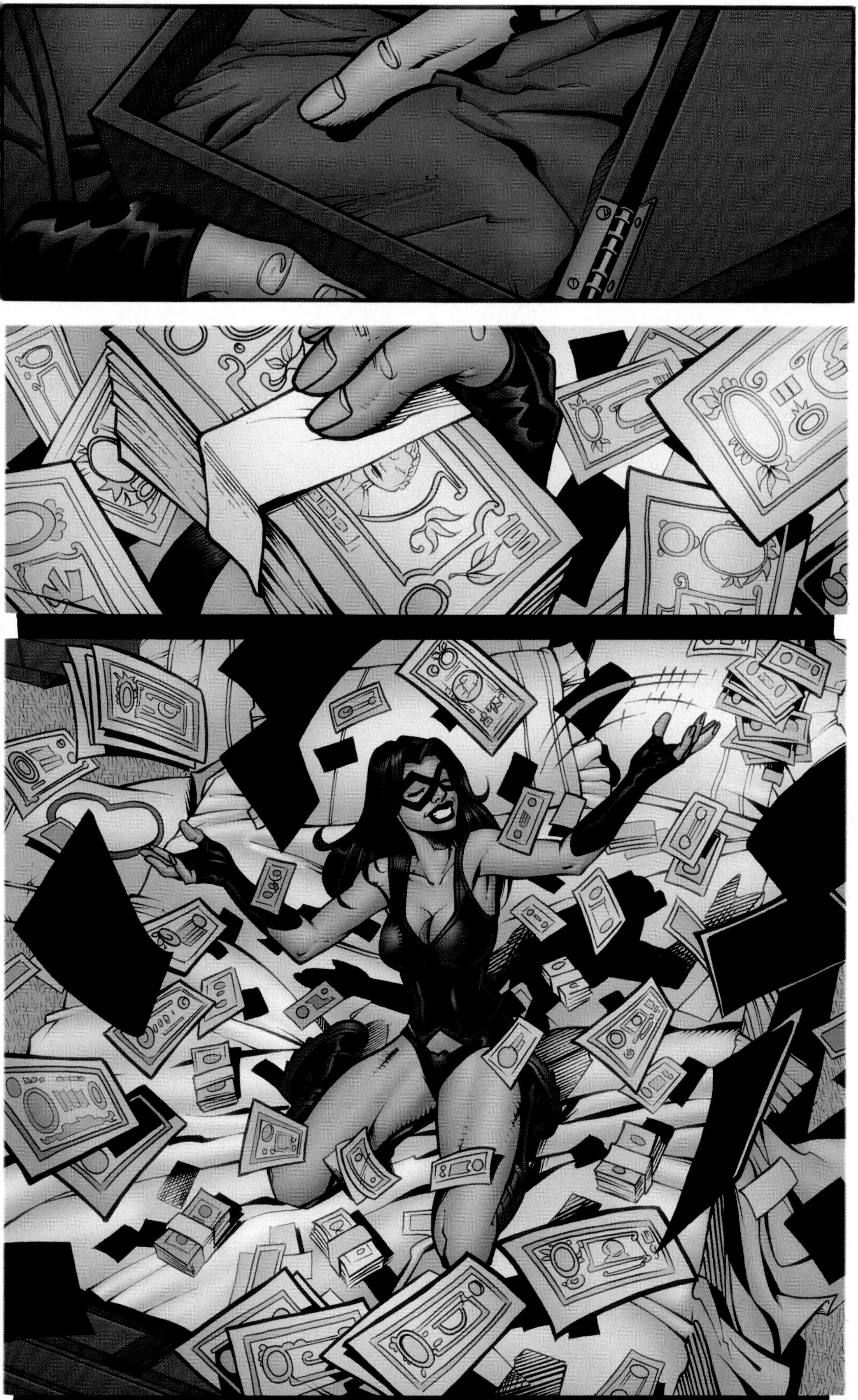

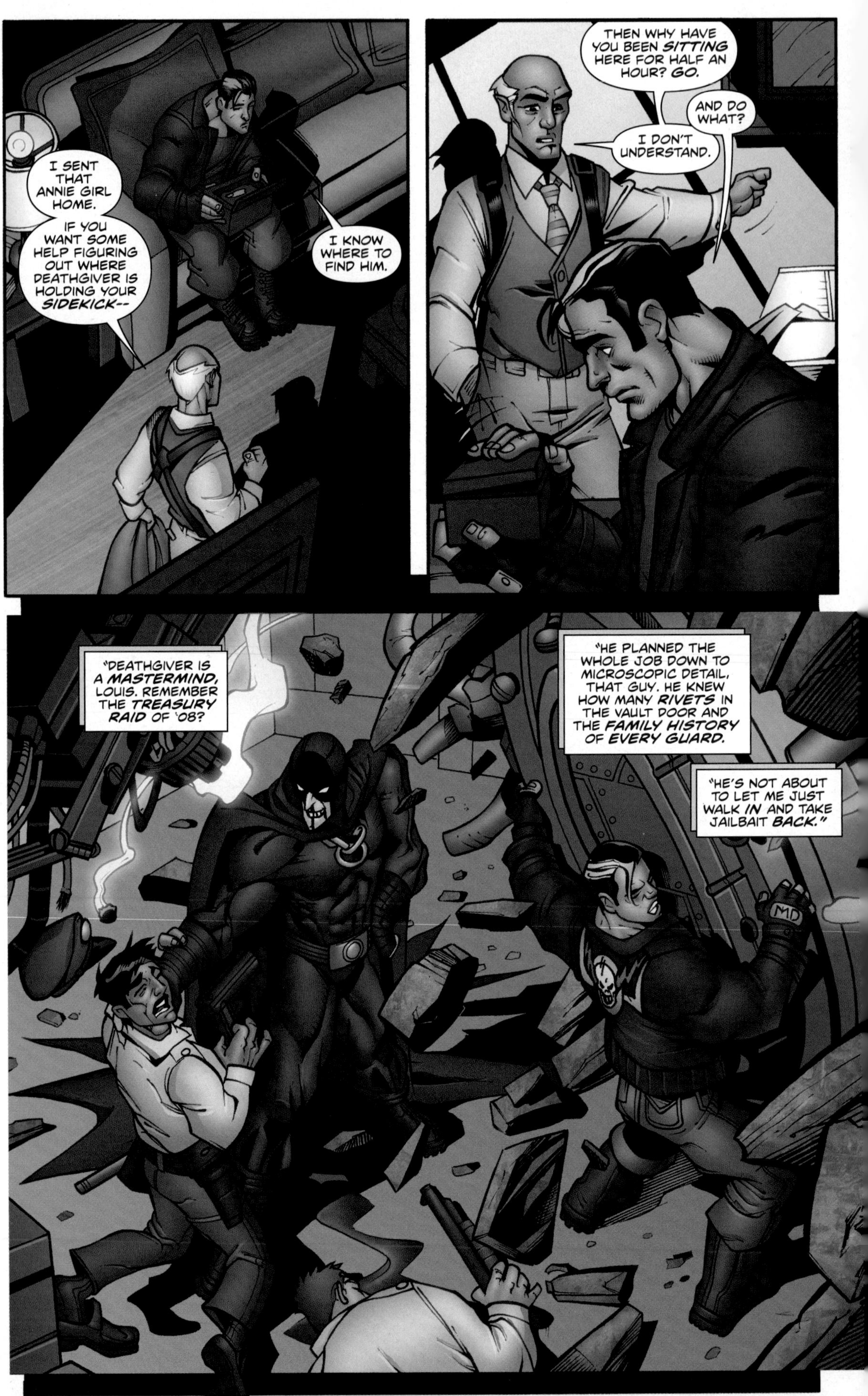
I SENT THAT ANNIE GIRL HOME.
IF YOU WANT SOME HELP FIGURING OUT WHERE DEATHGIVER IS HOLDING YOUR SIDEKICK--
I KNOW WHERE TO FIND HIM.
THEN WHY HAVE YOU BEEN SITTING HERE FOR HALF AN HOUR? GO.
I DON'T UNDERSTAND.
AND DO WHAT?
"DEATHGIVER IS A MASTERMIND, LOUIS. REMEMBER THE TREASURY RAID OF '08?
"HE PLANNED THE WHOLE JOB DOWN TO MICROSCOPIC DETAIL, THAT GUY. HE KNEW HOW MANY RIVETS IN THE VAULT DOOR AND THE FAMILY HISTORY OF EVERY GUARD.
"HE'S NOT ABOUT TO LET ME JUST WALK IN AND TAKE JAILBAIT BACK."

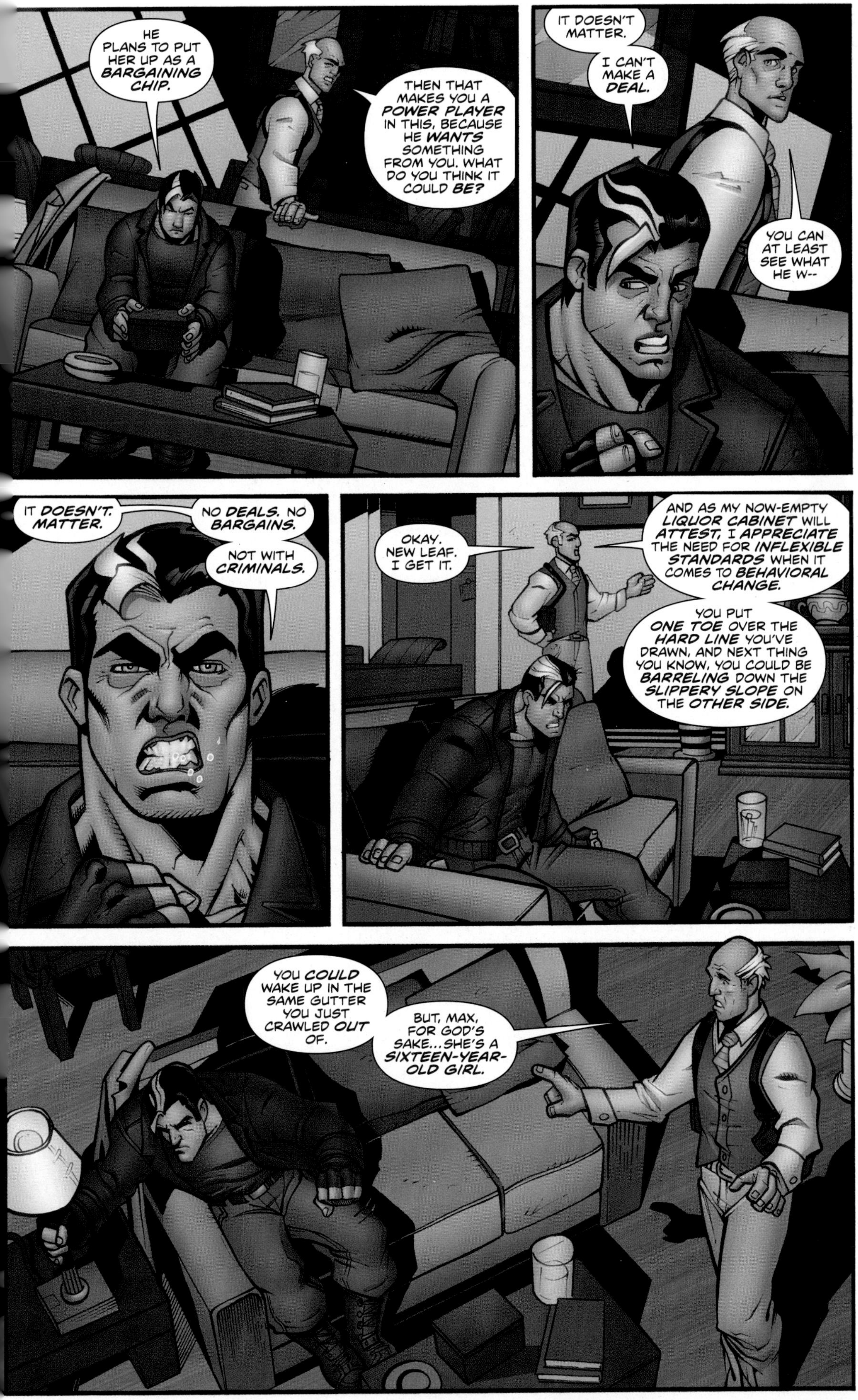

HE PLANS TO PUT HER UP AS A BARGAINING CHIP.
THEN THAT MAKES YOU A POWER PLAYER IN THIS, BECAUSE HE WANTS SOMETHING FROM YOU. WHAT DO YOU THINK IT COULD BE?
IT DOESN'T MATTER.
I CAN'T MAKE A DEAL.
YOU CAN AT LEAST SEE WHAT HE W--
IT DOESN'T. MATTER.
NO DEALS. NO BARGAINS.
NOT WITH CRIMINALS.
OKAY. NEW LEAF. I GET IT.
AND AS MY NOW-EMPTY LIQUOR CABINET WILL ATTEST, I APPRECIATE THE NEED FOR INFLEXIBLE STANDARDS WHEN IT COMES TO BEHAVIORAL CHANGE.
YOU PUT ONE TOE OVER THE HARD LINE YOU'VE DRAWN, AND NEXT THING YOU KNOW, YOU COULD BE BARRELING DOWN THE SLIPPERY SLOPE ON THE OTHER SIDE.
YOU COULD WAKE UP IN THE SAME GUTTER YOU JUST CRAWLED OUT OF.
BUT, MAX, FOR GOD'S SAKE...SHE'S A SIXTEEN-YEAR-OLD GIRL.

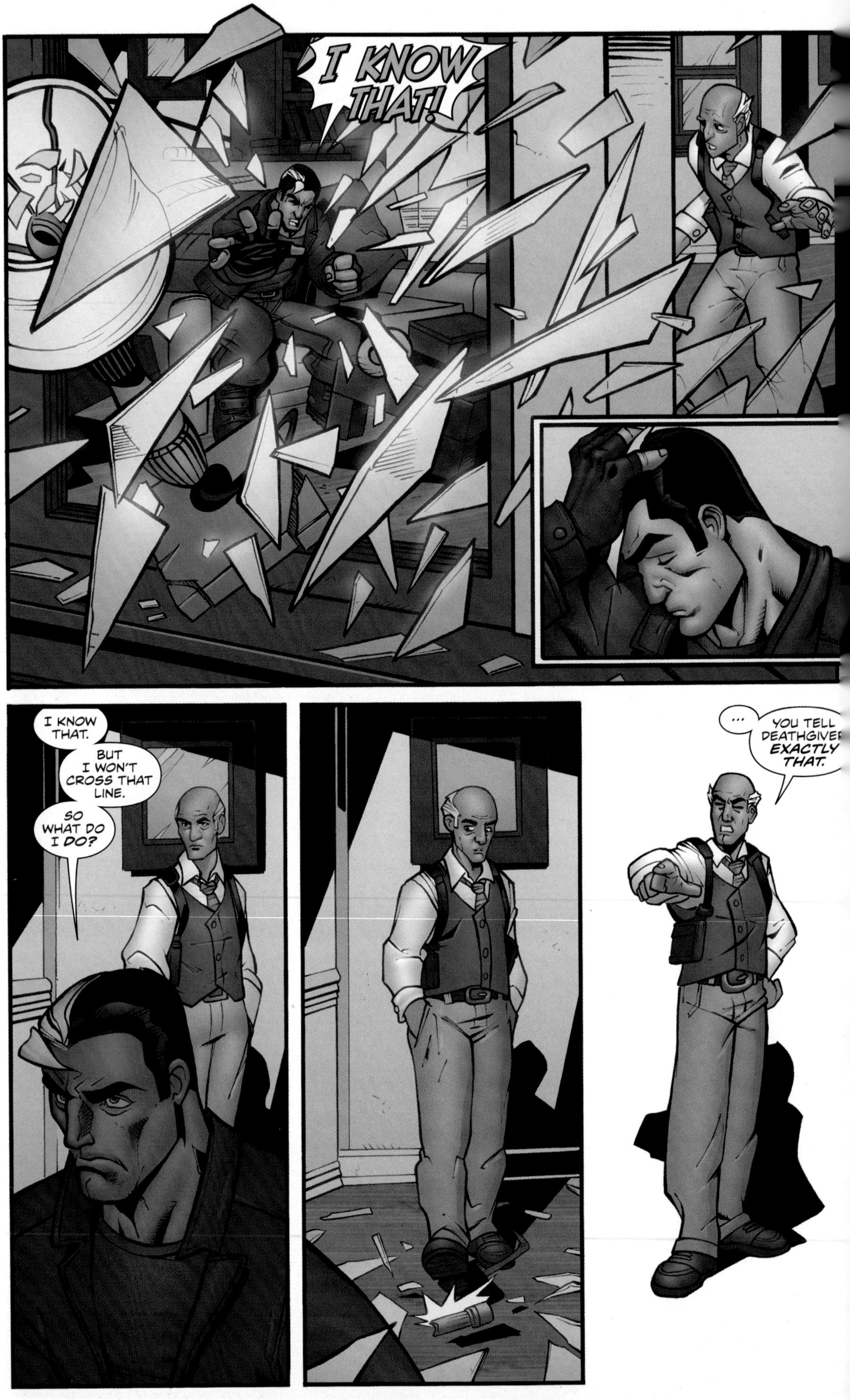
I KNOW THAT!
I KNOW THAT.
BUT I WON'T CROSS THAT LINE.
SO WHAT DO I DO?
...
YOU TELL DEATHGIVER EXACTLY THAT.

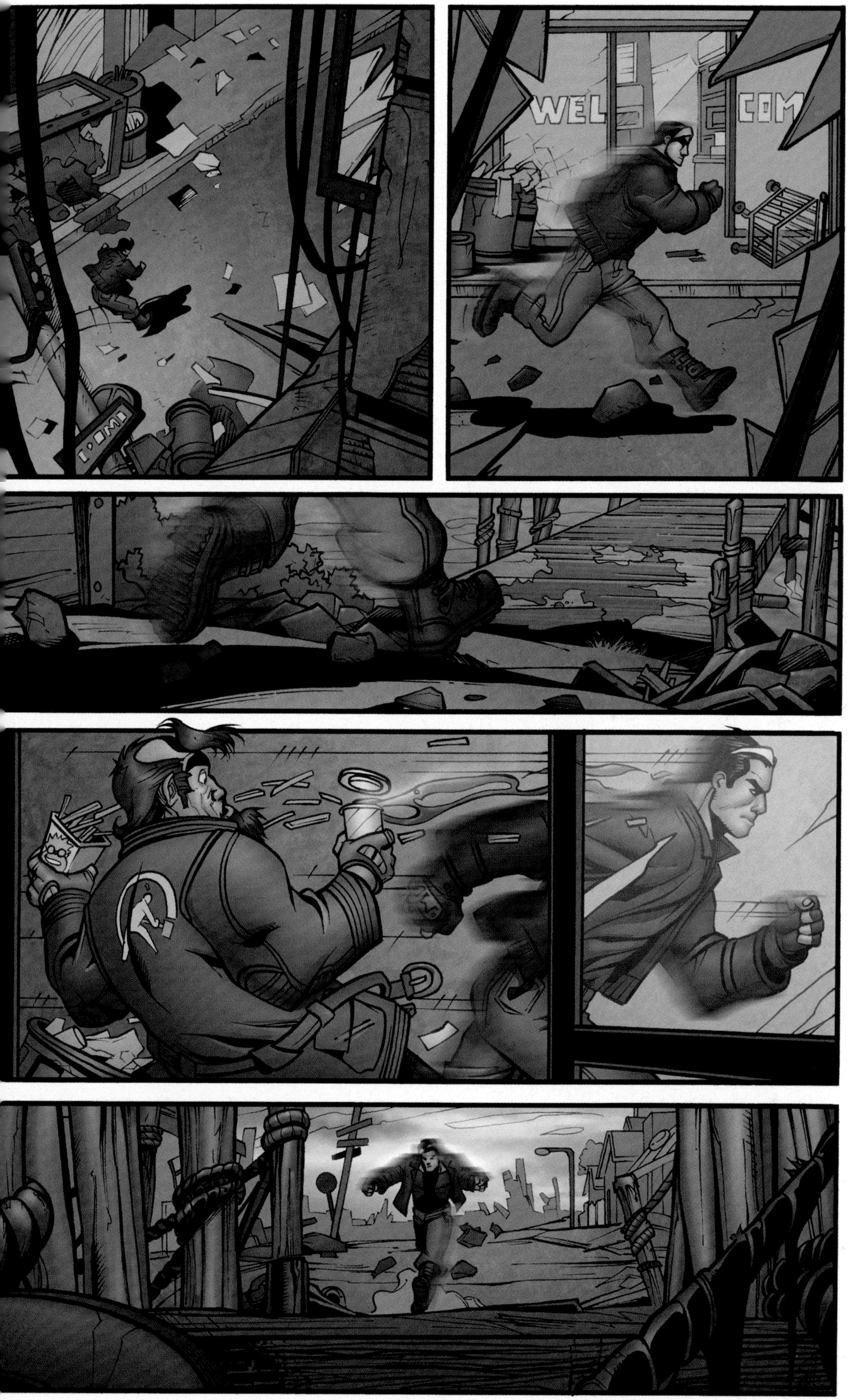
WEL
COM

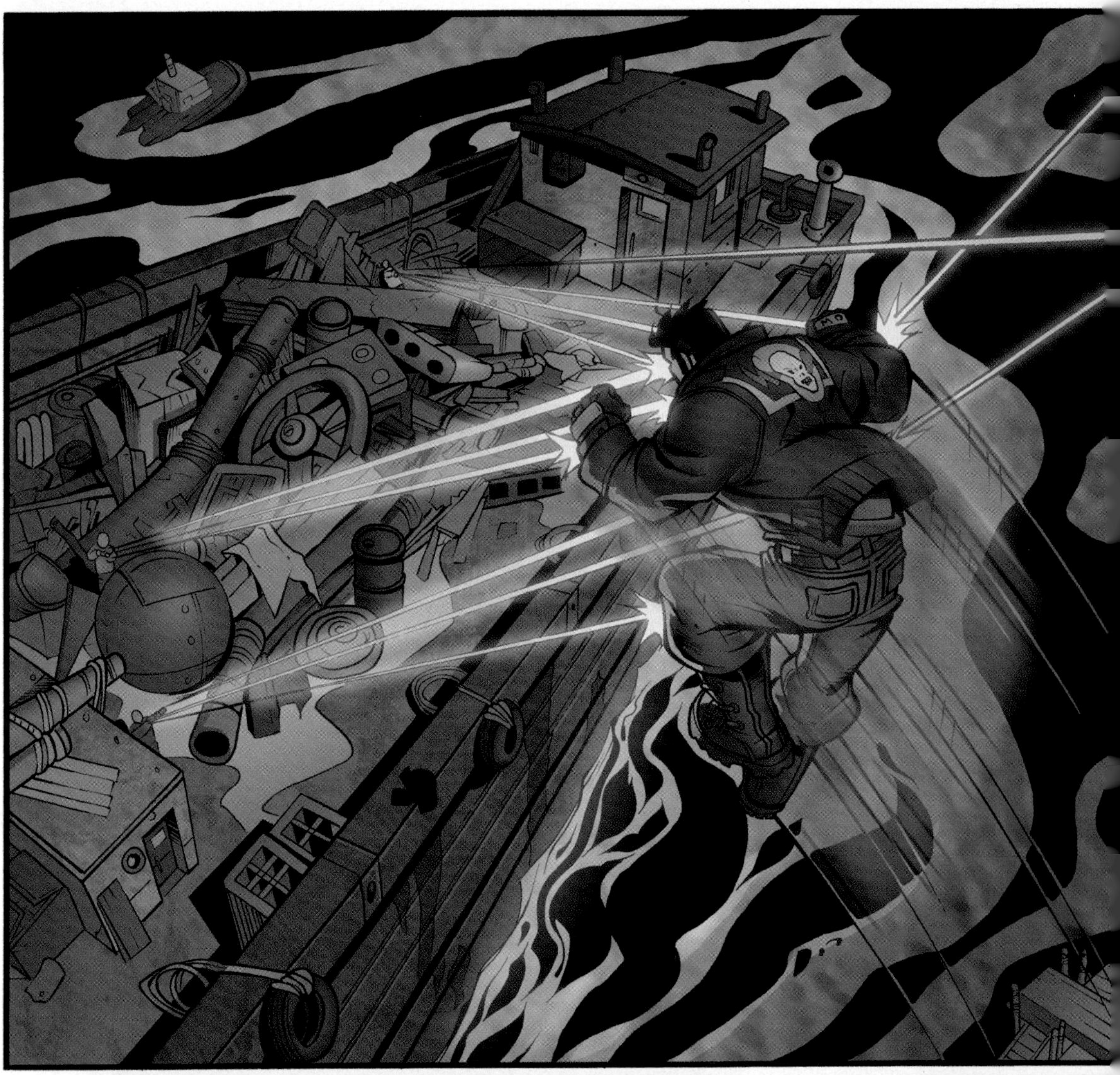

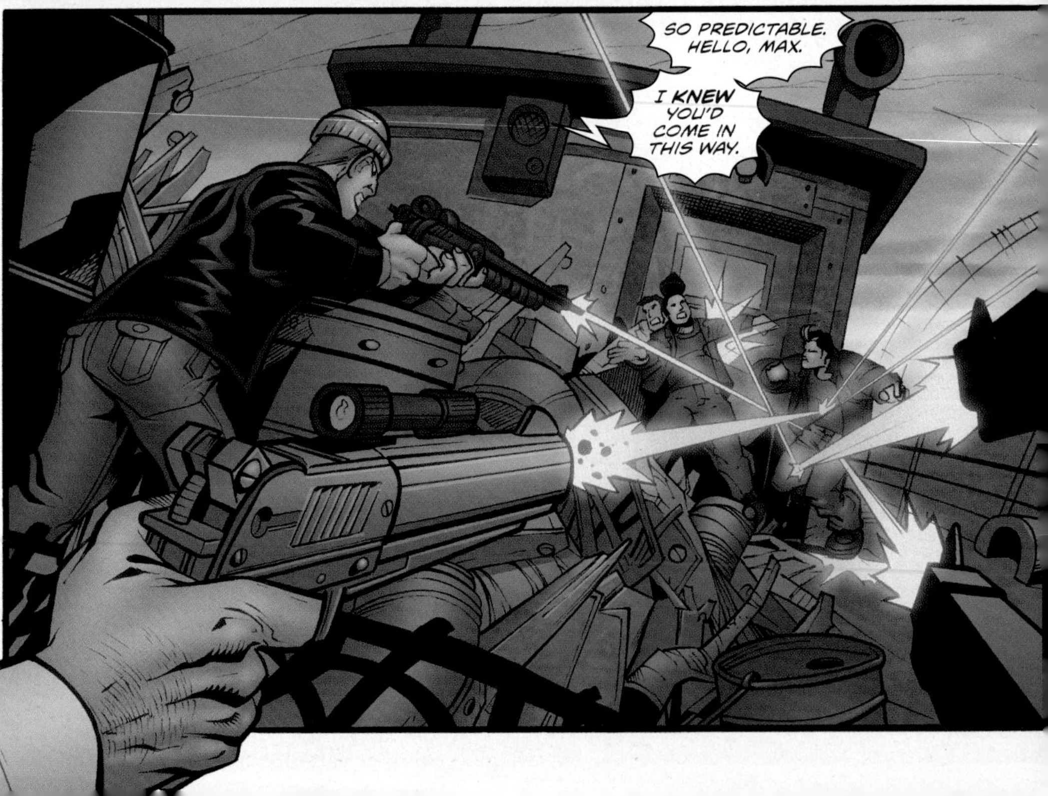
SO PREDICTABLE. HELLO, MAX.
I KNEW YOU'D COME IN THIS WAY.

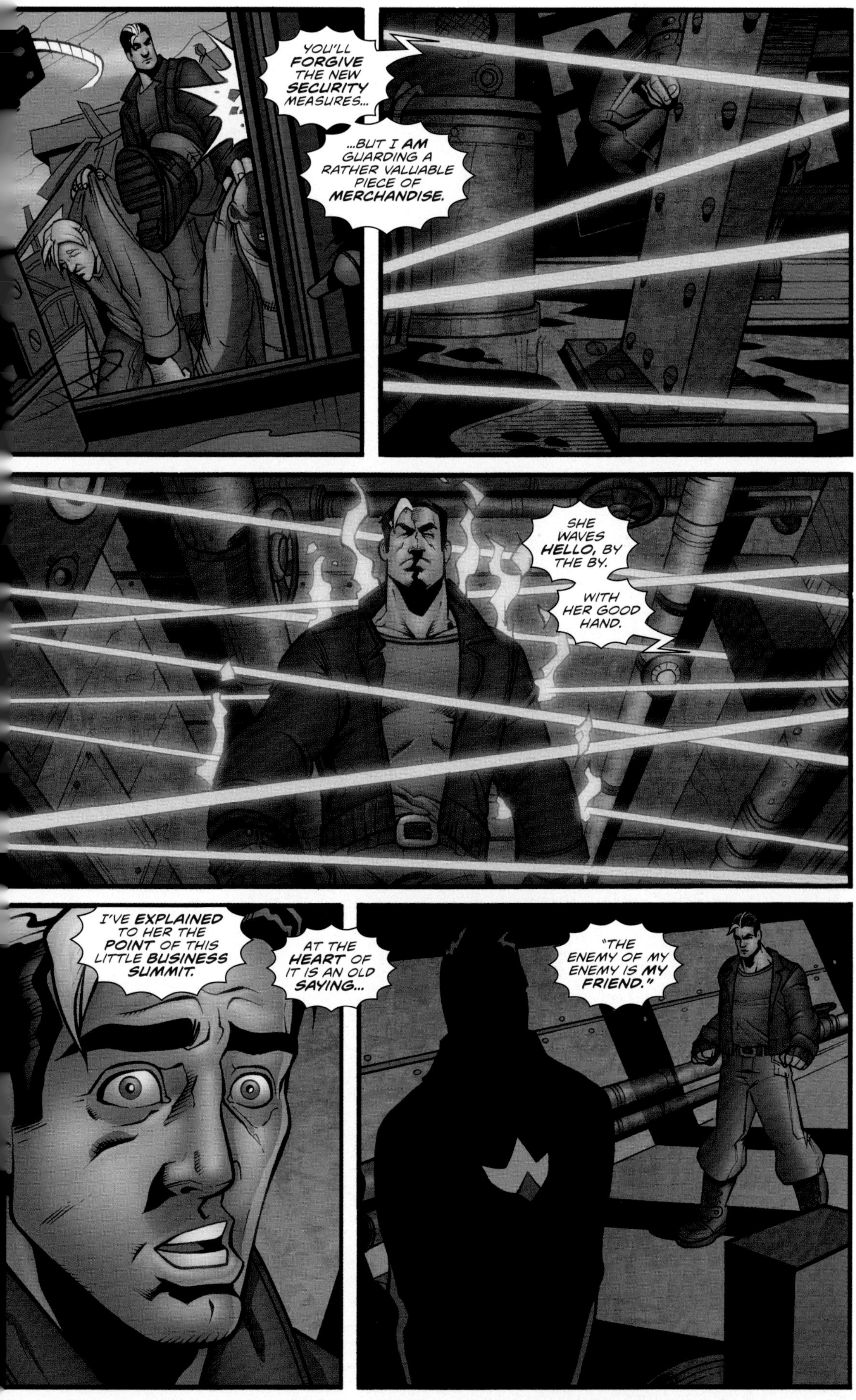
YOU'LL FORGIVE THE NEW SECURITY MEASURES...
...BUT I AM GUARDING A RATHER VALUABLE PIECE OF MERCHANDISE.
SHE WAVES HELLO, BY THE BY.
WITH HER GOOD HAND.
I'VE EXPLAINED TO HER THE POINT OF THIS LITTLE BUSINESS SUMMIT.
AT THE HEART OF IT IS AN OLD SAYING...
"THE ENEMY OF MY ENEMY IS MY FRIEND."

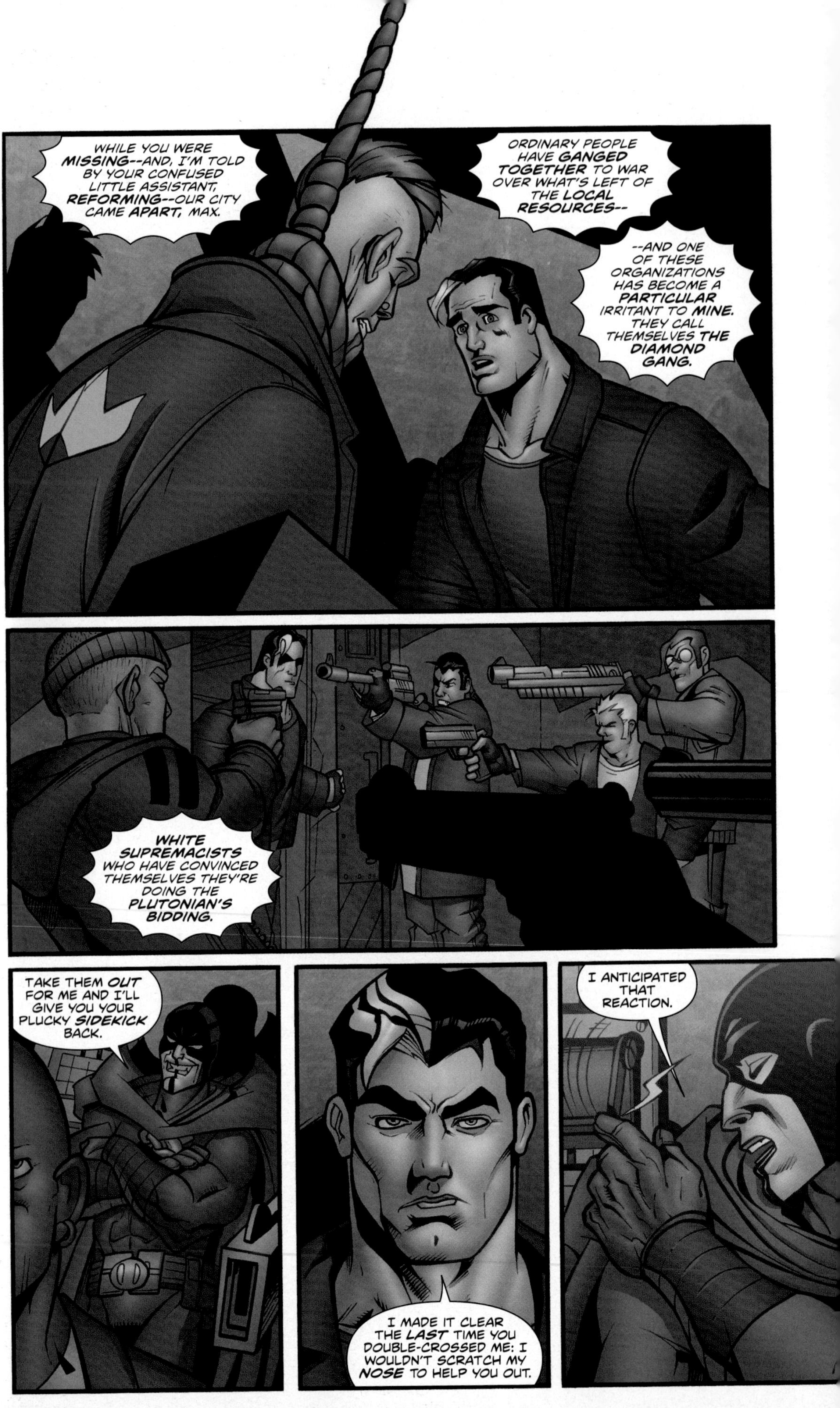
WHILE YOU WERE MISSING--AND, I'M TOLD BY YOUR CONFUSED LITTLE ASSISTANT, REFORMING--OUR CITY CAME APART, MAX.
ORDINARY PEOPLE HAVE GANGED TOGETHER TO WAR OVER WHAT'S LEFT OF THE LOCAL RESOURCES--
--AND ONE OF THESE ORGANIZATIONS HAS BECOME A PARTICULAR IRRITANT TO MINE. THEY CALL THEMSELVES THE DIAMOND GANG.
WHITE SUPREMACISTS WHO HAVE CONVINCED THEMSELVES THEY'RE DOING THE PLUTONIAN'S BIDDING.
TAKE THEM OUT FOR ME AND I'LL GIVE YOU YOUR PLUCKY SIDEKICK BACK.
I MADE IT CLEAR THE LAST TIME YOU DOUBLE-CROSSED ME: I WOULDN'T SCRATCH MY NOSE TO HELP YOU OUT.
I ANTICIPATED THAT REACTION.

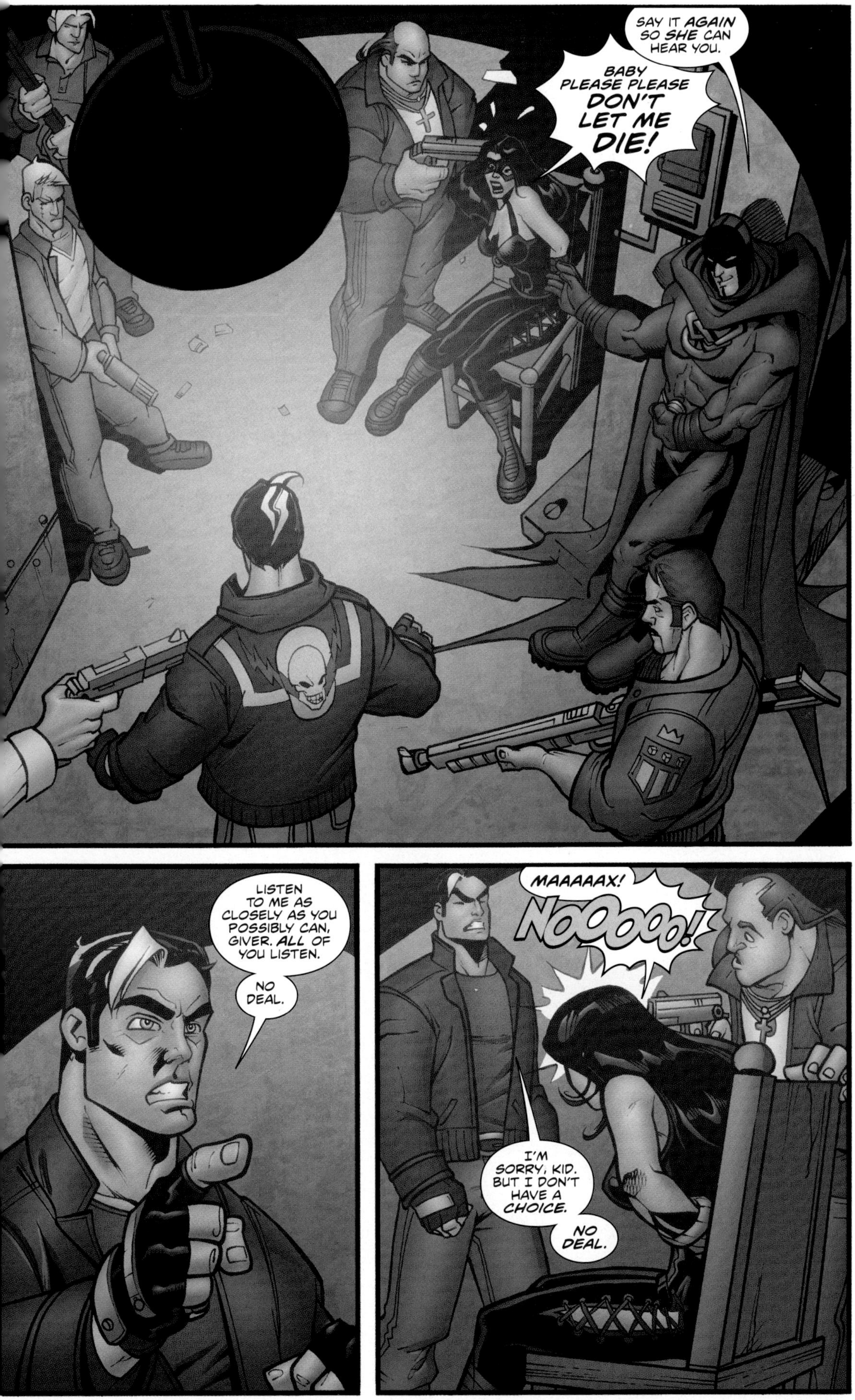

BABY PLEASE PLEASE DON'T LET ME DIE!
SAY IT AGAIN SO SHE CAN HEAR YOU.
LISTEN TO ME AS CLOSELY AS YOU POSSIBLY CAN, GIVER. ALL OF YOU LISTEN.
NO DEAL.
MAAAAAX!
NOOOOO!
I'M SORRY, KID. BUT I DON'T HAVE A CHOICE.
NO DEAL.

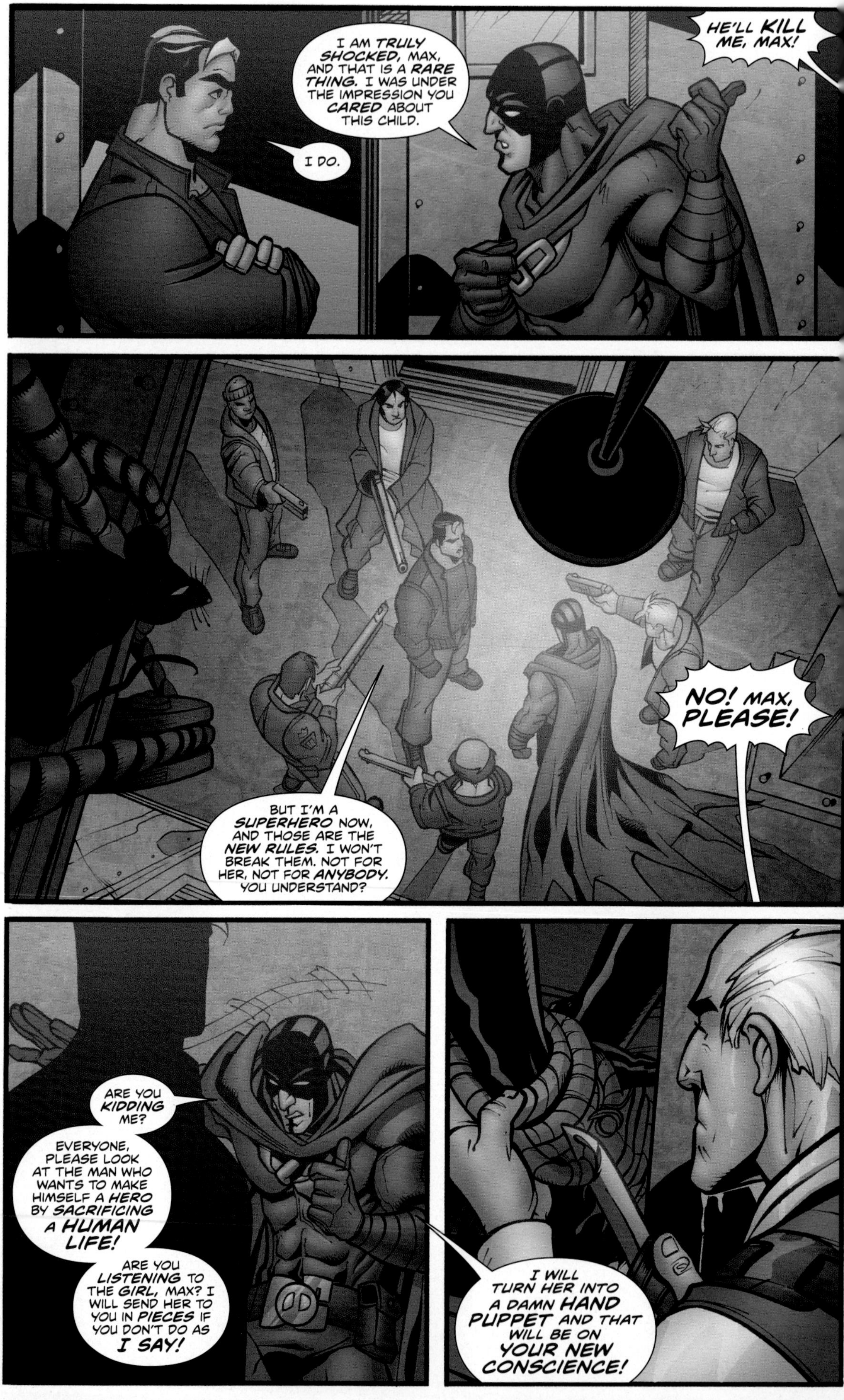
HE'LL KILL ME, MAX!
I AM TRULY SHOCKED, MAX, AND THAT IS A RARE THING. I WAS UNDER THE IMPRESSION YOU CARED ABOUT THIS CHILD.
I DO.
NO! MAX, PLEASE!
BUT I'M A SUPERHERO NOW, AND THOSE ARE THE NEW RULES. I WON'T BREAK THEM. NOT FOR HER, NOT FOR ANYBODY. YOU UNDERSTAND?
ARE YOU KIDDING ME?
EVERYONE, PLEASE LOOK AT THE MAN WHO WANTS TO MAKE HIMSELF A HERO BY SACRIFICING A HUMAN LIFE!
ARE YOU LISTENING TO THE GIRL, MAX? I WILL SEND HER TO YOU IN PIECES IF YOU DON'T DO AS I SAY!
I WILL TURN HER INTO A DAMN HAND PUPPET AND THAT WILL BE ON YOUR NEW CONSCIENCE!

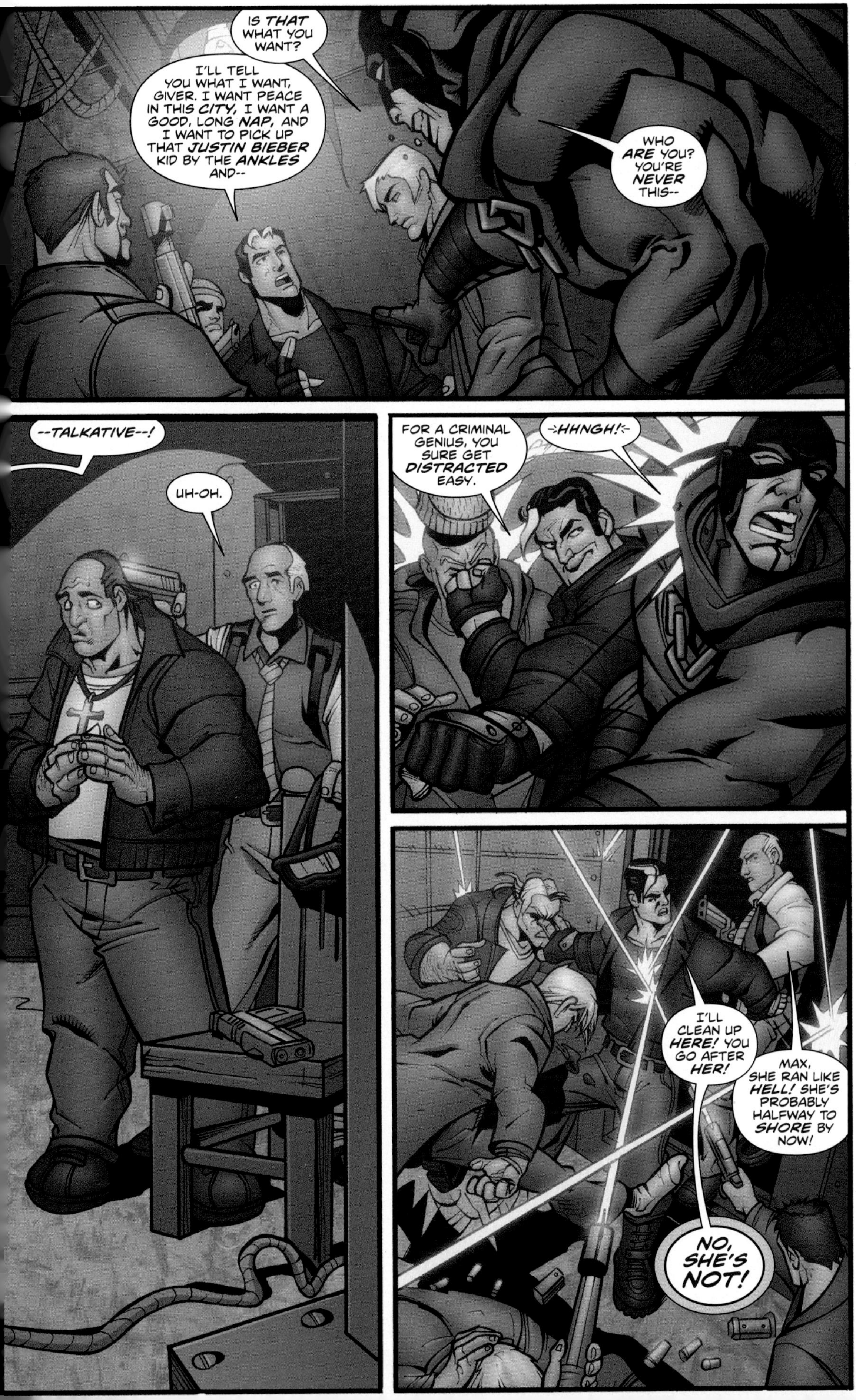
IS THAT WHAT YOU WANT?
I'LL TELL YOU WHAT I WANT, GIVER. I WANT PEACE IN THIS CITY, I WANT A GOOD, LONG NAP, AND I WANT TO PICK UP THAT JUSTIN BIEBER KID BY THE ANKLES AND--
WHO ARE YOU? YOU'RE NEVER THIS--
--TALKATIVE--!
UH-OH.
FOR A CRIMINAL GENIUS, YOU SURE GET DISTRACTED EASY.
HHNGH!
I'LL CLEAN UP HERE! YOU GO AFTER HER!
MAX, SHE RAN LIKE HELL! SHE'S PROBABLY HALFWAY TO SHORE BY NOW!
NO, SHE'S NOT!

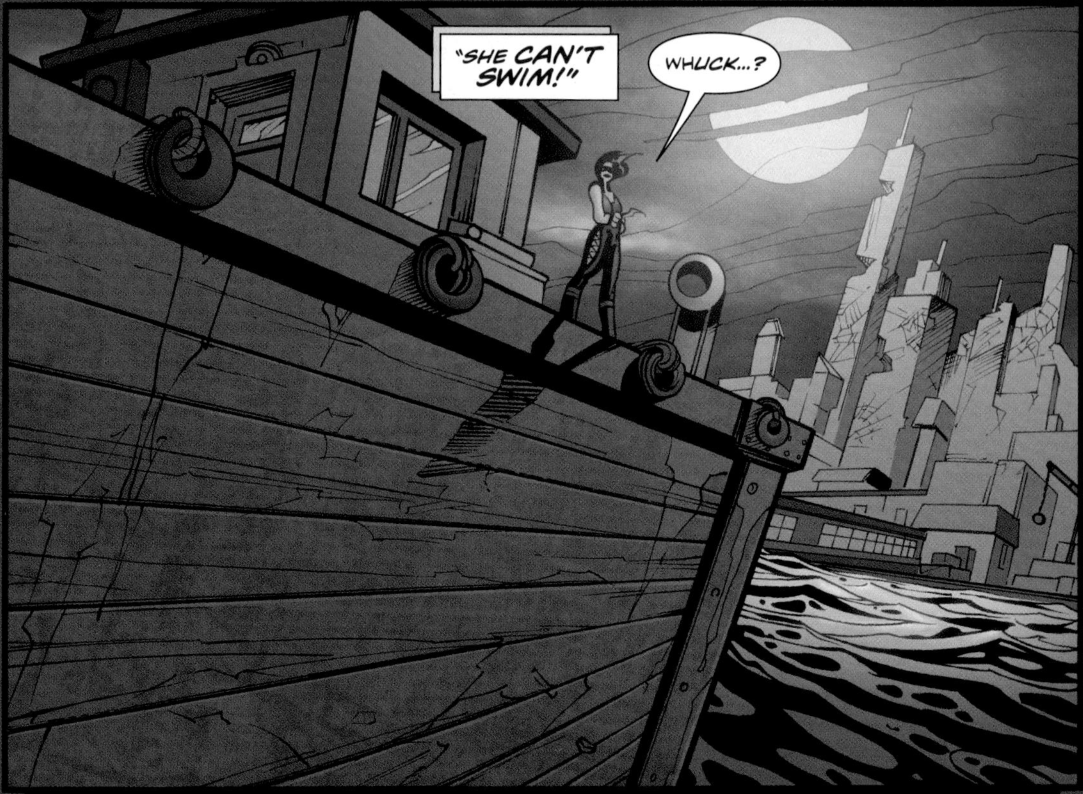
"SHE CAN'T SWIM!"
WHUCK...?

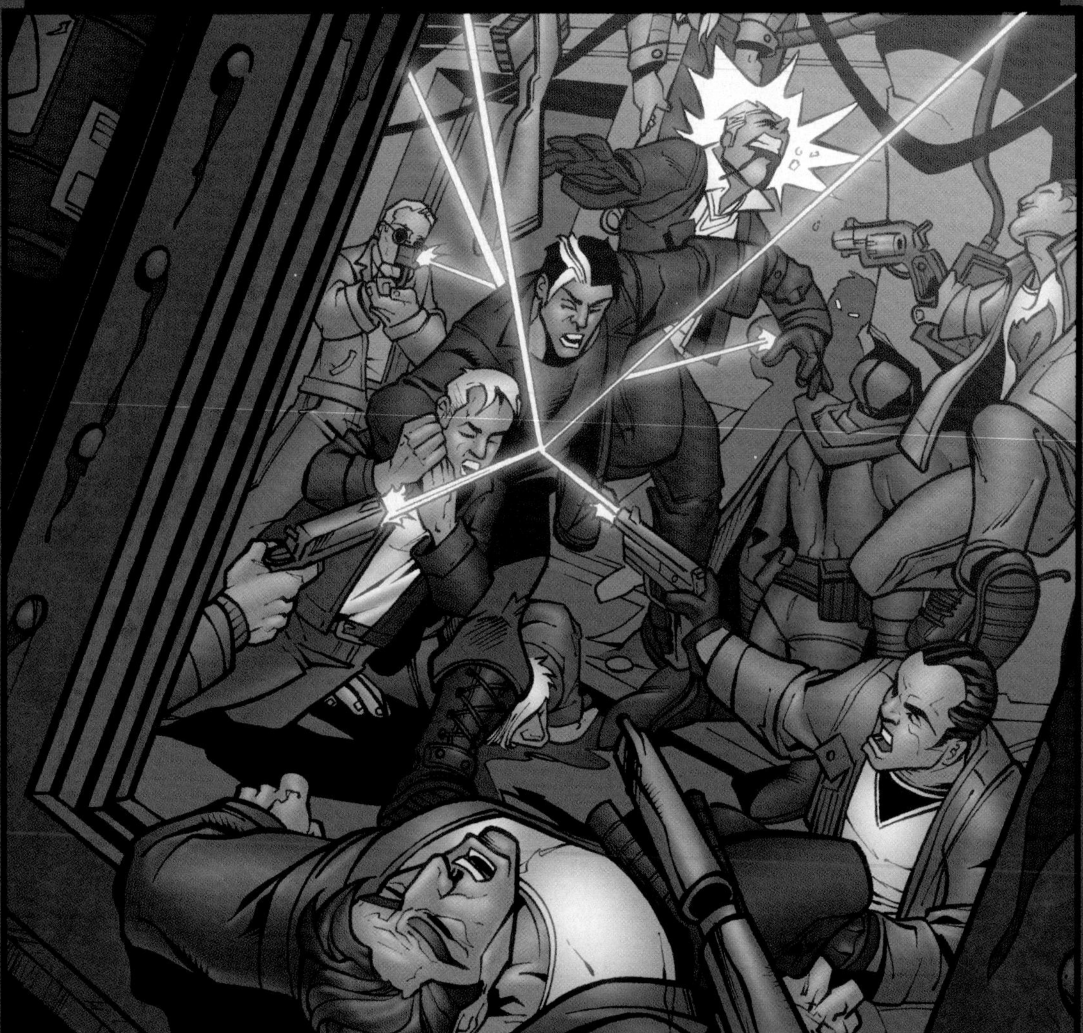

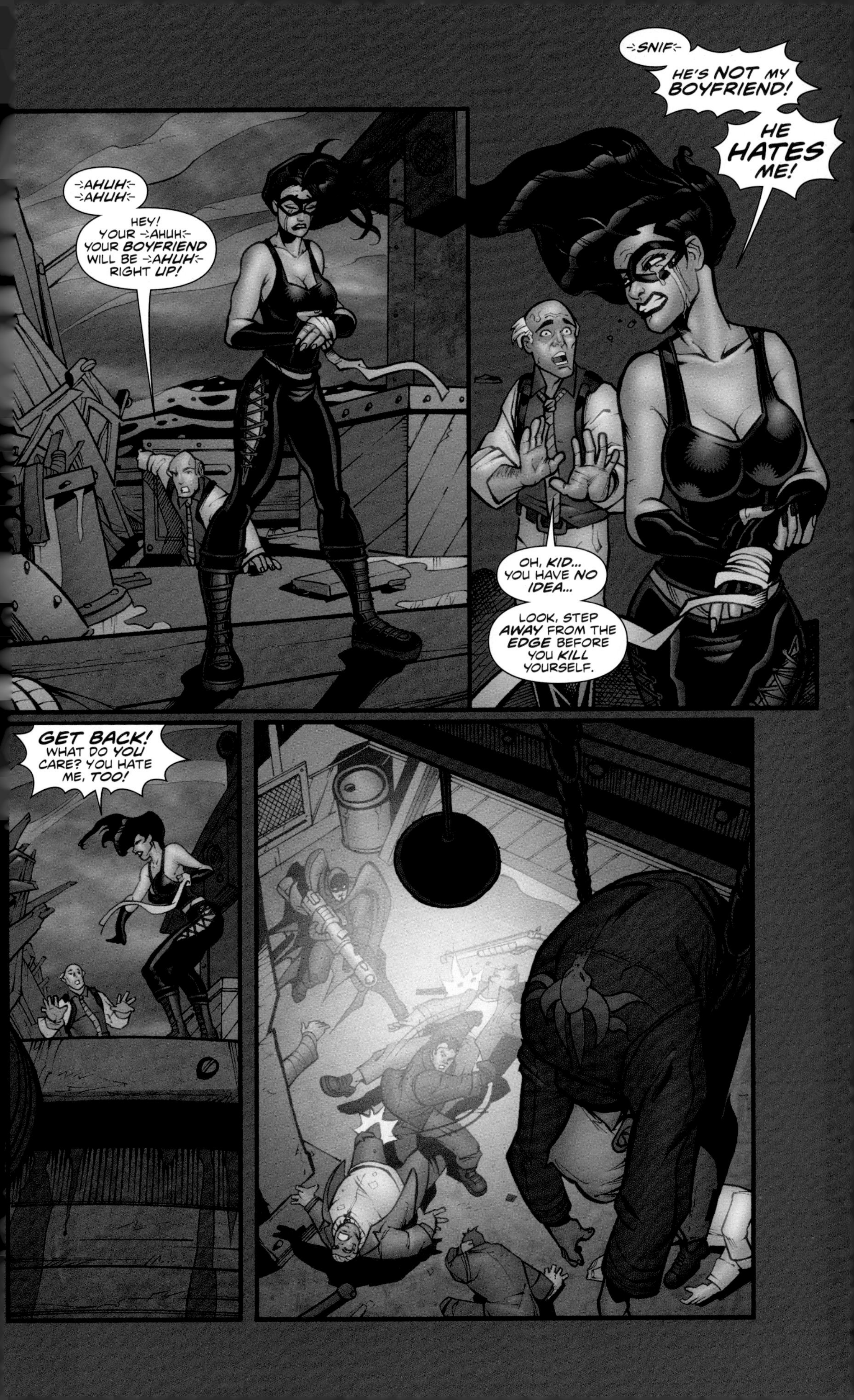

-AHUH-
-AHUH-
HEY! YOUR -AHUH- YOUR BOYFRIEND WILL BE -AHUH- RIGHT UP!
-SNIF-
HE'S NOT MY BOYFRIEND!
HE HATES ME!
OH, KID... YOU HAVE NO IDEA...
LOOK, STEP AWAY FROM THE EDGE BEFORE YOU KILL YOURSELF.
GET BACK! WHAT DO YOU CARE? YOU HATE ME, TOO!

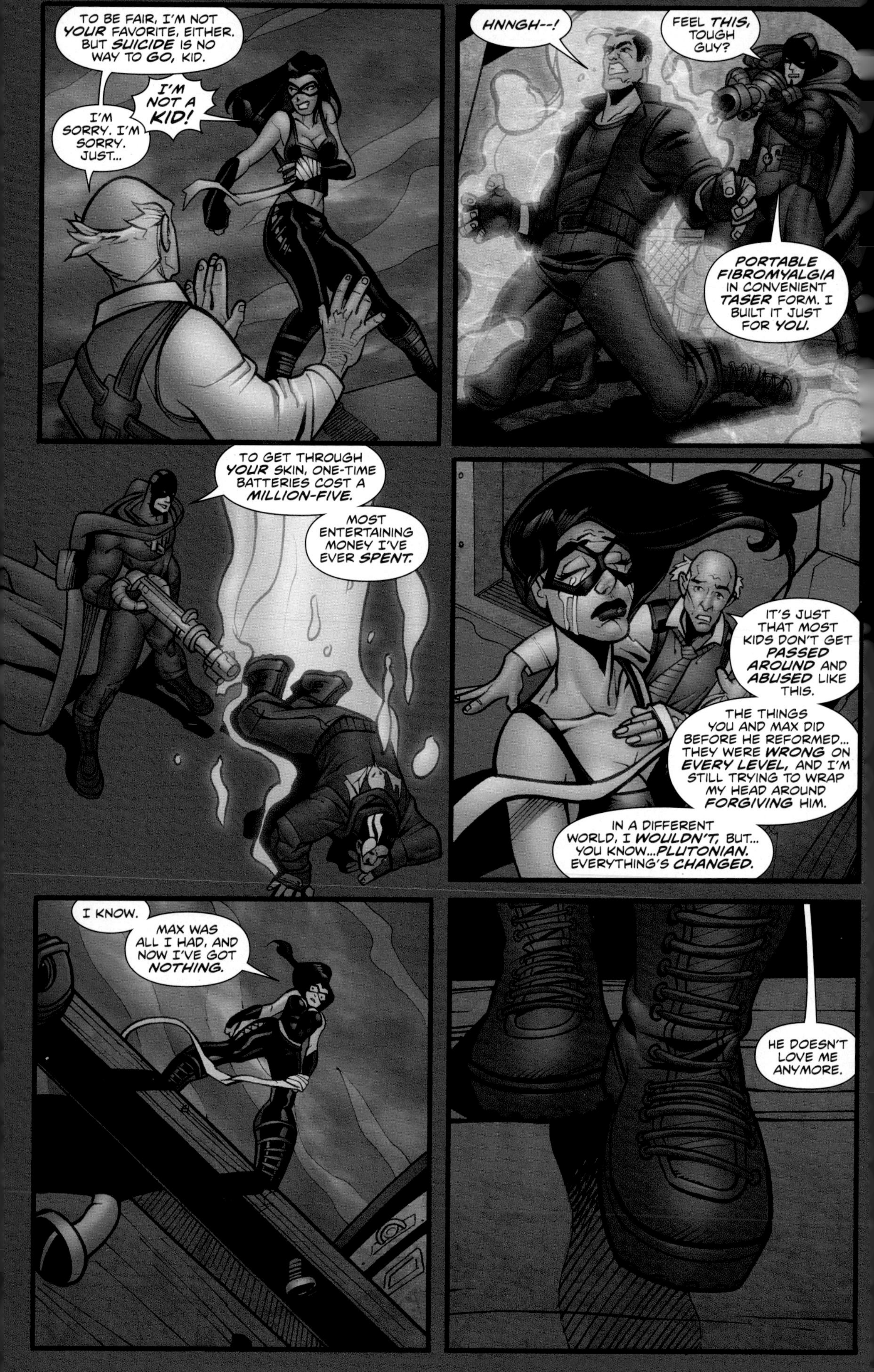

TO BE FAIR, I'M NOT YOUR FAVORITE, EITHER. BUT SUICIDE IS NO WAY TO GO, KID.
I'M NOT A KID!
I'M SORRY. I'M SORRY. JUST...
HNNGH--!
FEEL THIS, TOUGH GUY?
PORTABLE FIBROMYALGIA IN CONVENIENT TASER FORM. I BUILT IT JUST FOR YOU.
TO GET THROUGH YOUR SKIN, ONE-TIME BATTERIES COST A MILLION-FIVE.
MOST ENTERTAINING MONEY I'VE EVER SPENT.
IT'S JUST THAT MOST KIDS DON'T GET PASSED AROUND AND ABUSED LIKE THIS.
THE THINGS YOU AND MAX DID BEFORE HE REFORMED... THEY WERE WRONG ON EVERY LEVEL, AND I'M STILL TRYING TO WRAP MY HEAD AROUND FORGIVING HIM.
IN A DIFFERENT WORLD, I WOULDN'T, BUT... YOU KNOW...PLUTONIAN. EVERYTHING'S CHANGED.
I KNOW.
MAX WAS ALL I HAD, AND NOW I'VE GOT NOTHING.
HE DOESN'T LOVE ME ANYMORE.

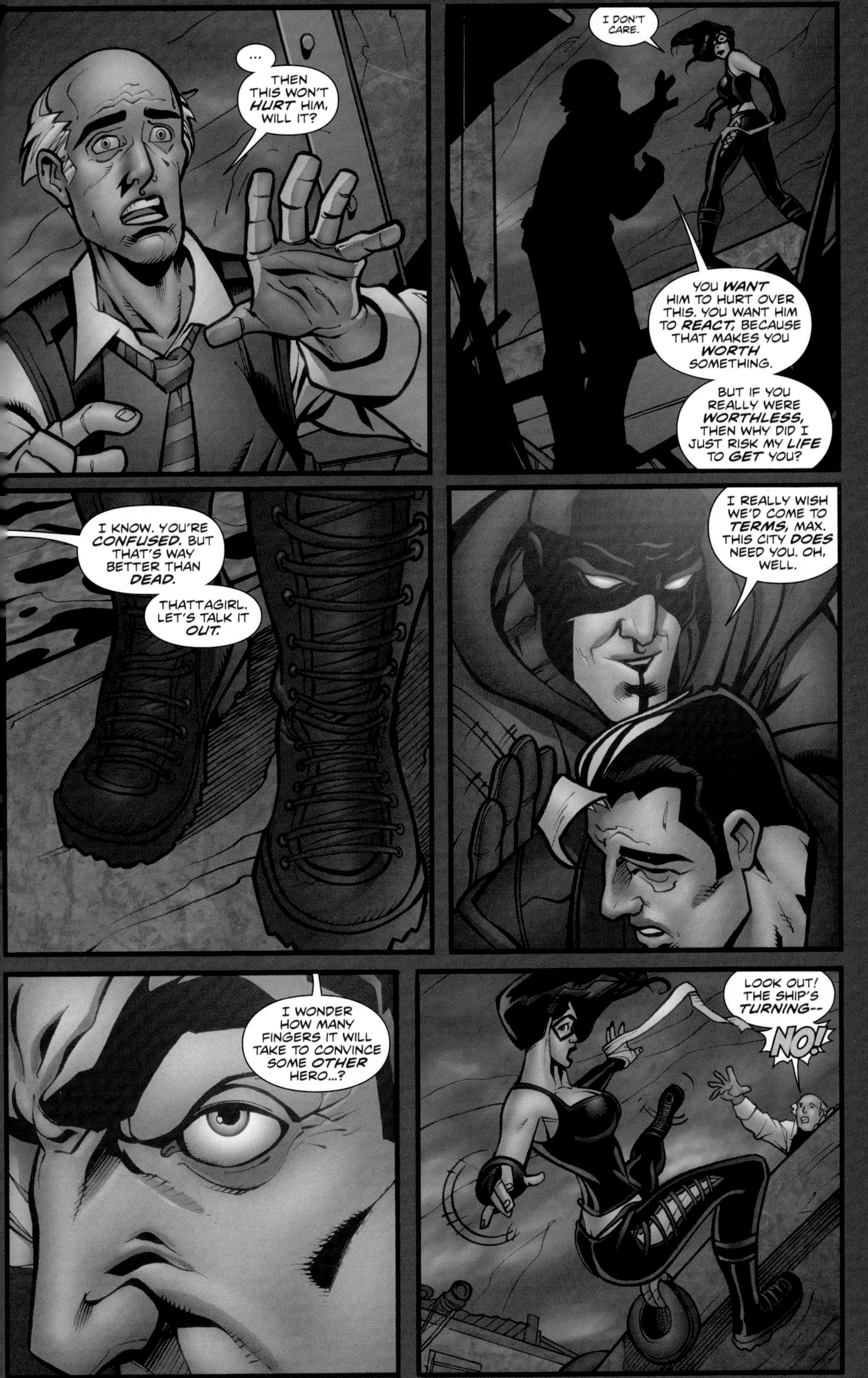
...
THEN THIS WON'T HURT HIM, WILL IT?
I DON'T CARE.
YOU WANT HIM TO HURT OVER THIS. YOU WANT HIM TO REACT, BECAUSE THAT MAKES YOU WORTH SOMETHING.
BUT IF YOU REALLY WERE WORTHLESS, THEN WHY DID I JUST RISK MY LIFE TO GET YOU?
I KNOW. YOU'RE CONFUSED. BUT THAT'S WAY BETTER THAN DEAD.
THATTAGIRL. LET'S TALK IT OUT.
I REALLY WISH WE'D COME TO TERMS, MAX. THIS CITY DOES NEED YOU. OH, WELL.
I WONDER HOW MANY FINGERS IT WILL TAKE TO CONVINCE SOME OTHER HERO...?
LOOK OUT! THE SHIP'S TURNING--
NO!

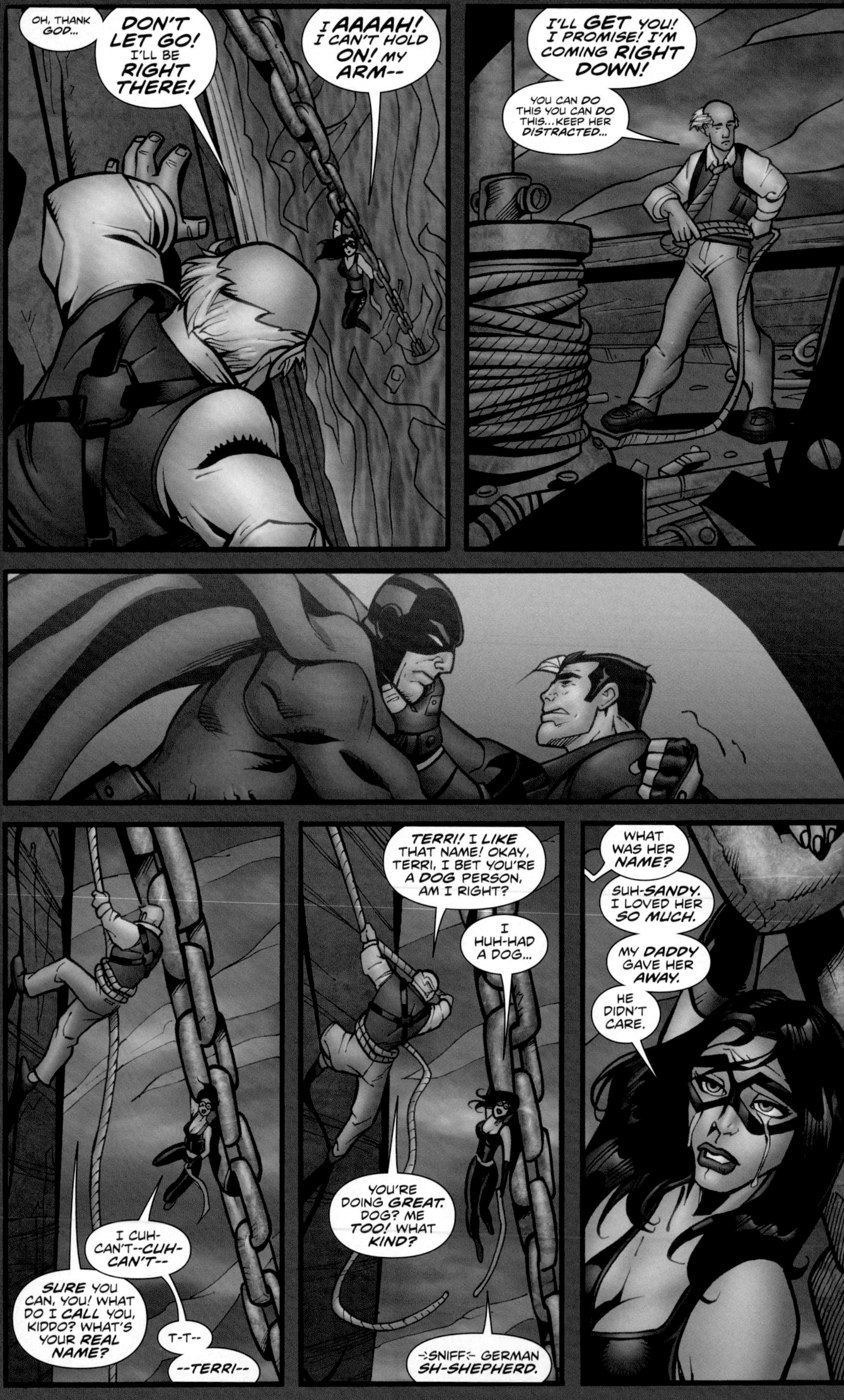
OH, THANK GOD...
DON'T LET GO! I'LL BE RIGHT THERE!
I AAAAH! I CAN'T HOLD ON! MY ARM--
I'LL GET YOU! I PROMISE! I'M COMING RIGHT DOWN!
YOU CAN DO THIS YOU CAN DO THIS...KEEP HER DISTRACTED...
I CUH-CAN'T--CUH-CAN'T--
SURE YOU CAN, YOU! WHAT DO I CALL YOU, KIDDO? WHAT'S YOUR REAL NAME?
T-T--
--TERRI--
TERRI! I LIKE THAT NAME! OKAY, TERRI, I BET YOU'RE A DOG PERSON, AM I RIGHT?
I HUH-HAD A DOG...
YOU'RE DOING GREAT. DOG? ME TOO! WHAT KIND?
-SNIFF- GERMAN SH-SHEPHERD.
WHAT WAS HER NAME?
SUH-SANDY. I LOVED HER SO MUCH.
MY DADDY GAVE HER AWAY.
HE DIDN'T CARE.

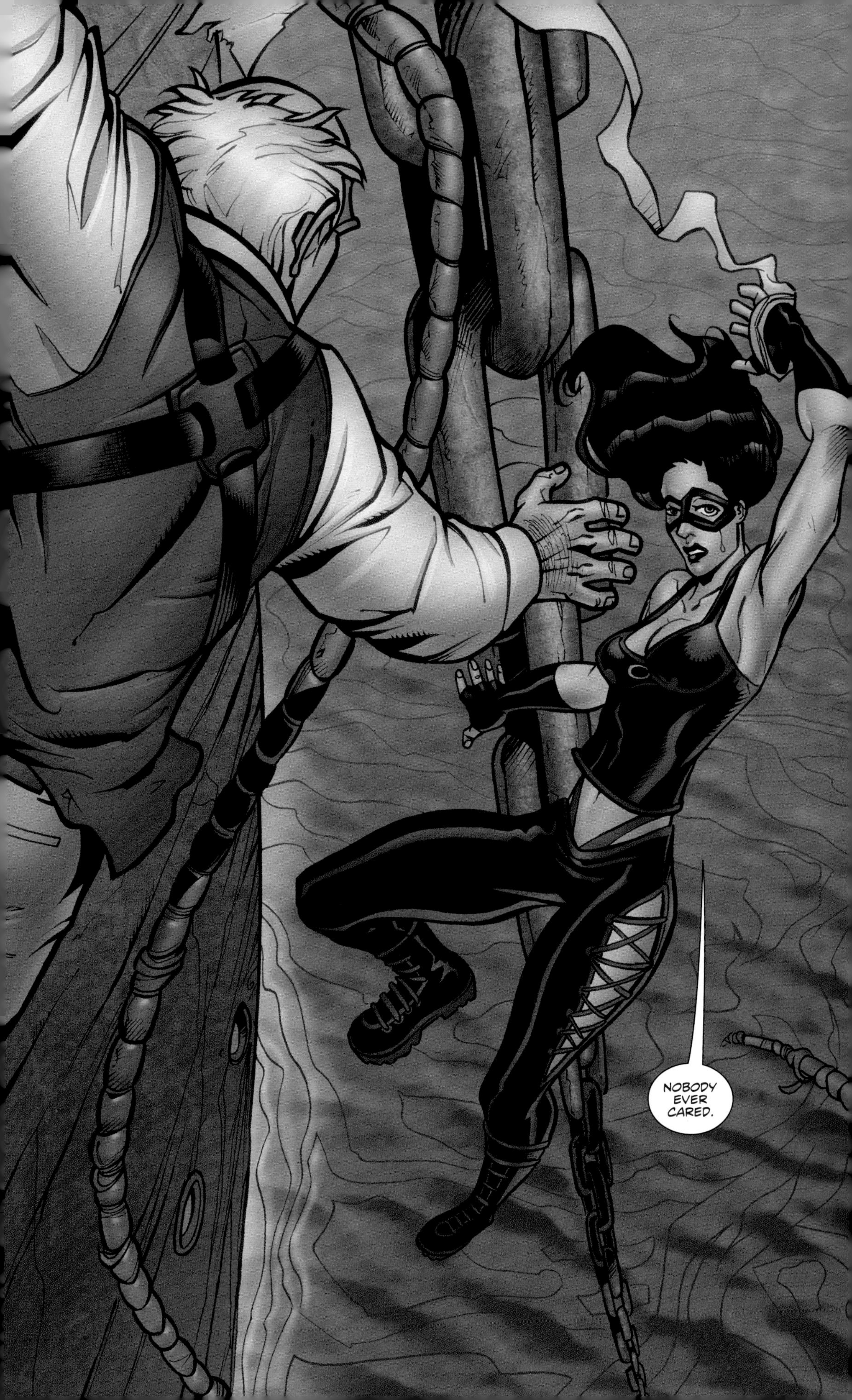
NOBODY EVER CARED.

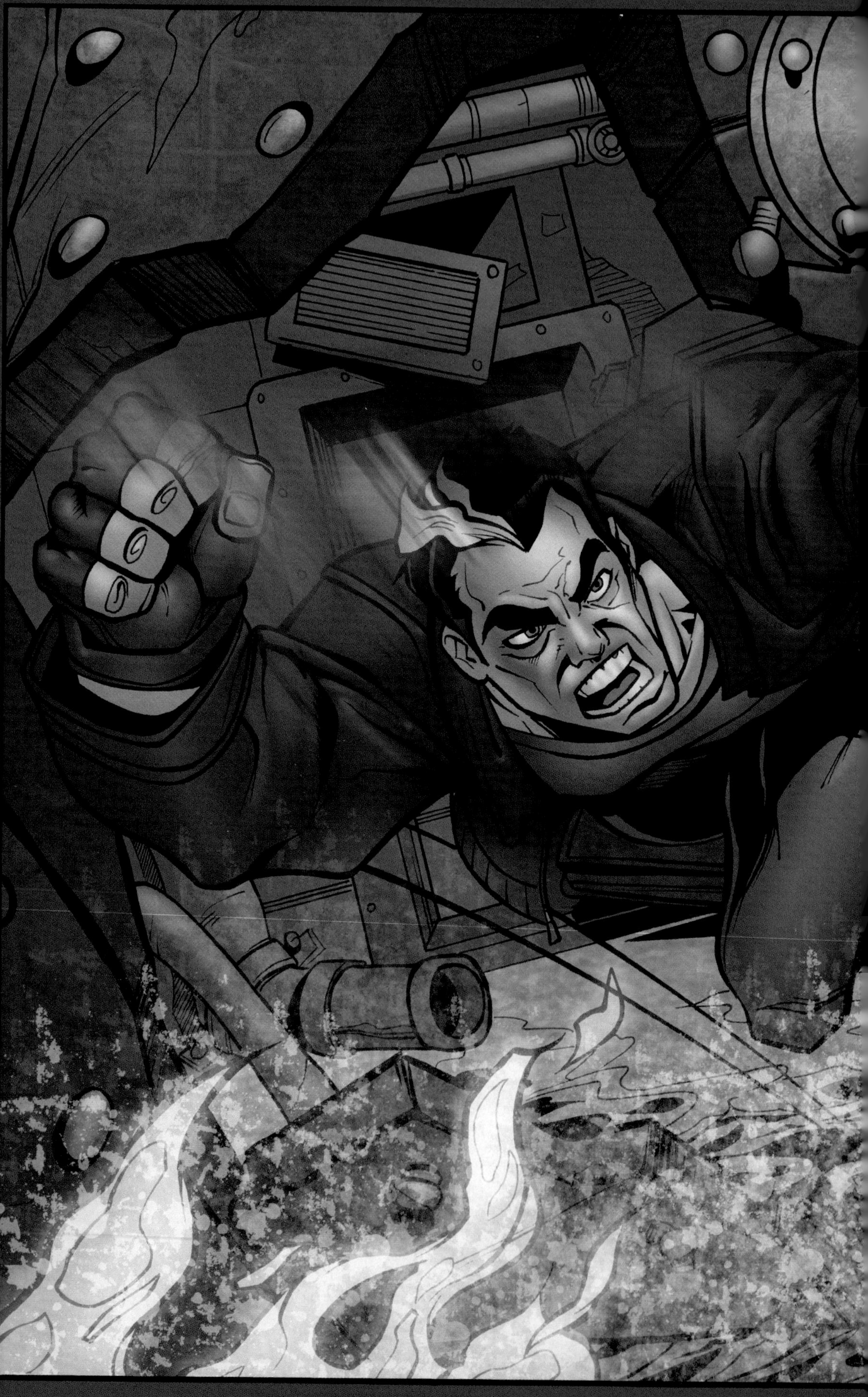

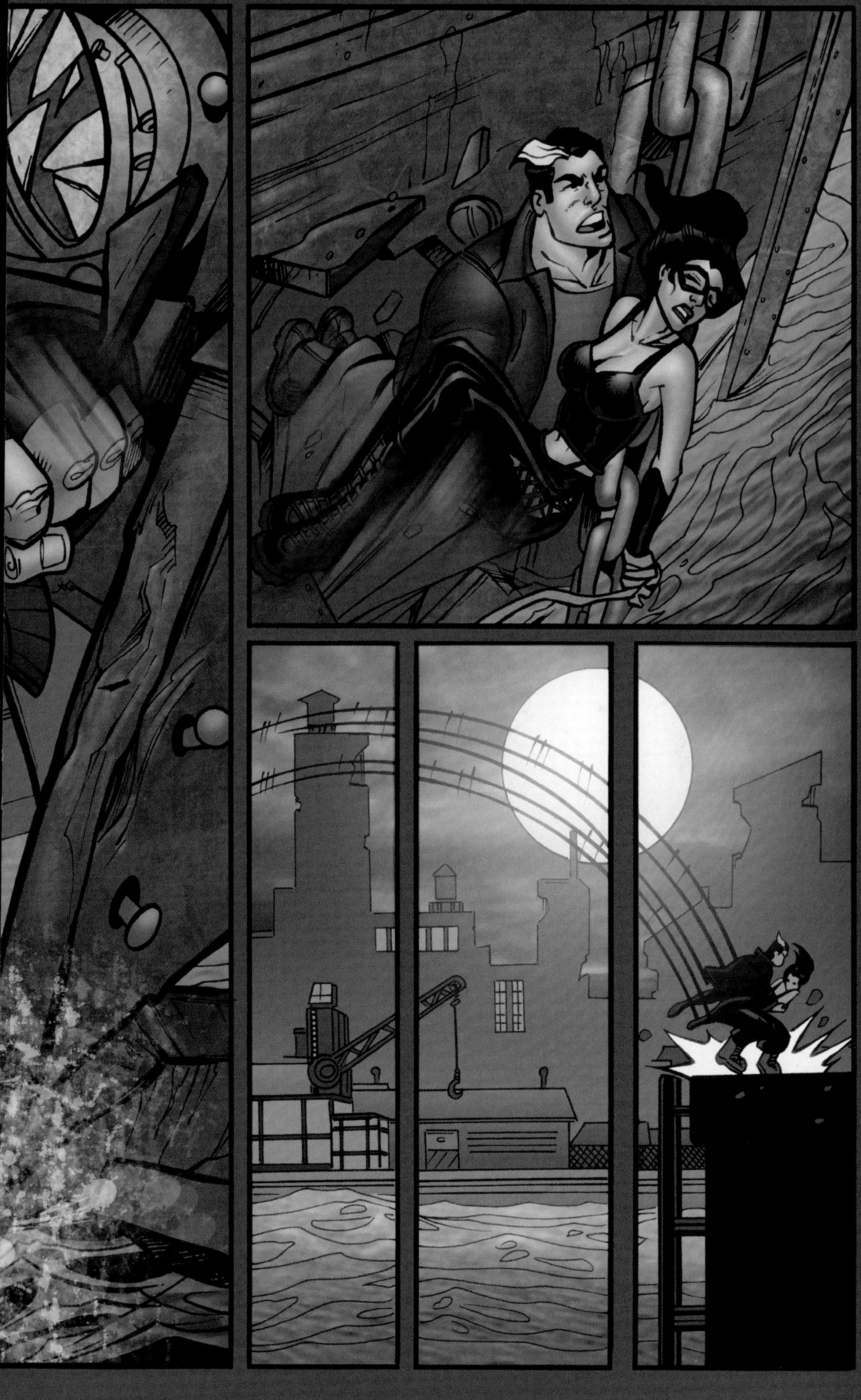

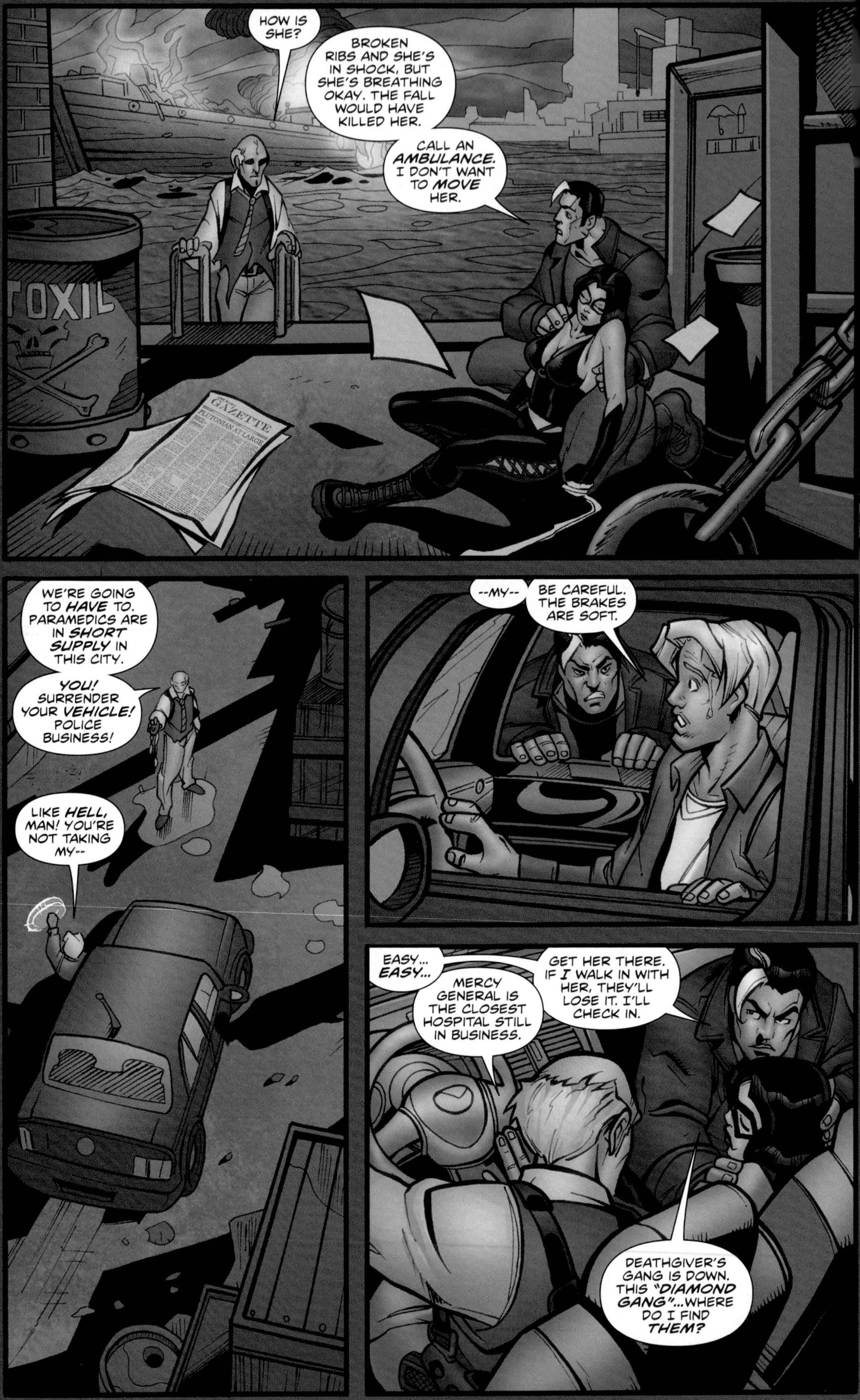
HOW IS SHE?
BROKEN RIBS AND SHE'S IN SHOCK, BUT SHE'S BREATHING OKAY. THE FALL WOULD HAVE KILLED HER.
CALL AN AMBULANCE. I DON'T WANT TO MOVE HER.
TOXIL
GAZETTE
PLUTONIAN AT LARGE
WE'RE GOING TO HAVE TO. PARAMEDICS ARE IN SHORT SUPPLY IN THIS CITY.
YOU! SURRENDER YOUR VEHICLE! POLICE BUSINESS!
LIKE HELL, MAN! YOU'RE NOT TAKING MY--
--MY--
BE CAREFUL. THE BRAKES ARE SOFT.
EASY... EASY...
MERCY GENERAL IS THE CLOSEST HOSPITAL STILL IN BUSINESS.
GET HER THERE. IF I WALK IN WITH HER, THEY'LL LOSE IT. I'LL CHECK IN.
DEATHGIVER'S GANG IS DOWN. THIS "DIAMOND GANG"...WHERE DO I FIND THEM?

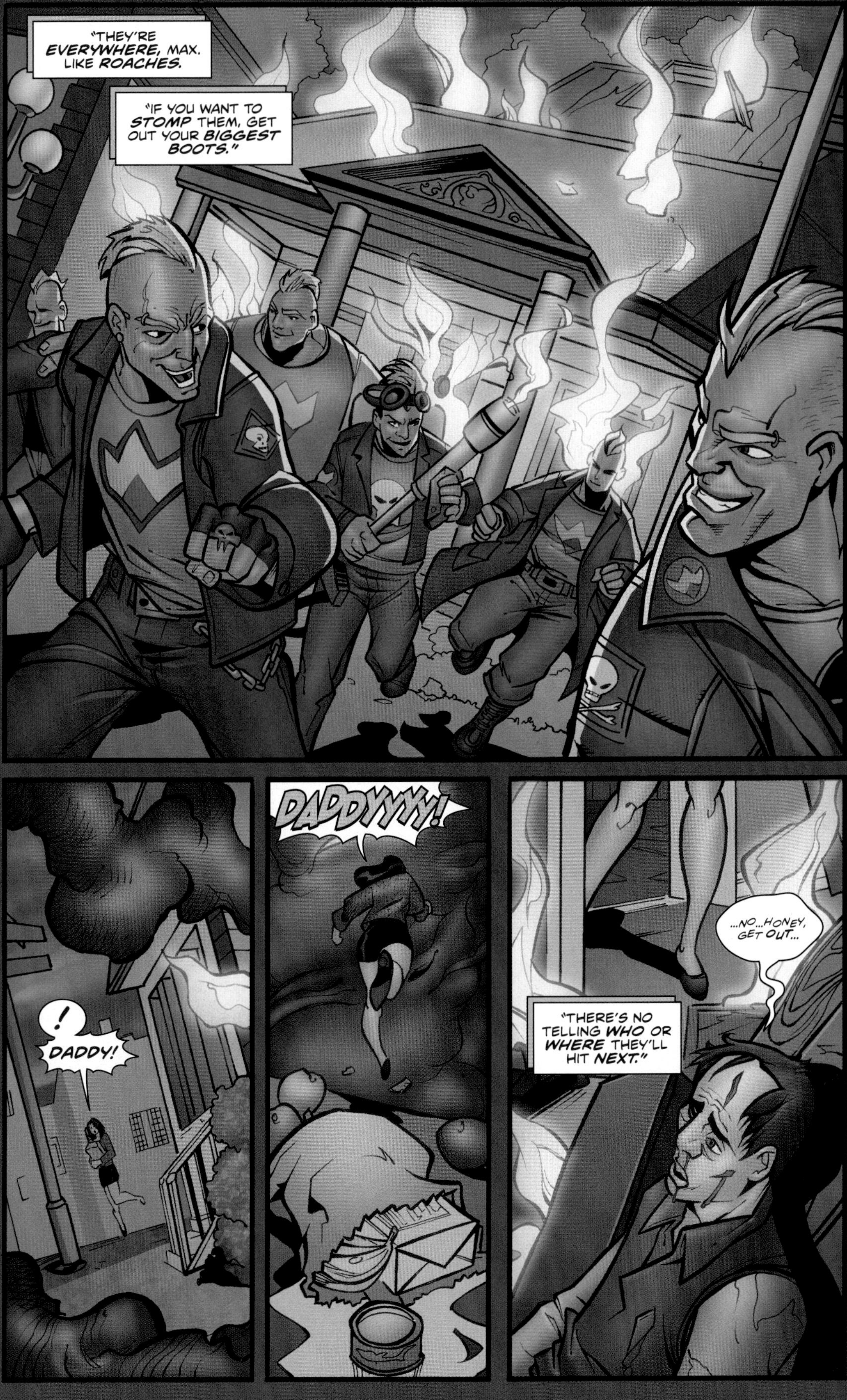
"THEY'RE EVERYWHERE, MAX. LIKE ROACHES.
"IF YOU WANT TO STOMP THEM, GET OUT YOUR BIGGEST BOOTS."
!
DADDY!
DADDYYYY!
...NO...HONEY, GET OUT...
"THERE'S NO TELLING WHO OR WHERE THEY'LL HIT NEXT."

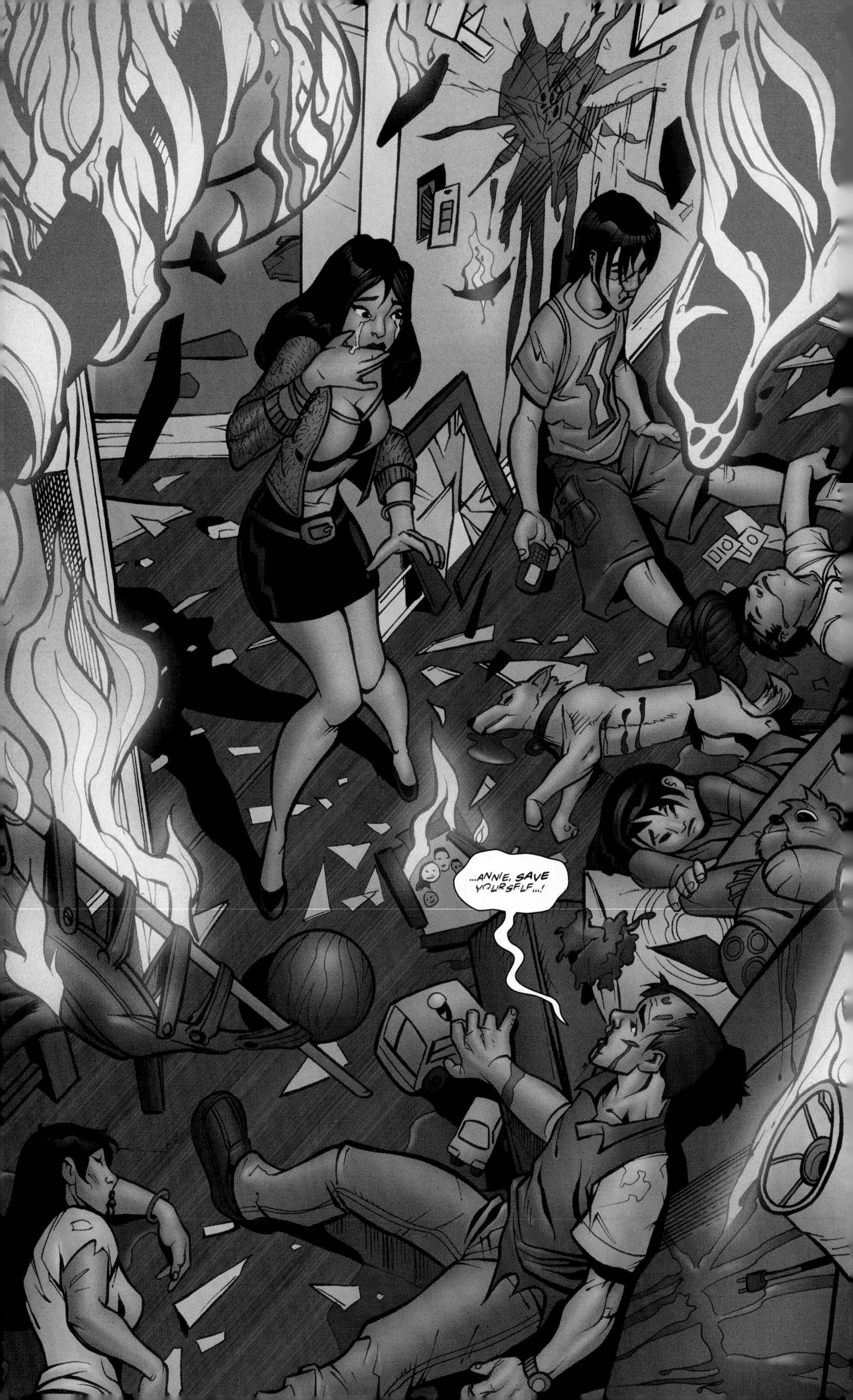
...ANNIE, SAVE YOURSELF...!

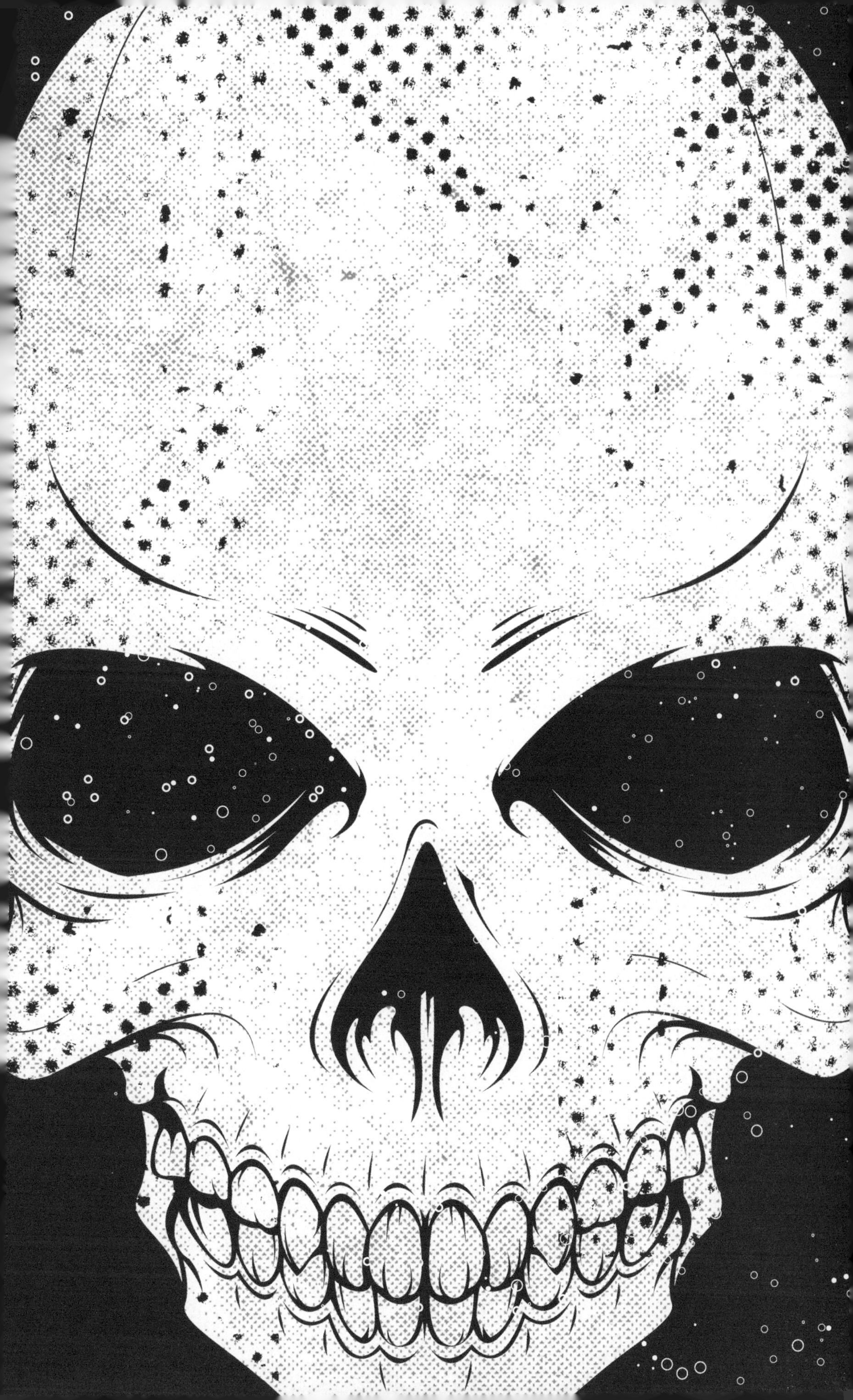

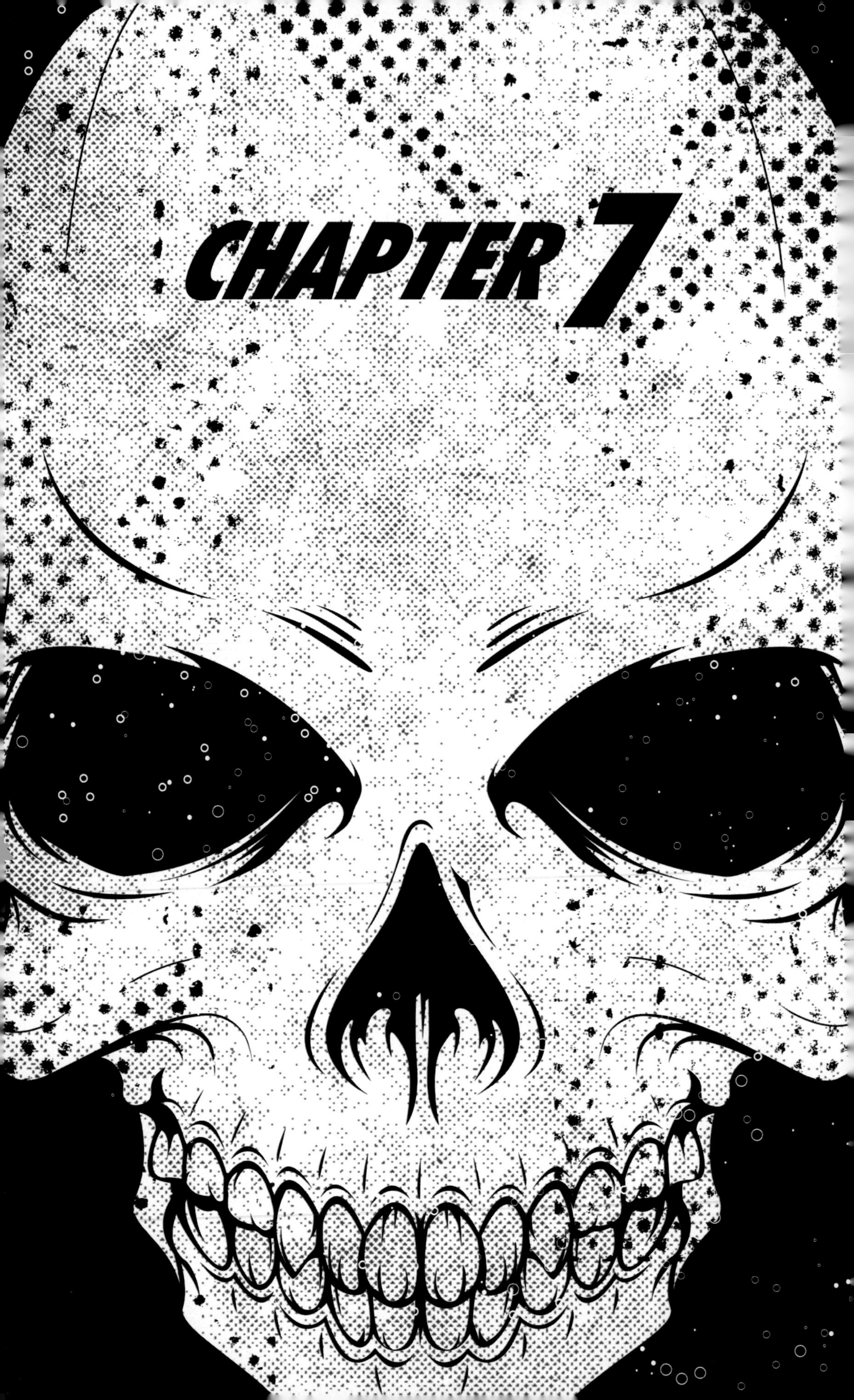
CHAPTER 7

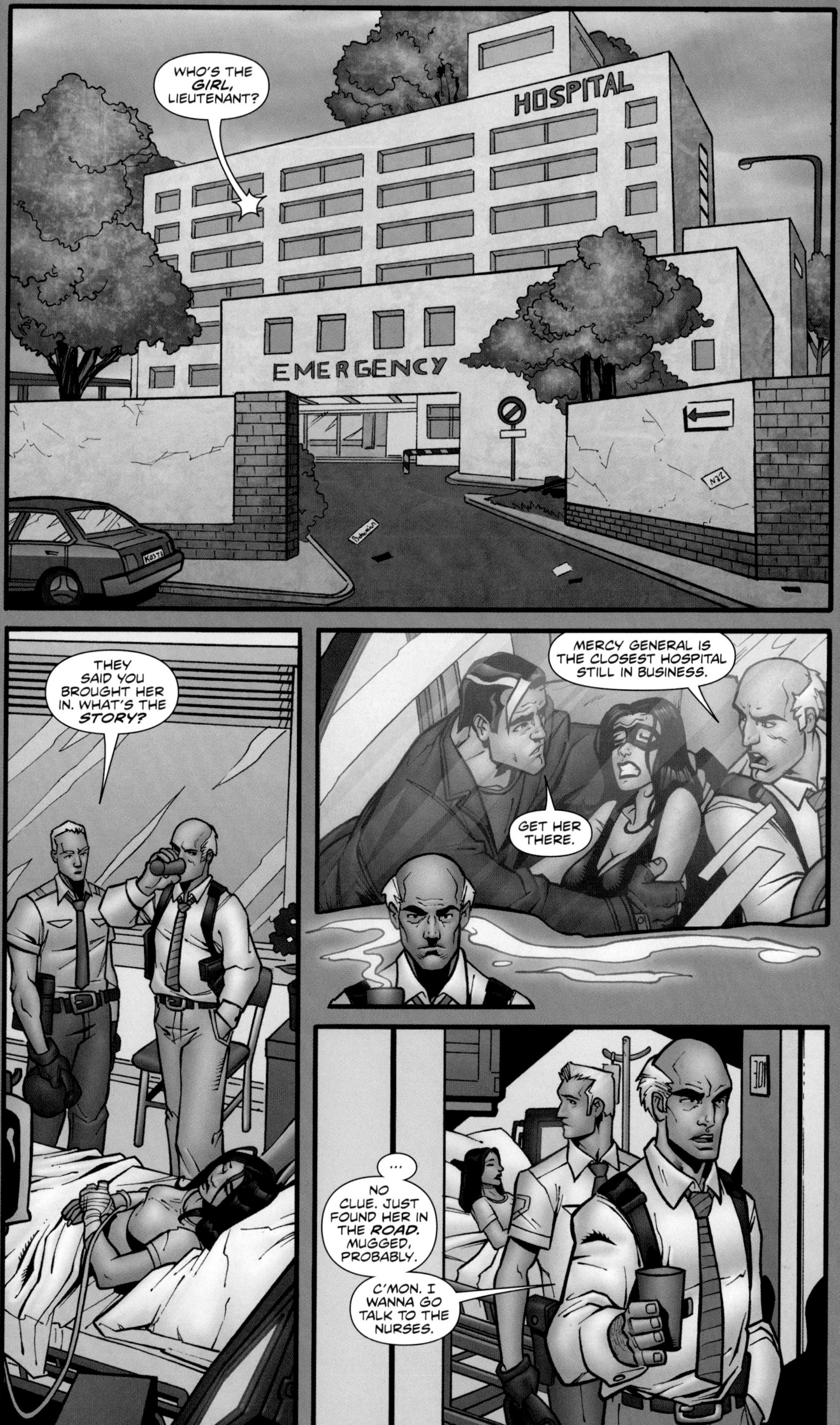
HOSPITAL
WHO'S THE *GIRL,* LIEUTENANT?
EMERGENCY
THEY SAID YOU BROUGHT HER IN. WHAT'S THE *STORY?*
MERCY GENERAL IS THE CLOSEST HOSPITAL STILL IN BUSINESS.
GET HER THERE.
...
NO CLUE. JUST FOUND HER IN THE *ROAD.* MUGGED, PROBABLY.
C'MON. I WANNA GO TALK TO THE NURSES.

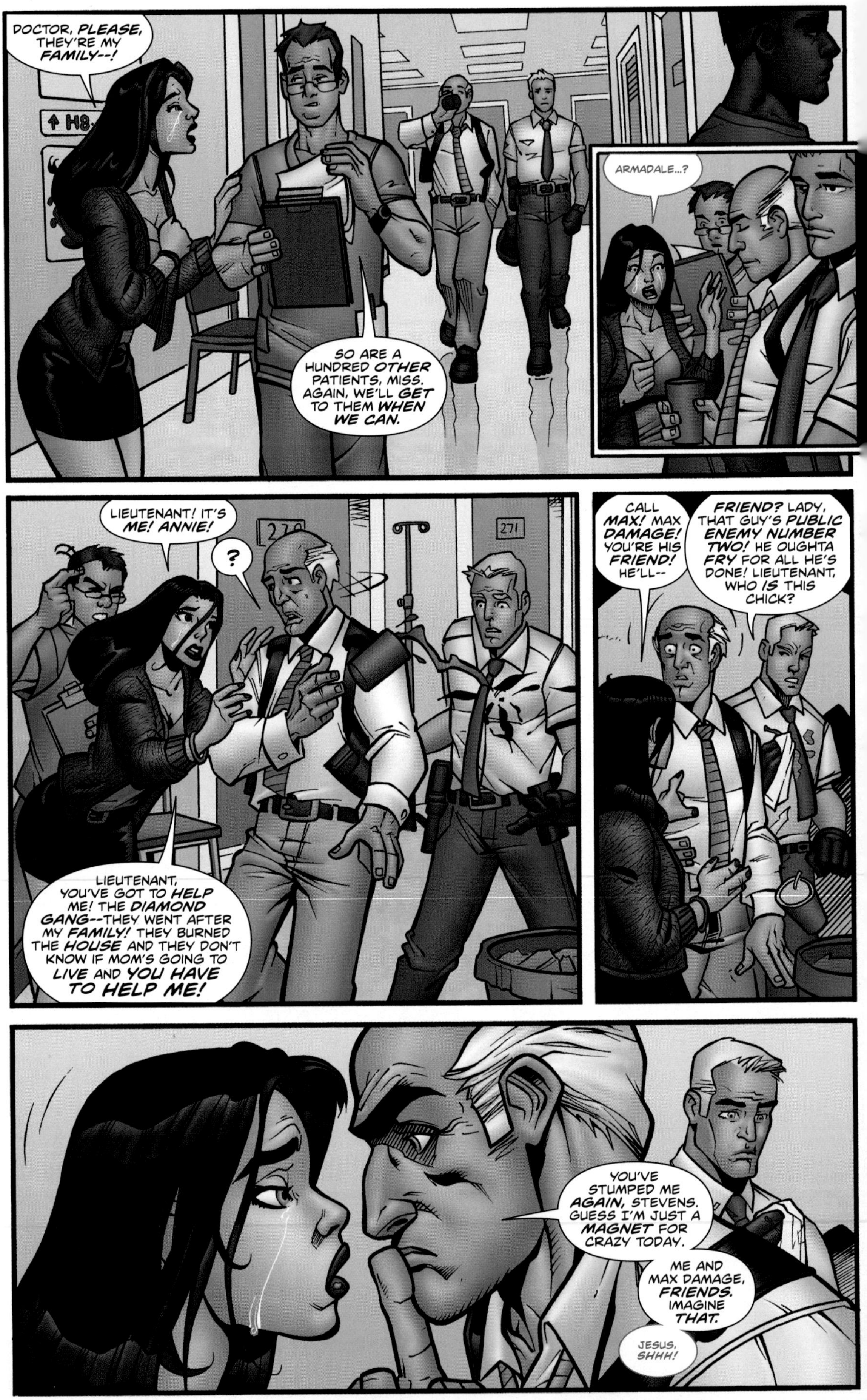

DOCTOR, PLEASE, THEY'RE MY FAMILY--!
SO ARE A HUNDRED OTHER PATIENTS, MISS. AGAIN, WE'LL GET TO THEM WHEN WE CAN.
ARMADALE...?
LIEUTENANT! IT'S ME! ANNIE!
?
LIEUTENANT, YOU'VE GOT TO HELP ME! THE DIAMOND GANG--THEY WENT AFTER MY FAMILY! THEY BURNED THE HOUSE AND THEY DON'T KNOW IF MOM'S GOING TO LIVE AND YOU HAVE TO HELP ME!
CALL MAX! MAX DAMAGE! YOU'RE HIS FRIEND! HE'LL--
FRIEND? LADY, THAT GUY'S PUBLIC ENEMY NUMBER TWO! HE OUGHTA FRY FOR ALL HE'S DONE! LIEUTENANT, WHO IS THIS CHICK?
YOU'VE STUMPED ME AGAIN, STEVENS. GUESS I'M JUST A MAGNET FOR CRAZY TODAY.
ME AND MAX DAMAGE, FRIENDS. IMAGINE THAT.
JESUS, SHHH!

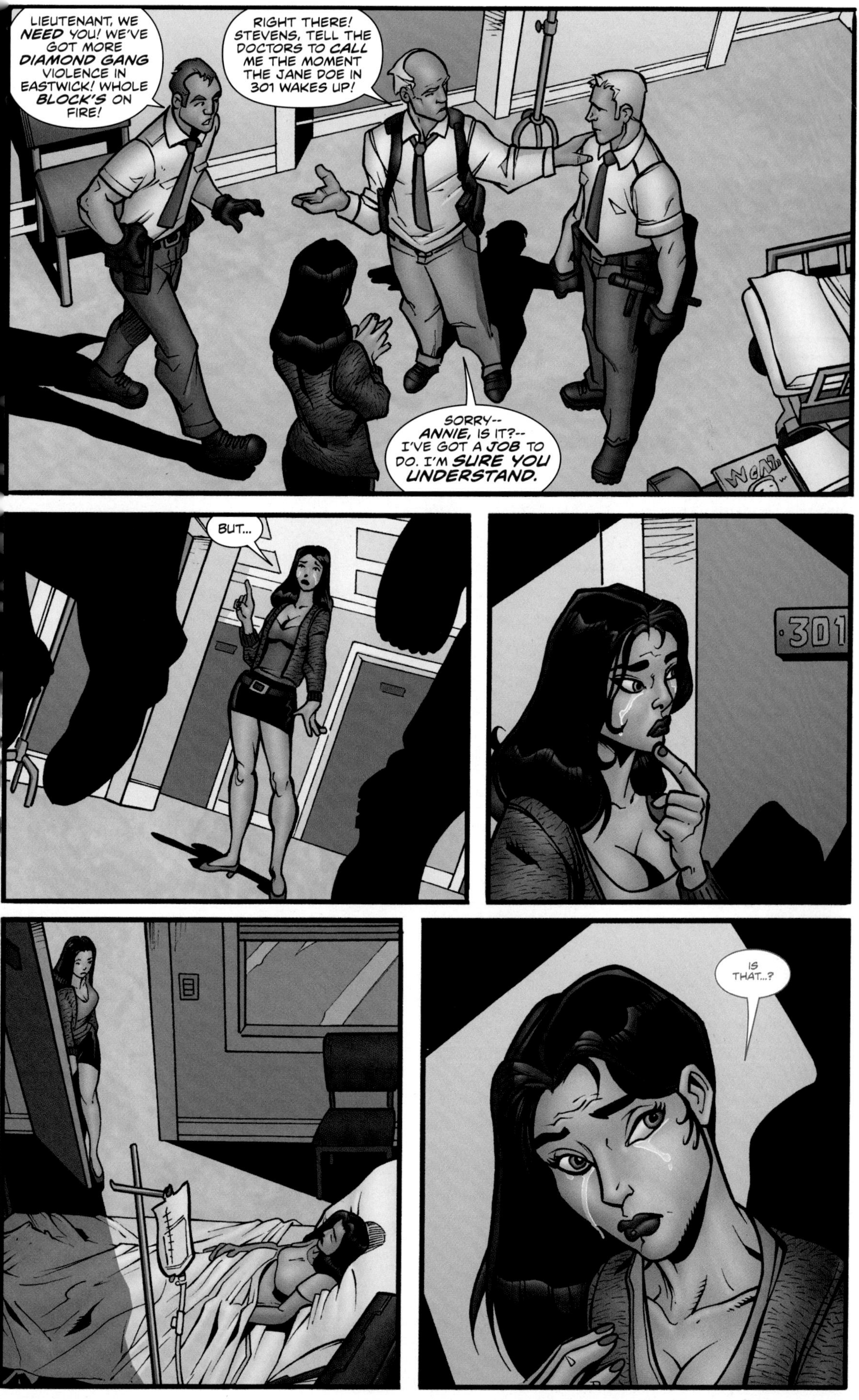
LIEUTENANT, WE NEED YOU! WE'VE GOT MORE DIAMOND GANG VIOLENCE IN EASTWICK! WHOLE BLOCK'S ON FIRE!
RIGHT THERE! STEVENS, TELL THE DOCTORS TO CALL ME THE MOMENT THE JANE DOE IN 301 WAKES UP!
SORRY-- ANNIE, IS IT?-- I'VE GOT A JOB TO DO. I'M SURE YOU UNDERSTAND.
BUT...
301
IS THAT...?

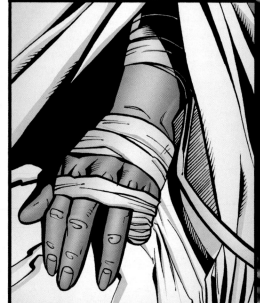

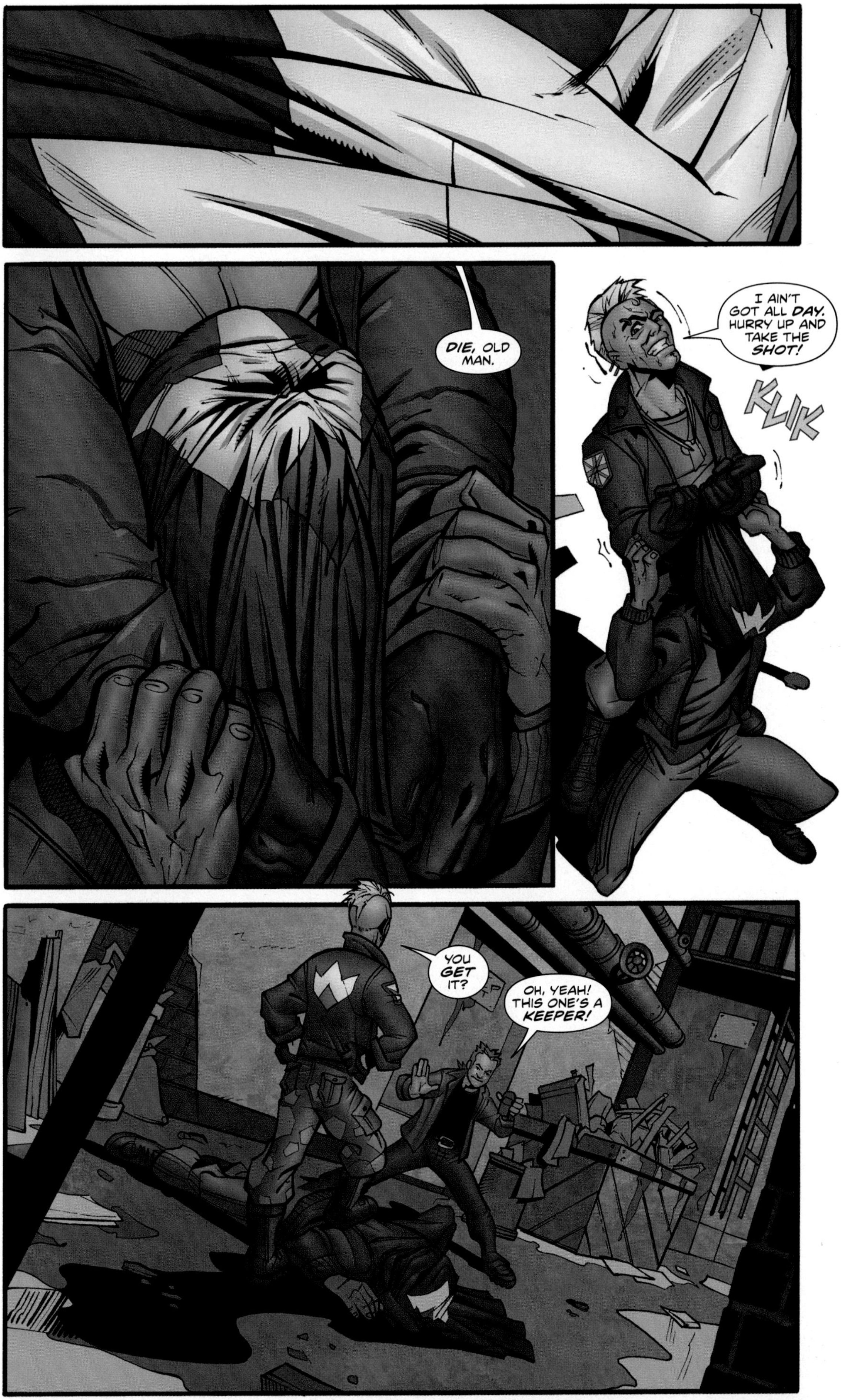
DIE, OLD MAN.
I AIN'T GOT ALL DAY. HURRY UP AND TAKE THE SHOT!
KLIK
YOU GET IT?
OH, YEAH! THIS ONE'S A KEEPER!

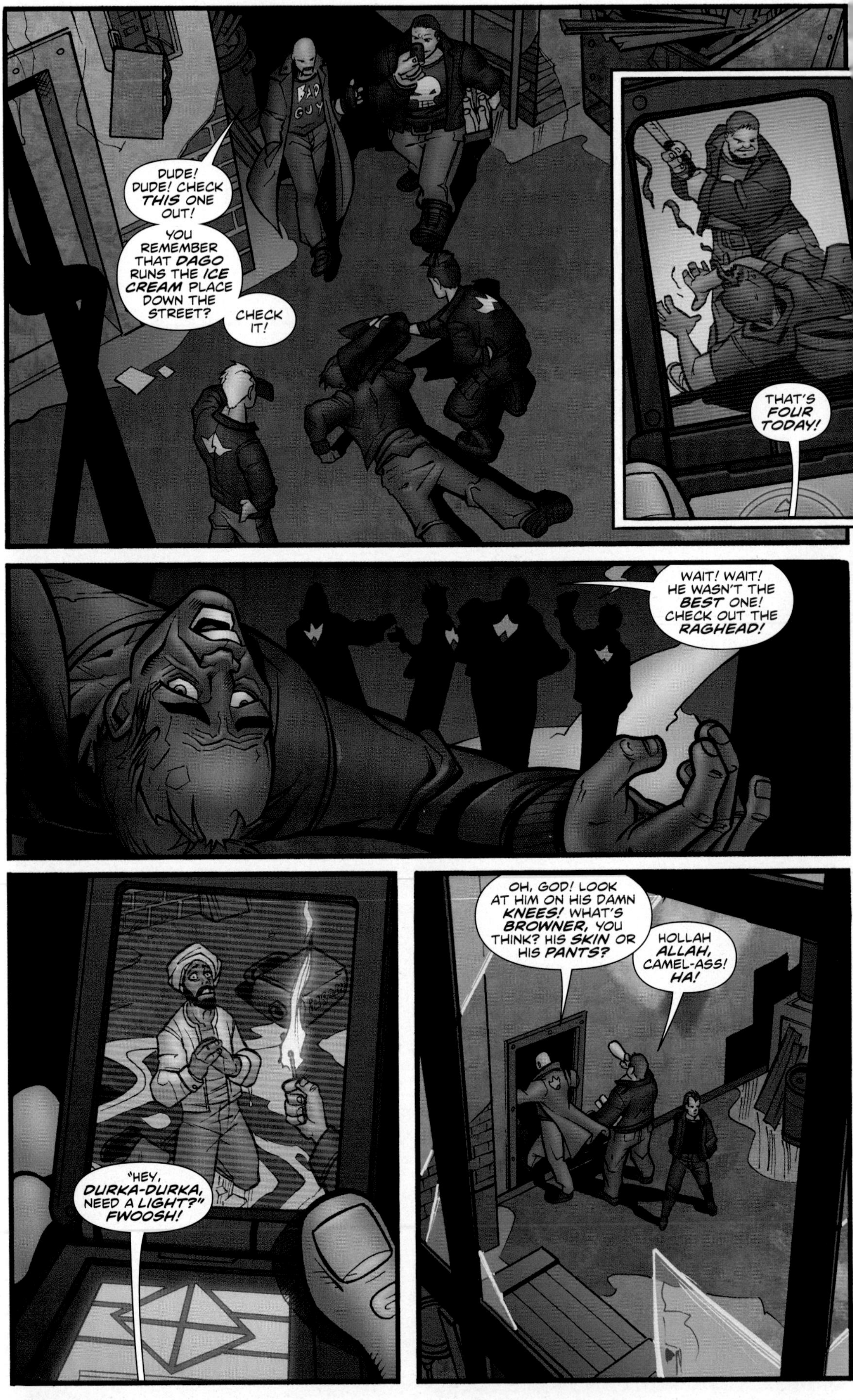
BAD GUY
DUDE! DUDE! CHECK *THIS* ONE OUT!
YOU REMEMBER THAT *DAGO* RUNS THE *ICE CREAM* PLACE DOWN THE STREET?
CHECK IT!
THAT'S *FOUR TODAY!*
WAIT! WAIT! HE WASN'T THE *BEST* ONE! CHECK OUT THE *RAGHEAD!*
"HEY, *DURKA-DURKA,* NEED A *LIGHT?*" *FWOOSH!*
OH, GOD! LOOK AT HIM ON HIS DAMN *KNEES!* WHAT'S *BROWNER,* YOU THINK? HIS *SKIN* OR HIS *PANTS?*
HOLLAH *ALLAH,* CAMEL-ASS! *HA!*

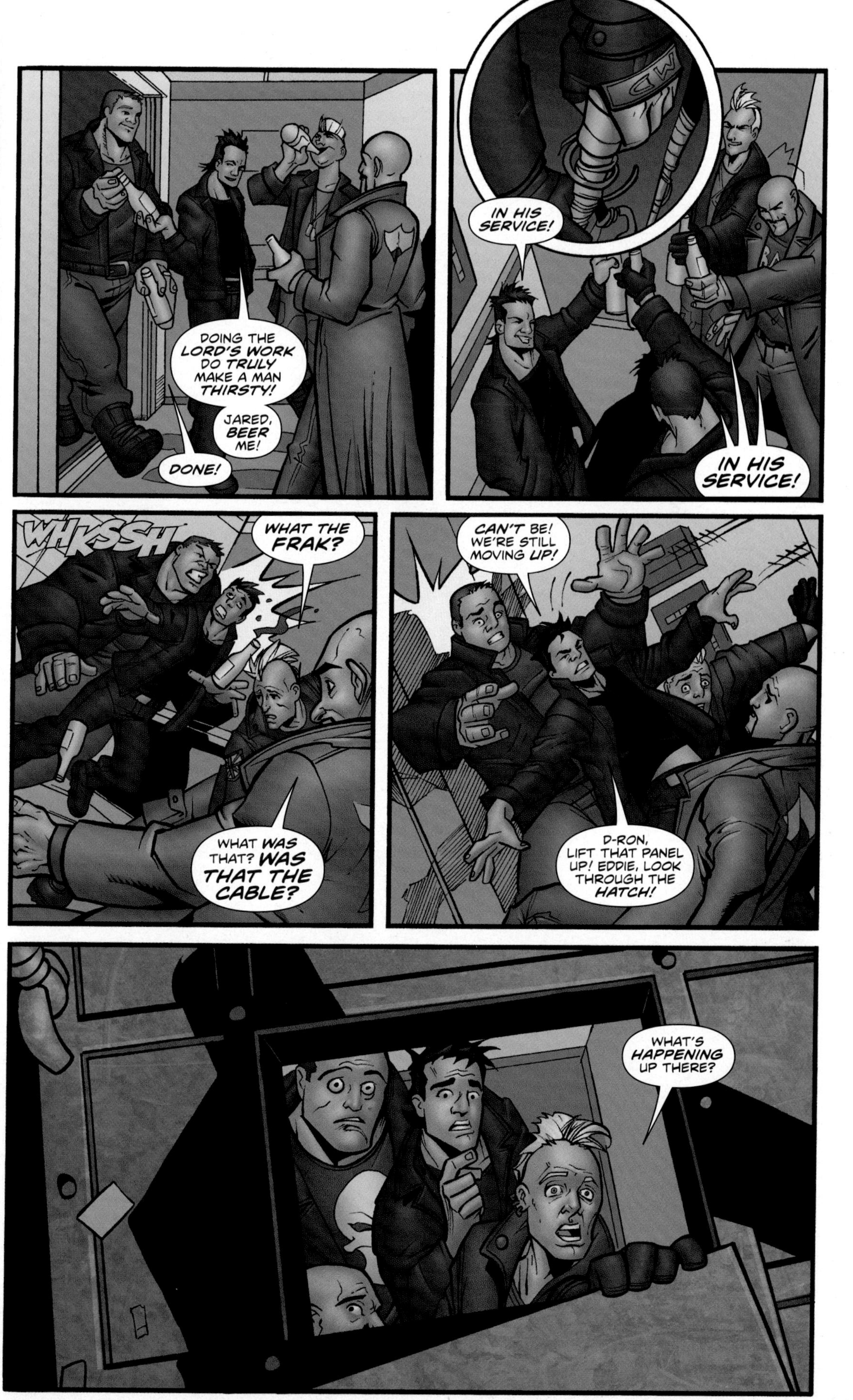
DOING THE LORD'S WORK DO TRULY MAKE A MAN THIRSTY!
JARED, BEER ME!
DONE!
IN HIS SERVICE!
IN HIS SERVICE!
WHKSSH
WHAT THE FRAK?
WHAT WAS THAT? WAS THAT THE CABLE?
CAN'T BE! WE'RE STILL MOVING UP!
D-RON, LIFT THAT PANEL UP! EDDIE, LOOK THROUGH THE HATCH!
WHAT'S HAPPENING UP THERE?

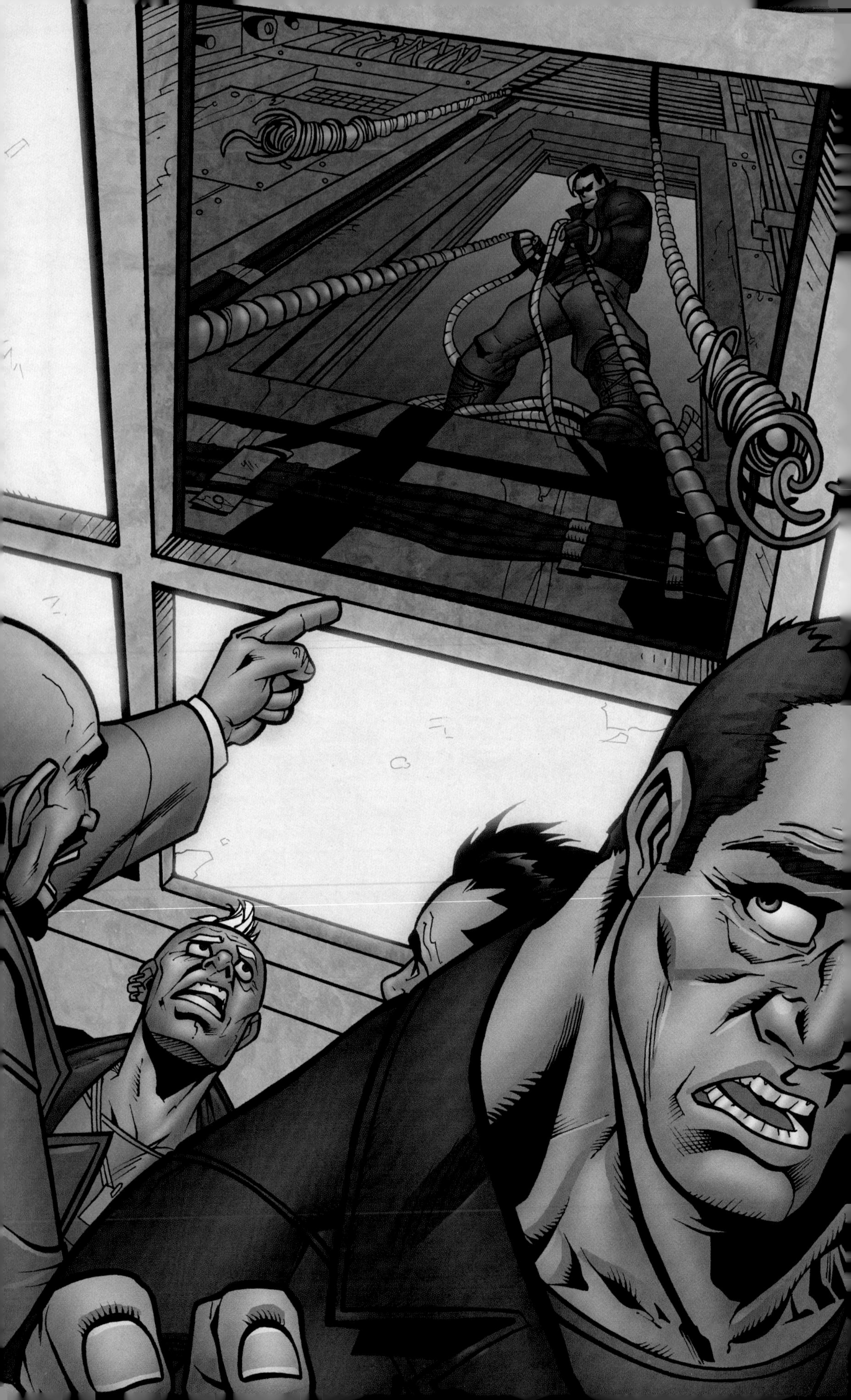

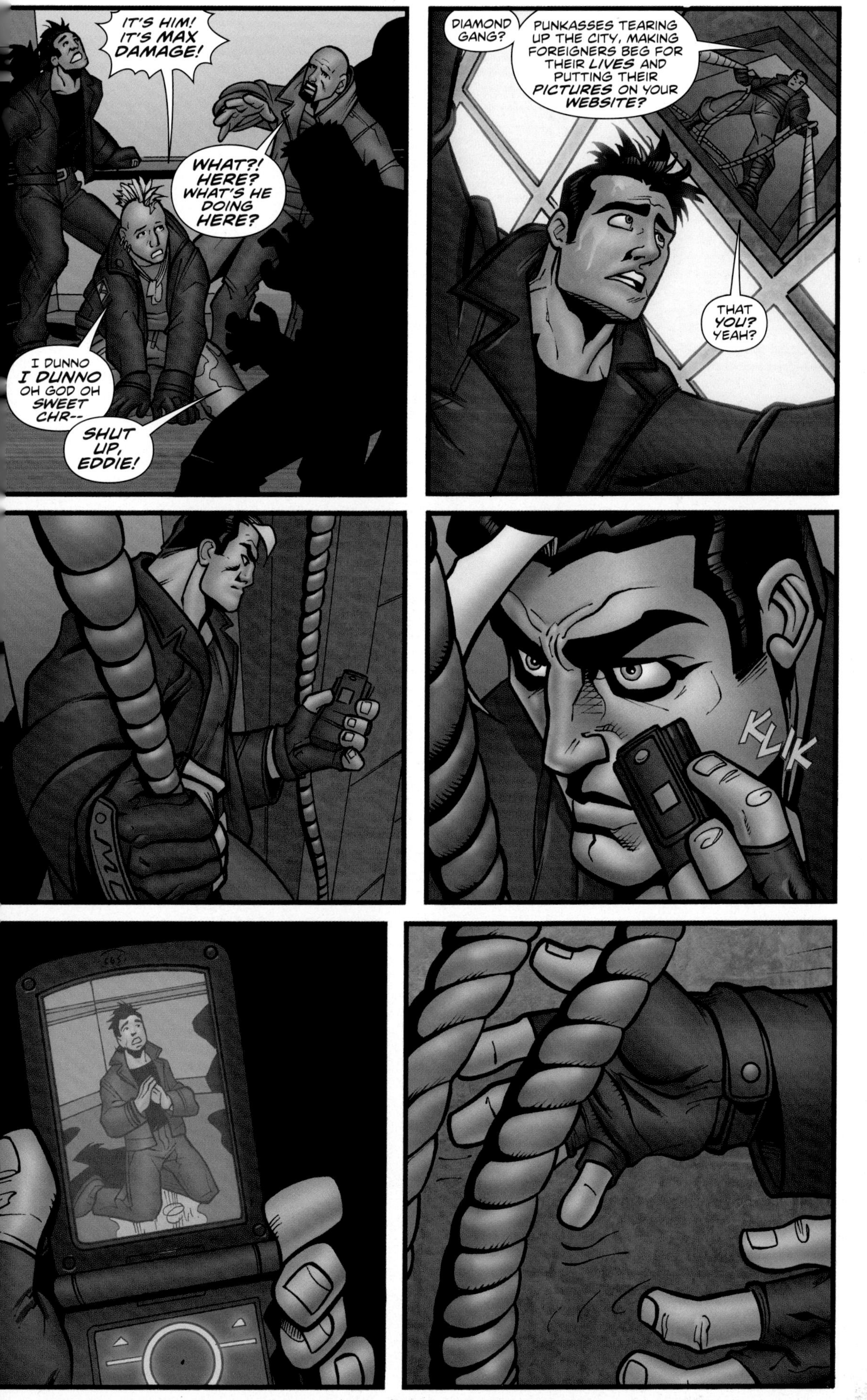
IT'S HIM! IT'S MAX DAMAGE!
WHAT?! HERE? WHAT'S HE DOING HERE?
I DUNNO I DUNNO OH GOD OH SWEET CHR--
SHUT UP, EDDIE!
DIAMOND GANG?
PUNKASSES TEARING UP THE CITY, MAKING FOREIGNERS BEG FOR THEIR LIVES AND PUTTING THEIR PICTURES ON YOUR WEBSITE?
THAT YOU? YEAH?
KLIK

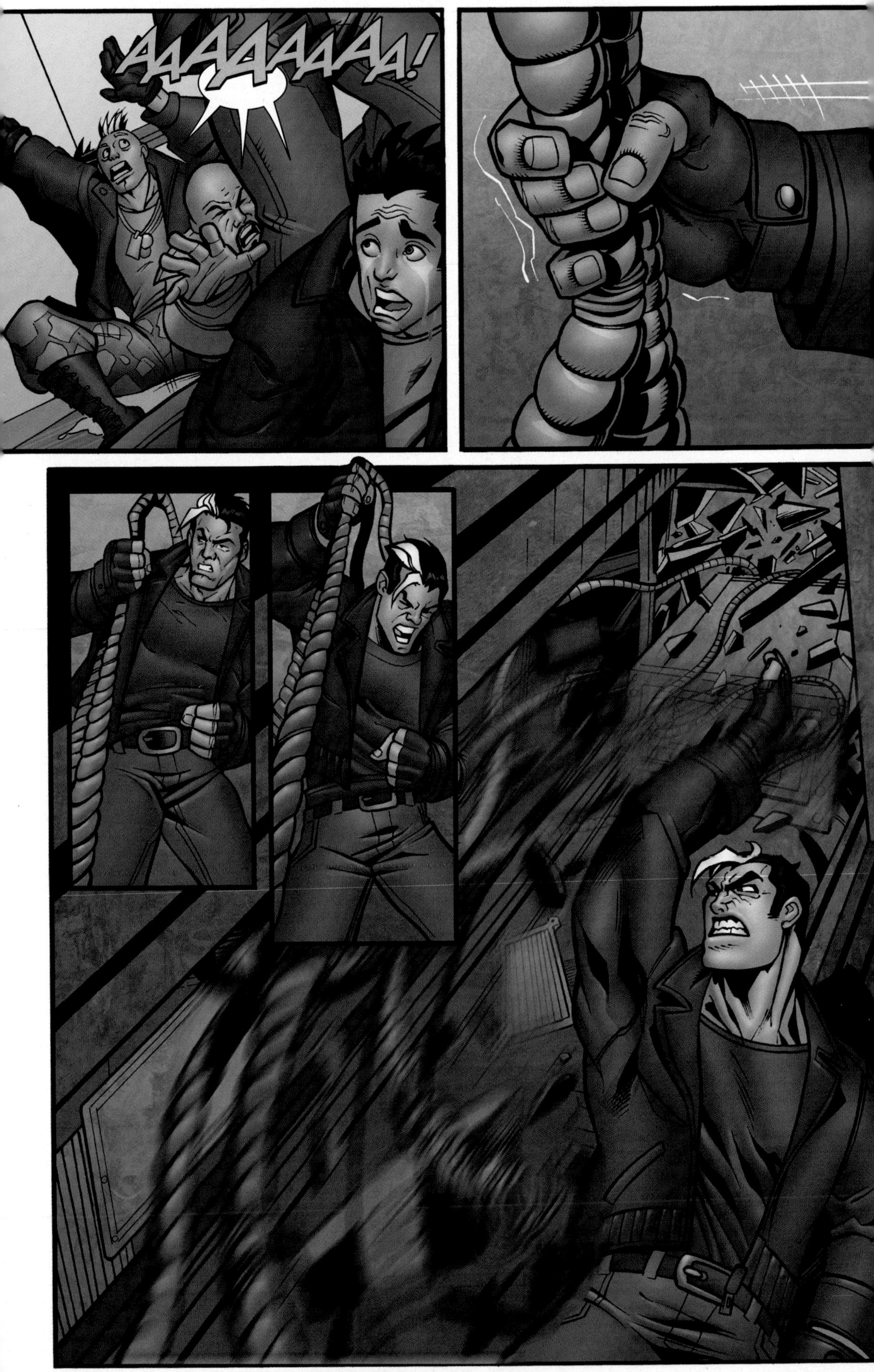
AAAAAAAA!

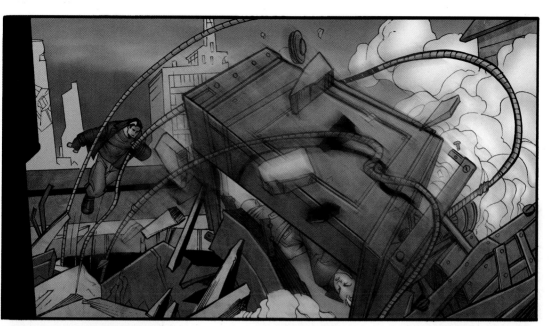

...UNNNNNH...

-:KOFF:-

...HNNNGH...

WHY?

WHY -:KOFF:- WHAT? WHY PLUTONIAN'S *BRAND?* MAN'S GOTTA STAND FOR *SOMETHIN'.*

WE'RE LIKE *HIM.* TOUGH. PURE. *WHITE.* LIKE *DIAMONDS.*

WE GET THE *MESSAGE,* MAN. GOD'S ON A TEAR, AND HE DOESN'T LIKE *COLOR.*

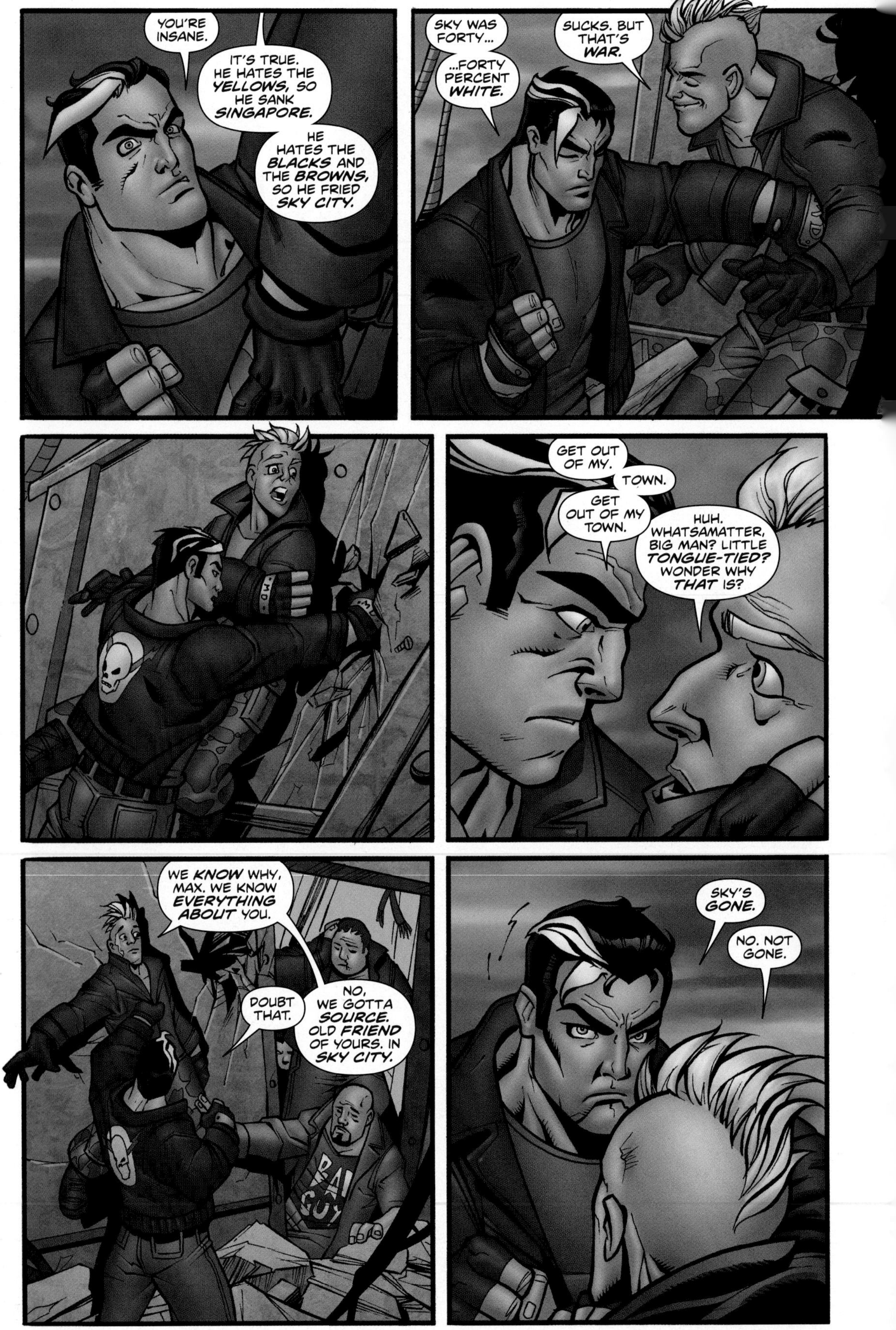
YOU'RE INSANE.
IT'S TRUE. HE HATES THE YELLOWS, SO HE SANK SINGAPORE.
HE HATES THE BLACKS AND THE BROWNS, SO HE FRIED SKY CITY.
SKY WAS FORTY...
...FORTY PERCENT WHITE.
SUCKS. BUT THAT'S WAR.
GET OUT OF MY.
TOWN.
GET OUT OF MY TOWN.
HUH. WHATSAMATTER, BIG MAN? LITTLE TONGUE-TIED? WONDER WHY THAT IS?
WE KNOW WHY, MAX. WE KNOW EVERYTHING ABOUT YOU.
DOUBT THAT.
NO, WE GOTTA SOURCE. OLD FRIEND OF YOURS. IN SKY CITY.
SKY'S GONE.
NO. NOT GONE.

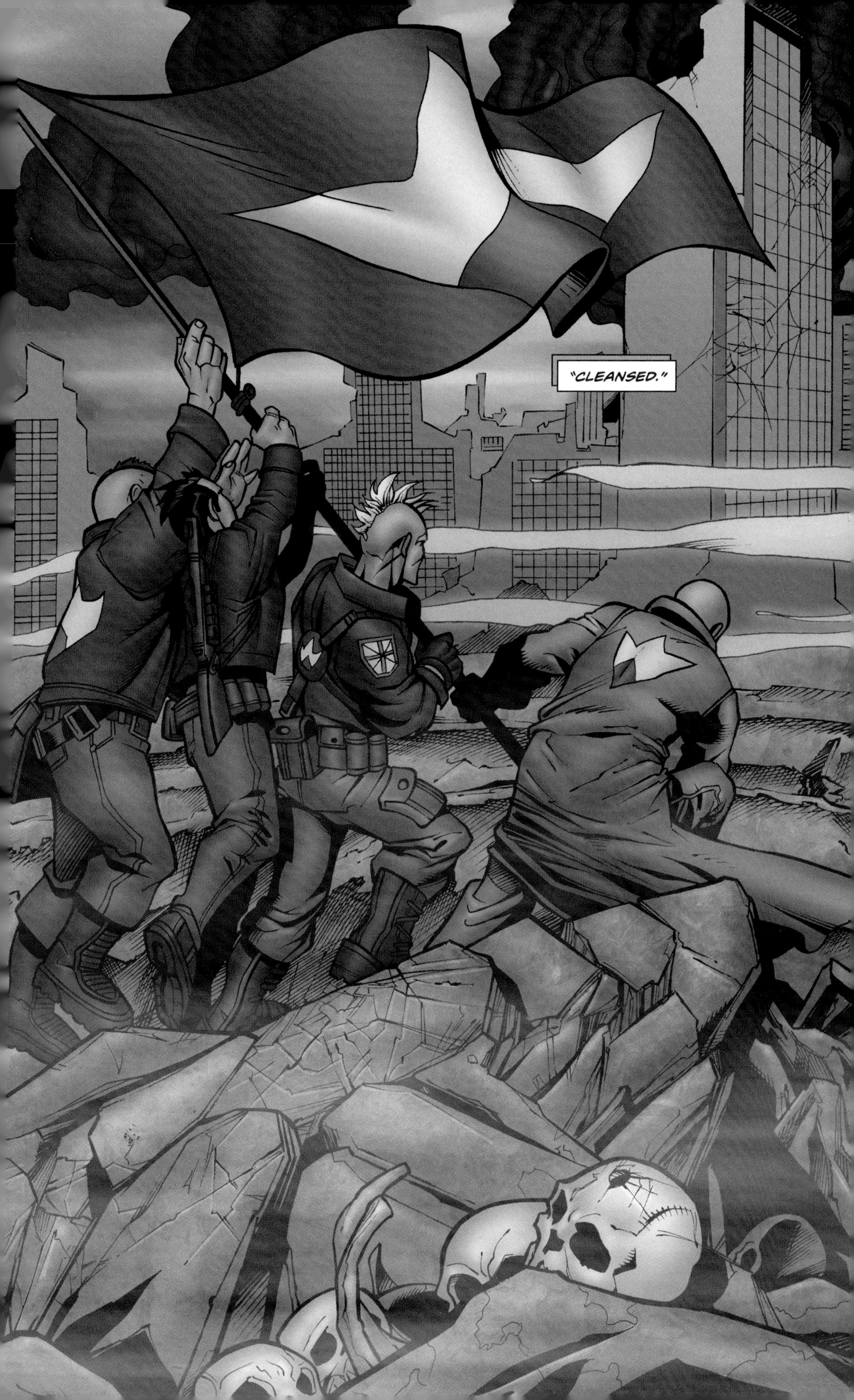
"CLEANSED."

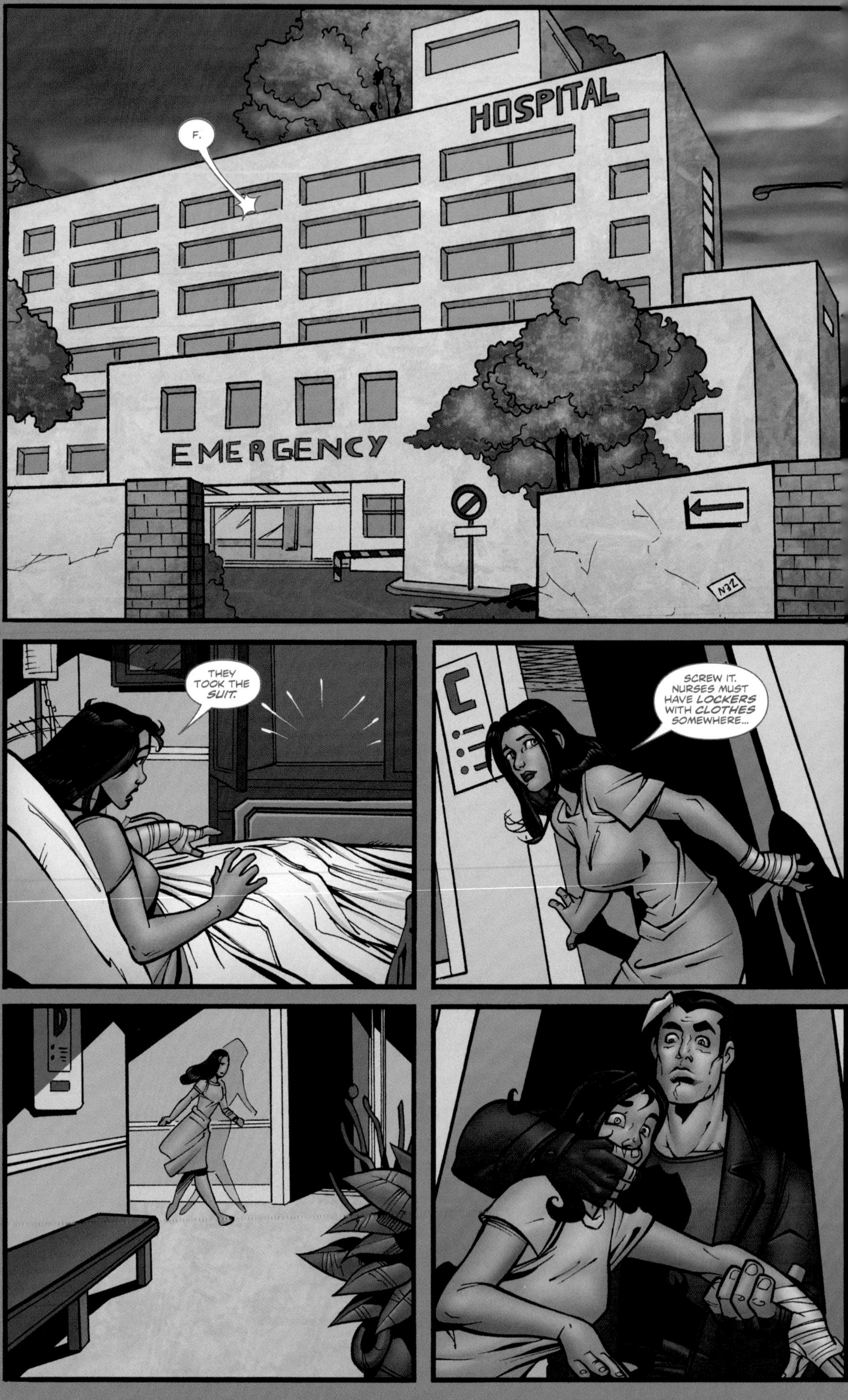
HOSPITAL
F.
EMERGENCY
THEY TOOK THE SUIT.
SCREW IT. NURSES MUST HAVE LOCKERS WITH CLOTHES SOMEWHERE...

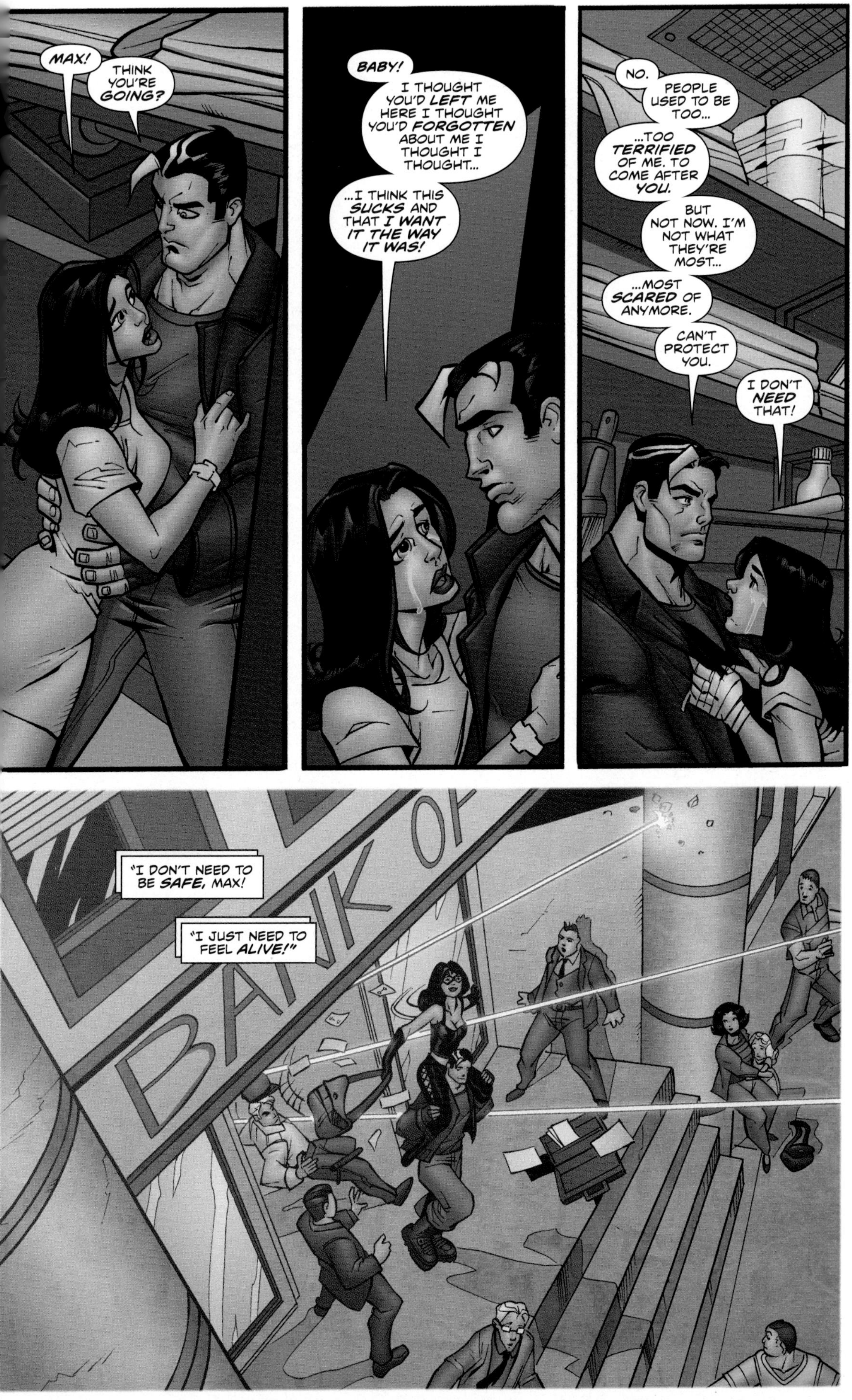
MAX!
THINK YOU'RE GOING?
BABY!
I THOUGHT YOU'D LEFT ME HERE I THOUGHT YOU'D FORGOTTEN ABOUT ME I THOUGHT I THOUGHT...
...I THINK THIS SUCKS AND THAT I WANT IT THE WAY IT WAS!
NO.
PEOPLE USED TO BE TOO...
...TOO TERRIFIED OF ME. TO COME AFTER YOU.
BUT NOT NOW. I'M NOT WHAT THEY'RE MOST...
...MOST SCARED OF ANYMORE.
CAN'T PROTECT YOU.
I DON'T NEED THAT!
"I DON'T NEED TO BE SAFE, MAX!
"I JUST NEED TO FEEL ALIVE!"

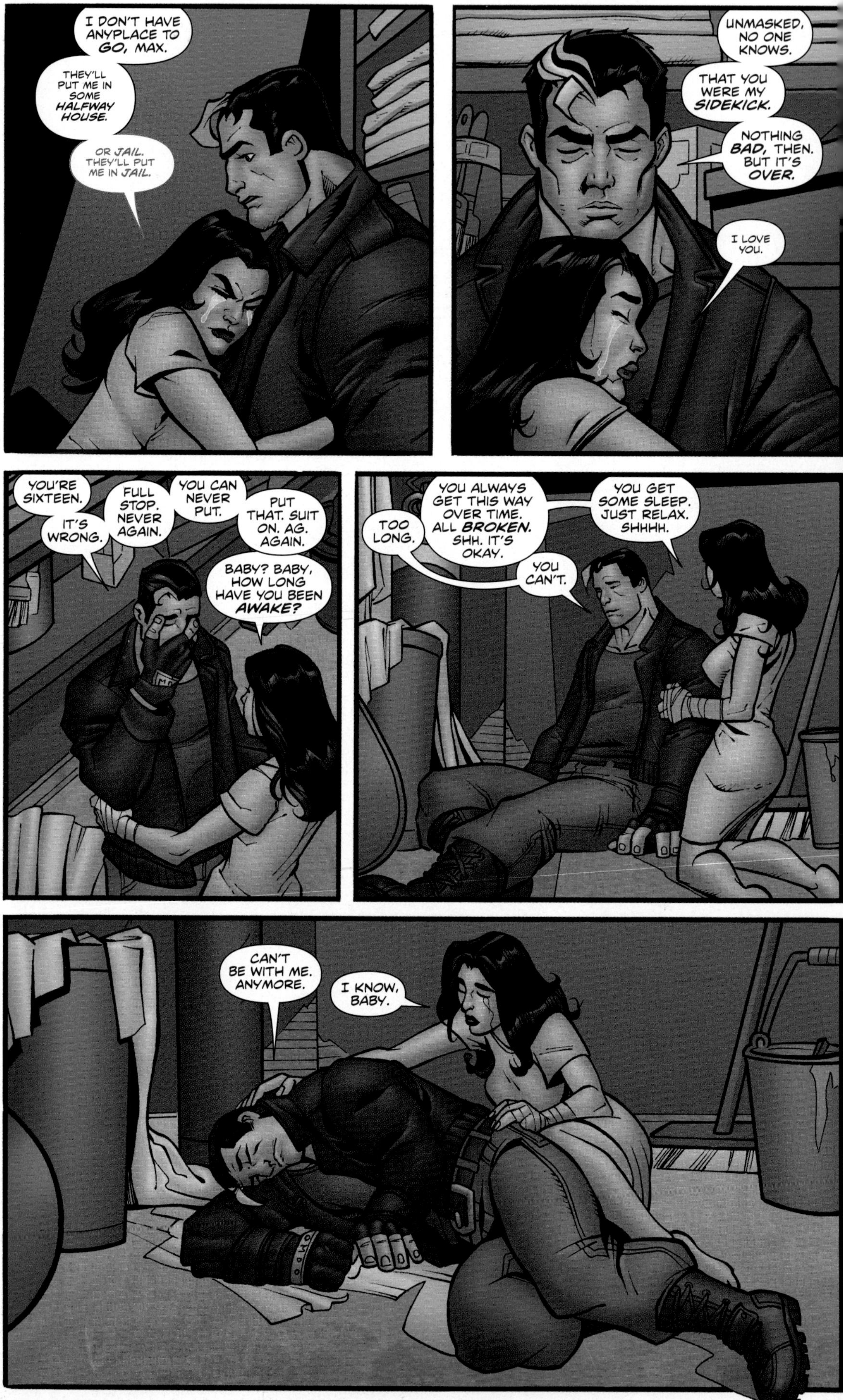
I DON'T HAVE ANYPLACE TO GO, MAX.
THEY'LL PUT ME IN SOME HALFWAY HOUSE.
OR JAIL. THEY'LL PUT ME IN JAIL.
UNMASKED, NO ONE KNOWS.
THAT YOU WERE MY SIDEKICK.
NOTHING BAD, THEN. BUT IT'S OVER.
I LOVE YOU.
YOU'RE SIXTEEN.
IT'S WRONG.
FULL STOP. NEVER AGAIN.
YOU CAN NEVER PUT.
PUT THAT. SUIT ON. AG. AGAIN.
BABY? BABY, HOW LONG HAVE YOU BEEN AWAKE?
TOO LONG.
YOU ALWAYS GET THIS WAY OVER TIME. ALL BROKEN. SHH. IT'S OKAY.
YOU GET SOME SLEEP. JUST RELAX. SHHHH.
YOU CAN'T.
CAN'T BE WITH ME. ANYMORE.
I KNOW, BABY.

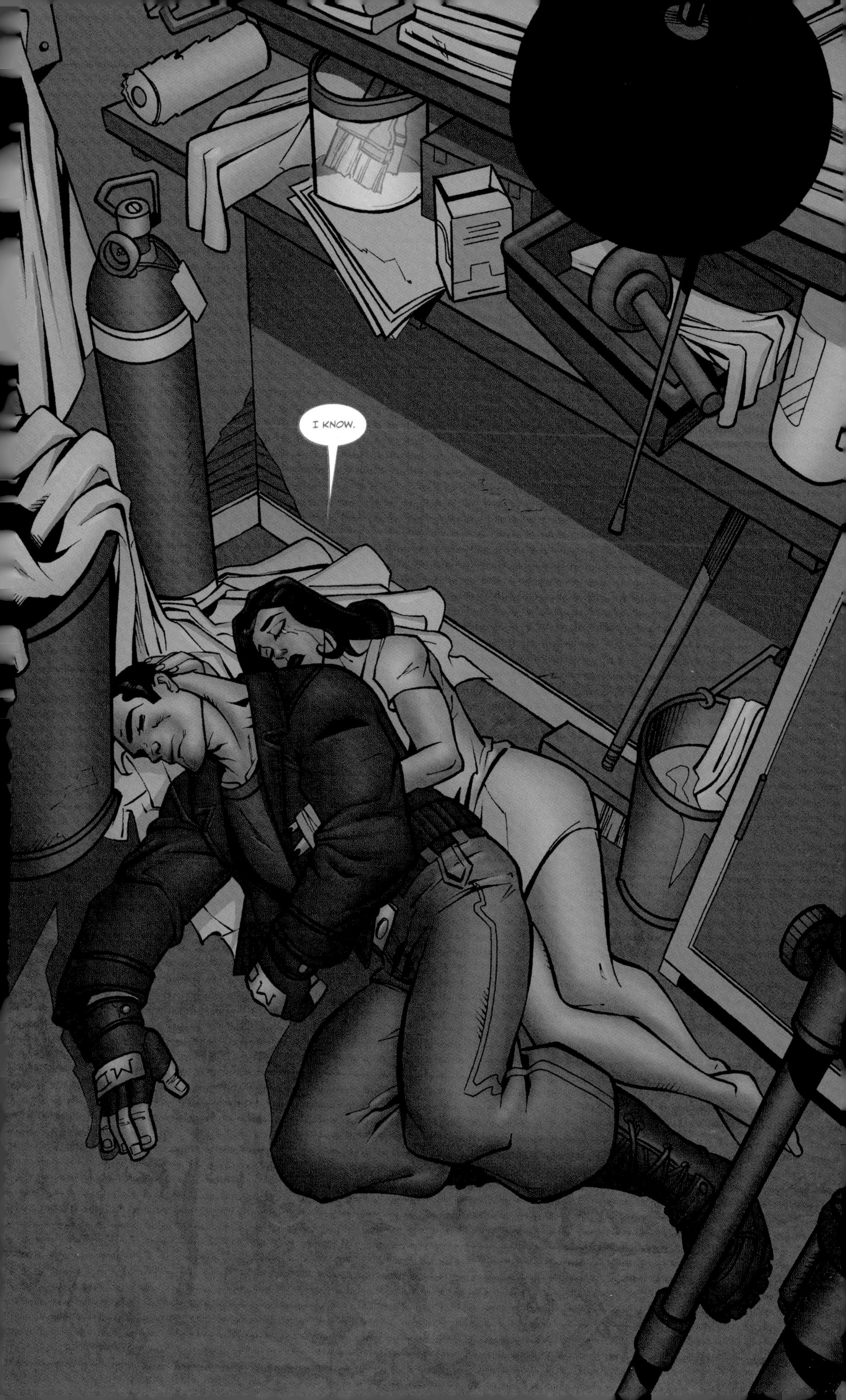
I KNOW.

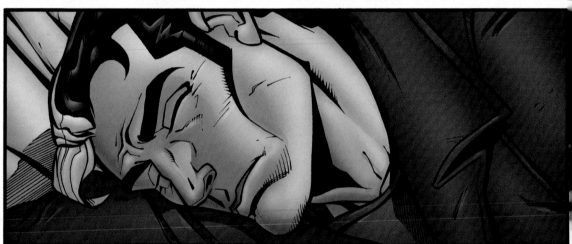

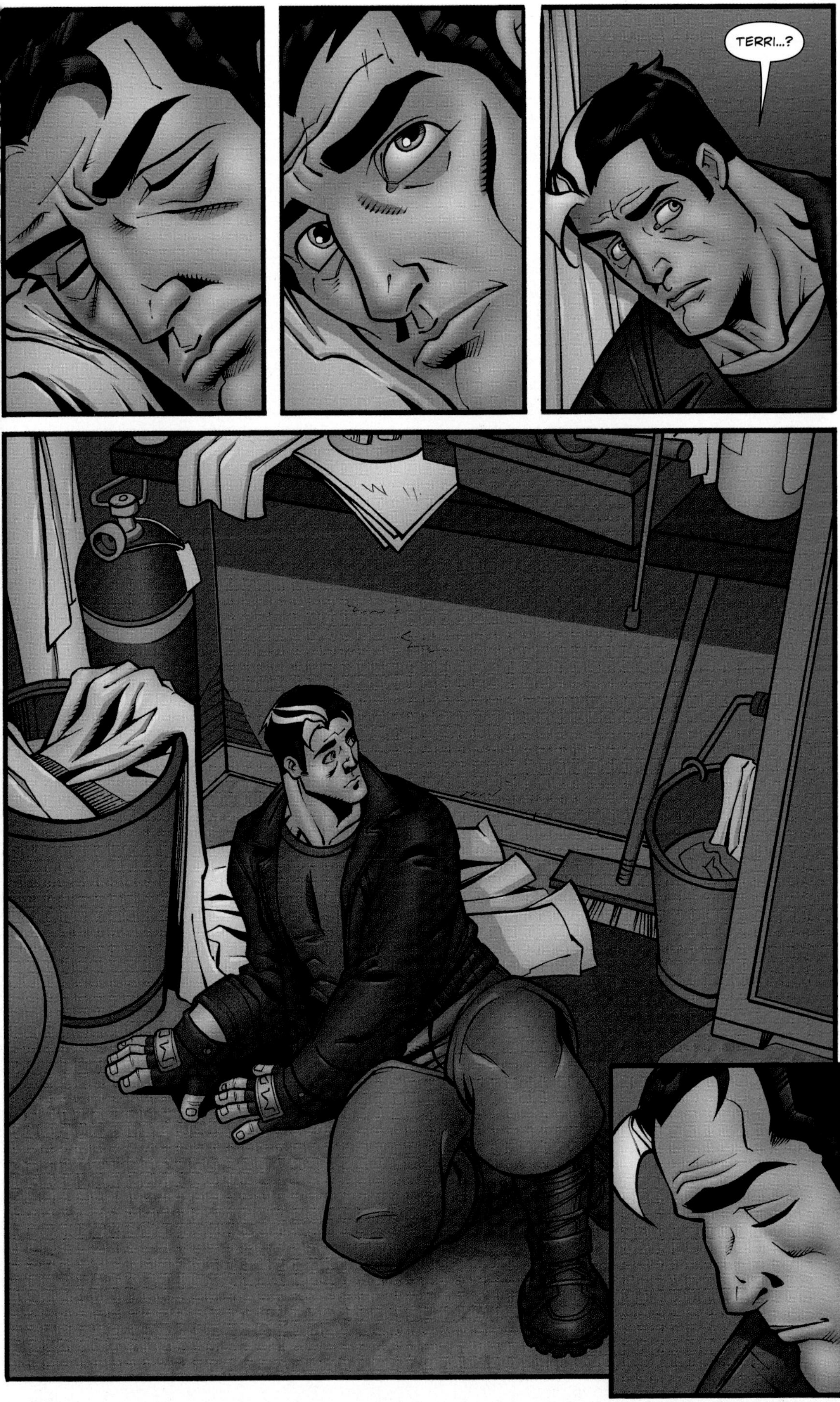
TERRI...?

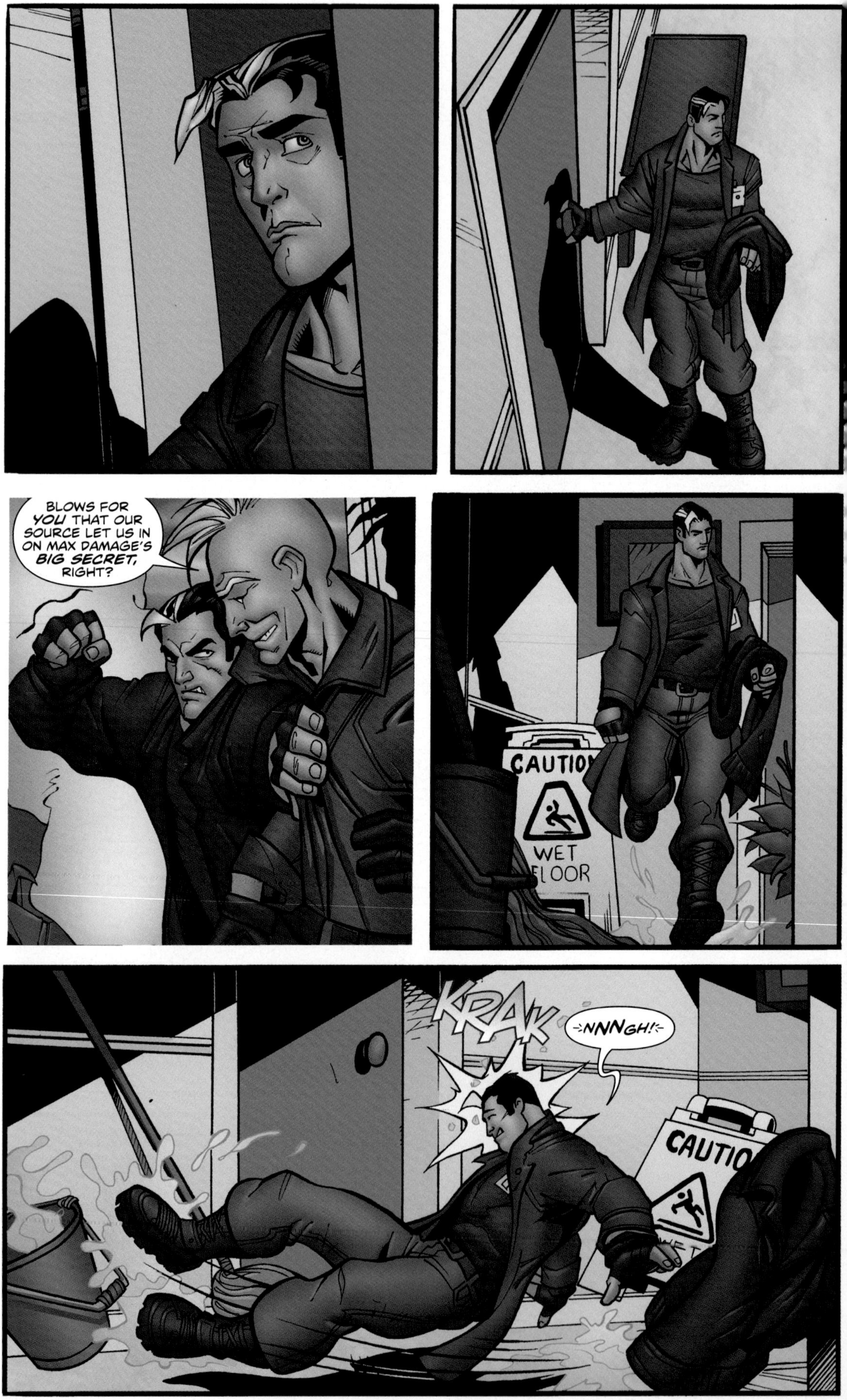
BLOWS FOR YOU THAT OUR SOURCE LET US IN ON MAX DAMAGE'S BIG SECRET, RIGHT?
CAUTION
WET FLOOR
KRAK
-NNNGH!-
CAUTION

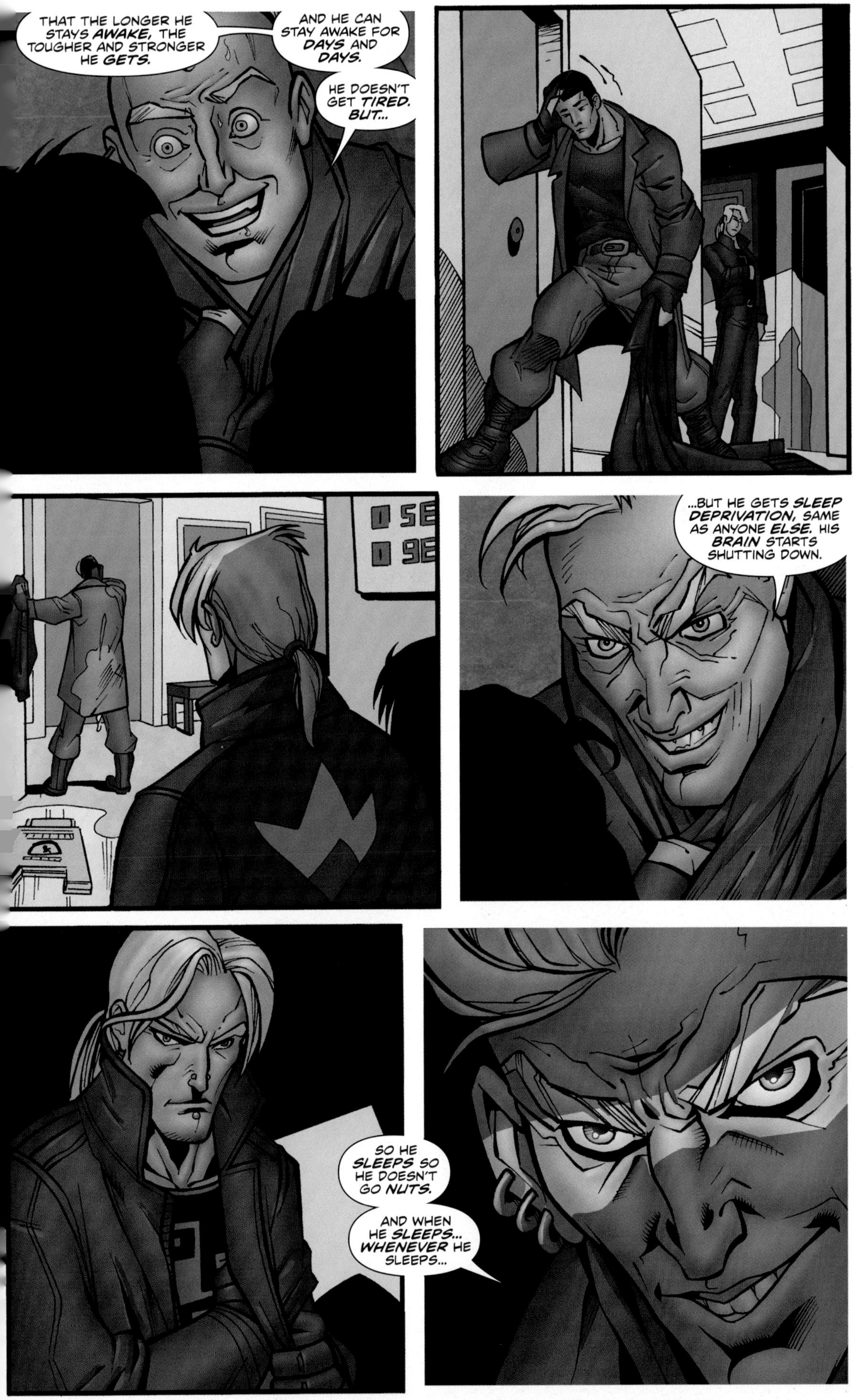
THAT THE LONGER HE STAYS AWAKE, THE TOUGHER AND STRONGER HE GETS.
AND HE CAN STAY AWAKE FOR DAYS AND DAYS.
HE DOESN'T GET TIRED. BUT...
...BUT HE GETS SLEEP DEPRIVATION, SAME AS ANYONE ELSE. HIS BRAIN STARTS SHUTTING DOWN.
SO HE SLEEPS SO HE DOESN'T GO NUTS.
AND WHEN HE SLEEPS... WHENEVER HE SLEEPS...

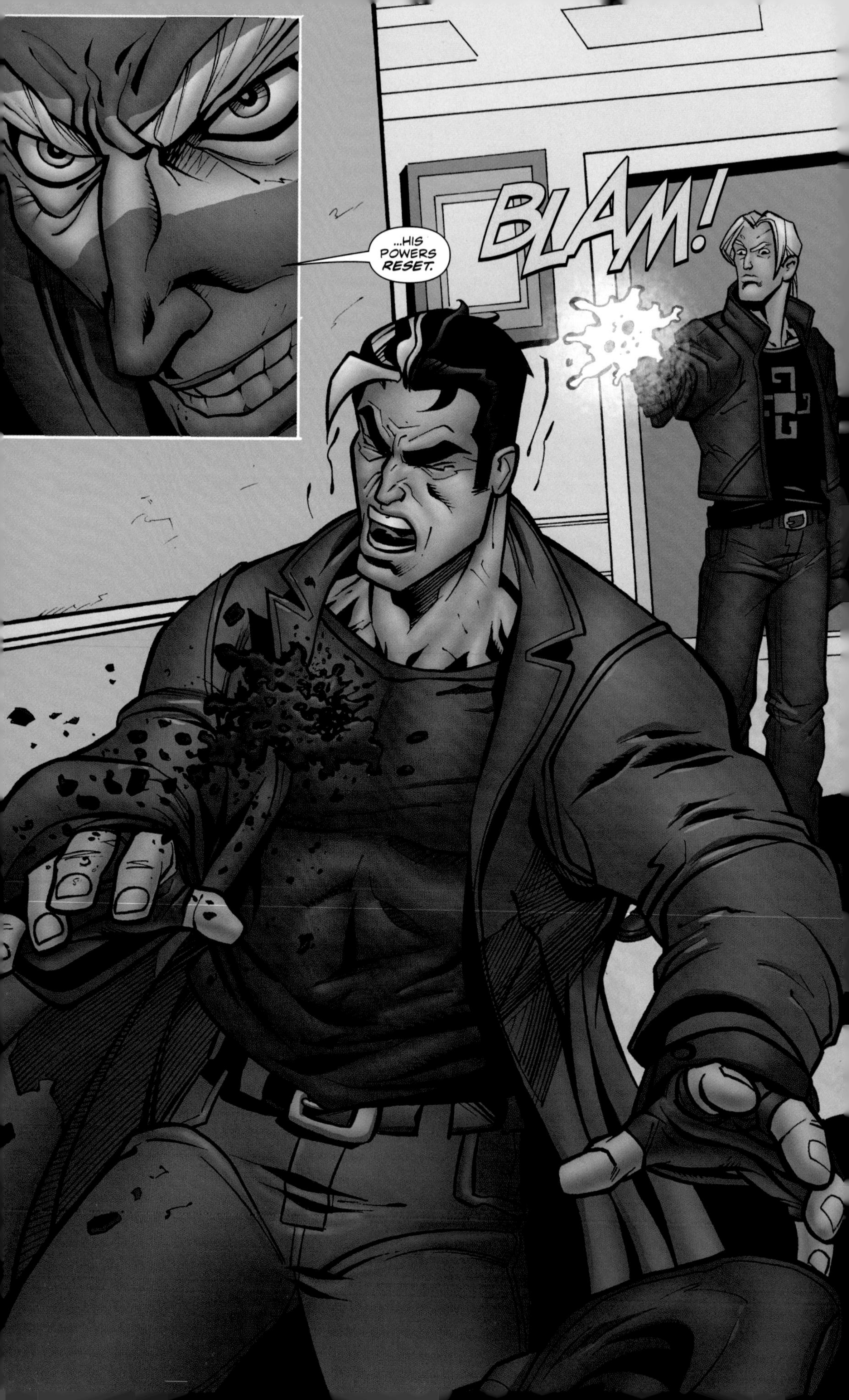
...HIS POWERS RESET.
BLAM!

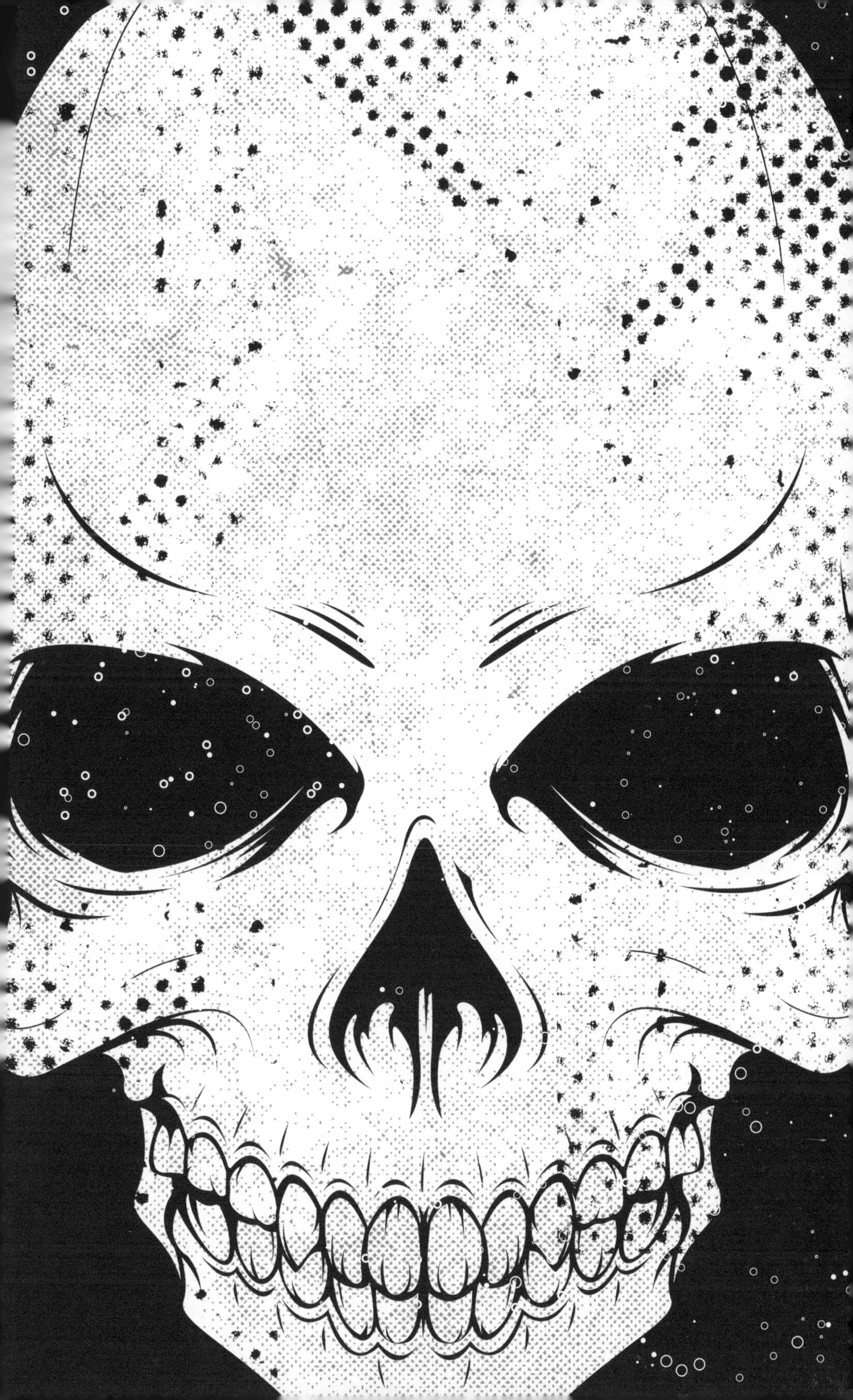

CHAPTER 8

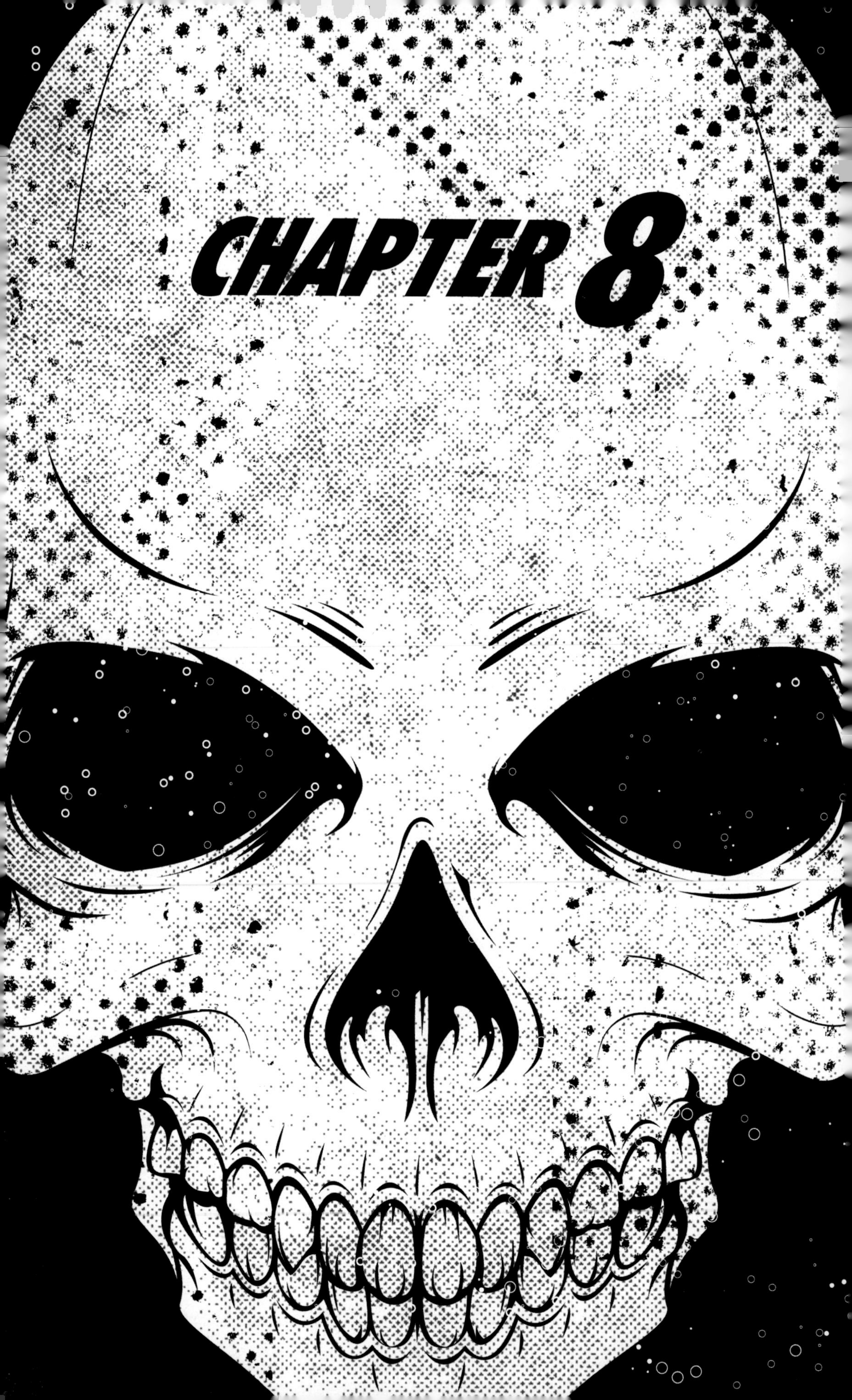

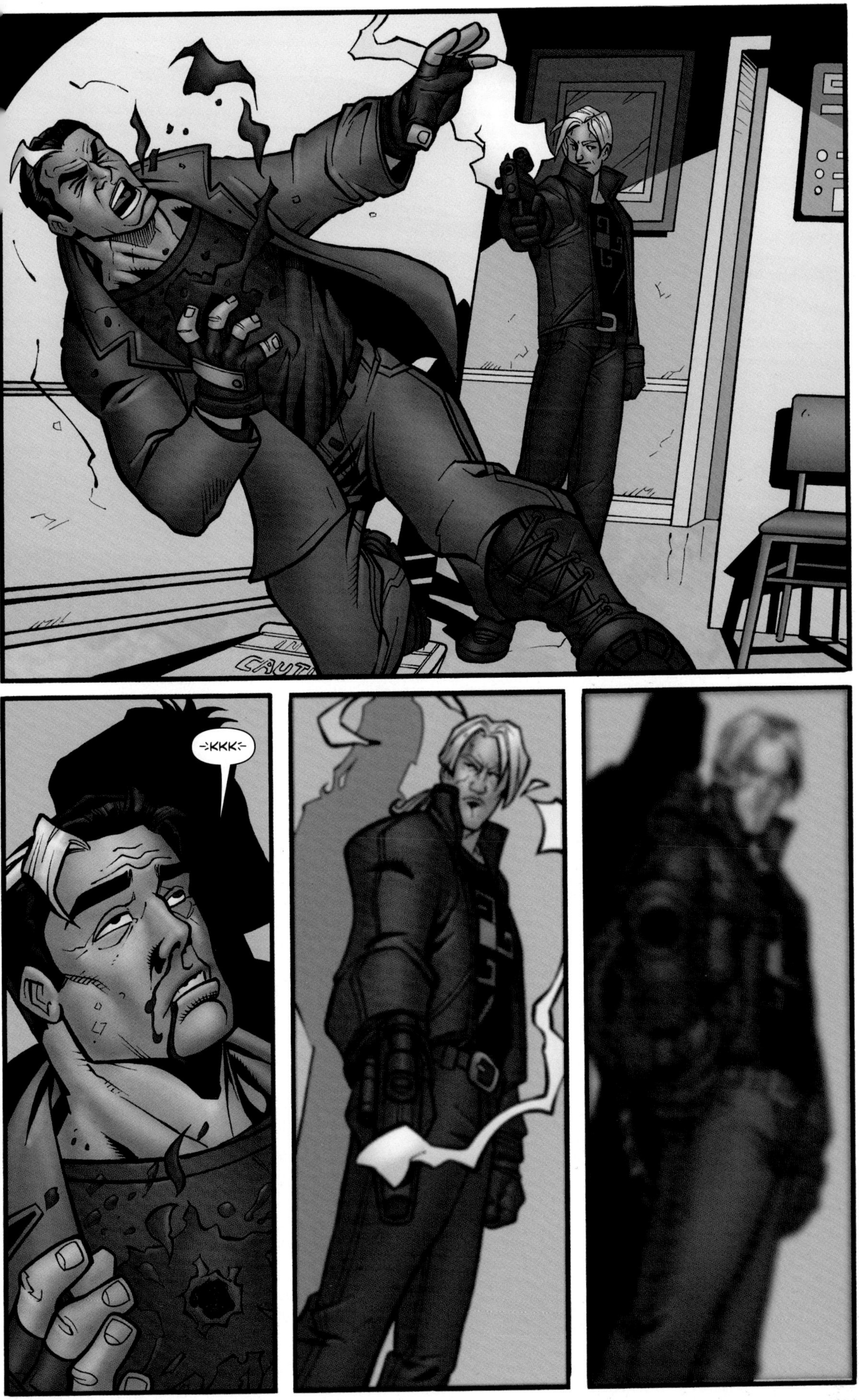
-KKK-

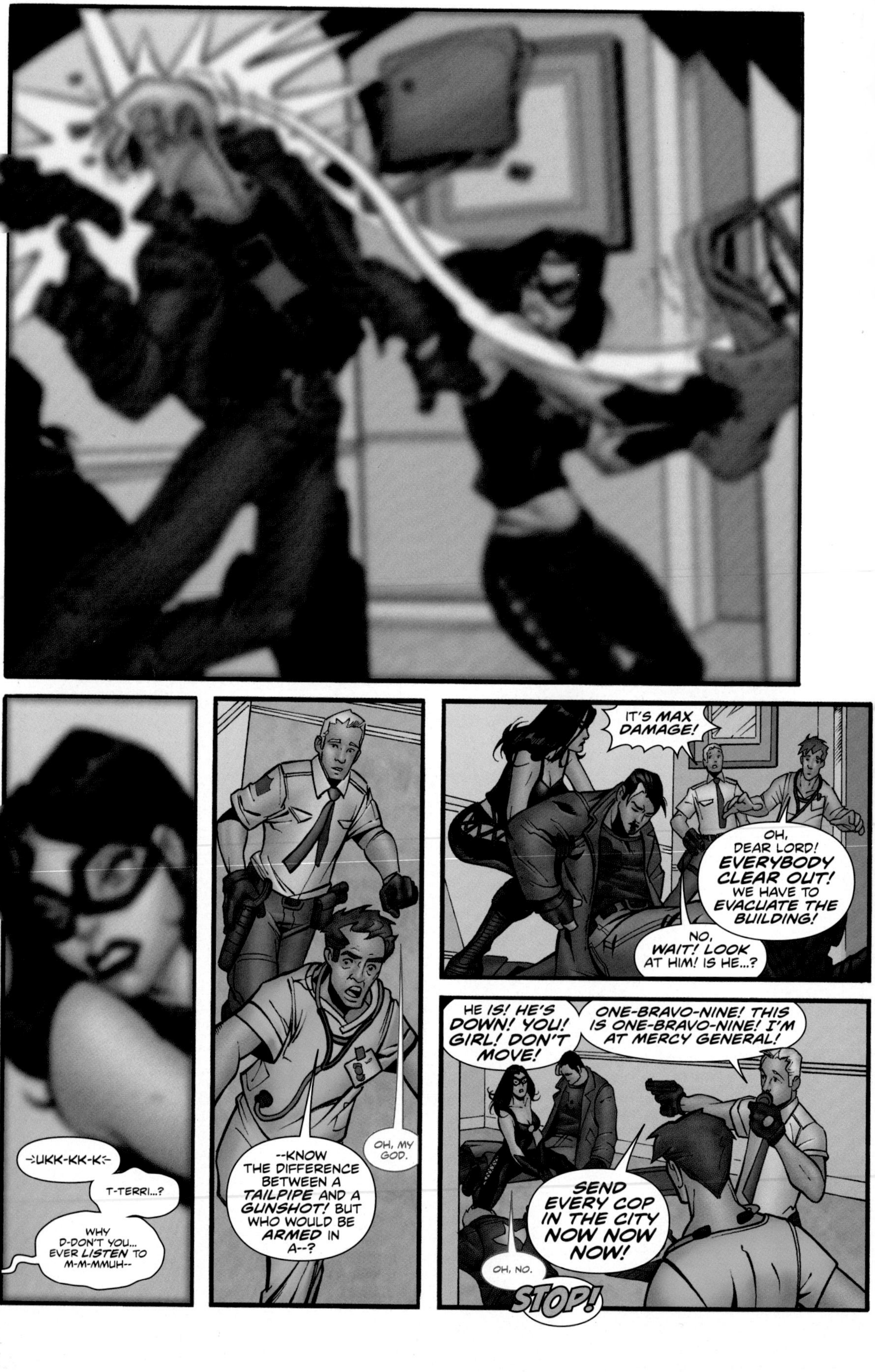
-UKK-KK-K-
T-TERRI...?
WHY D-DON'T YOU... EVER LISTEN TO M-M-MMUH--
--KNOW THE DIFFERENCE BETWEEN A TAILPIPE AND A GUNSHOT! BUT WHO WOULD BE ARMED IN A--?
OH, MY GOD.
IT'S MAX DAMAGE!
OH, DEAR LORD! EVERYBODY CLEAR OUT! WE HAVE TO EVACUATE THE BUILDING!
NO, WAIT! LOOK AT HIM! IS HE...?
HE IS! HE'S DOWN! YOU! GIRL! DON'T MOVE!
ONE-BRAVO-NINE! THIS IS ONE-BRAVO-NINE! I'M AT MERCY GENERAL!
SEND EVERY COP IN THE CITY NOW NOW NOW!
OH, NO.
STOP!

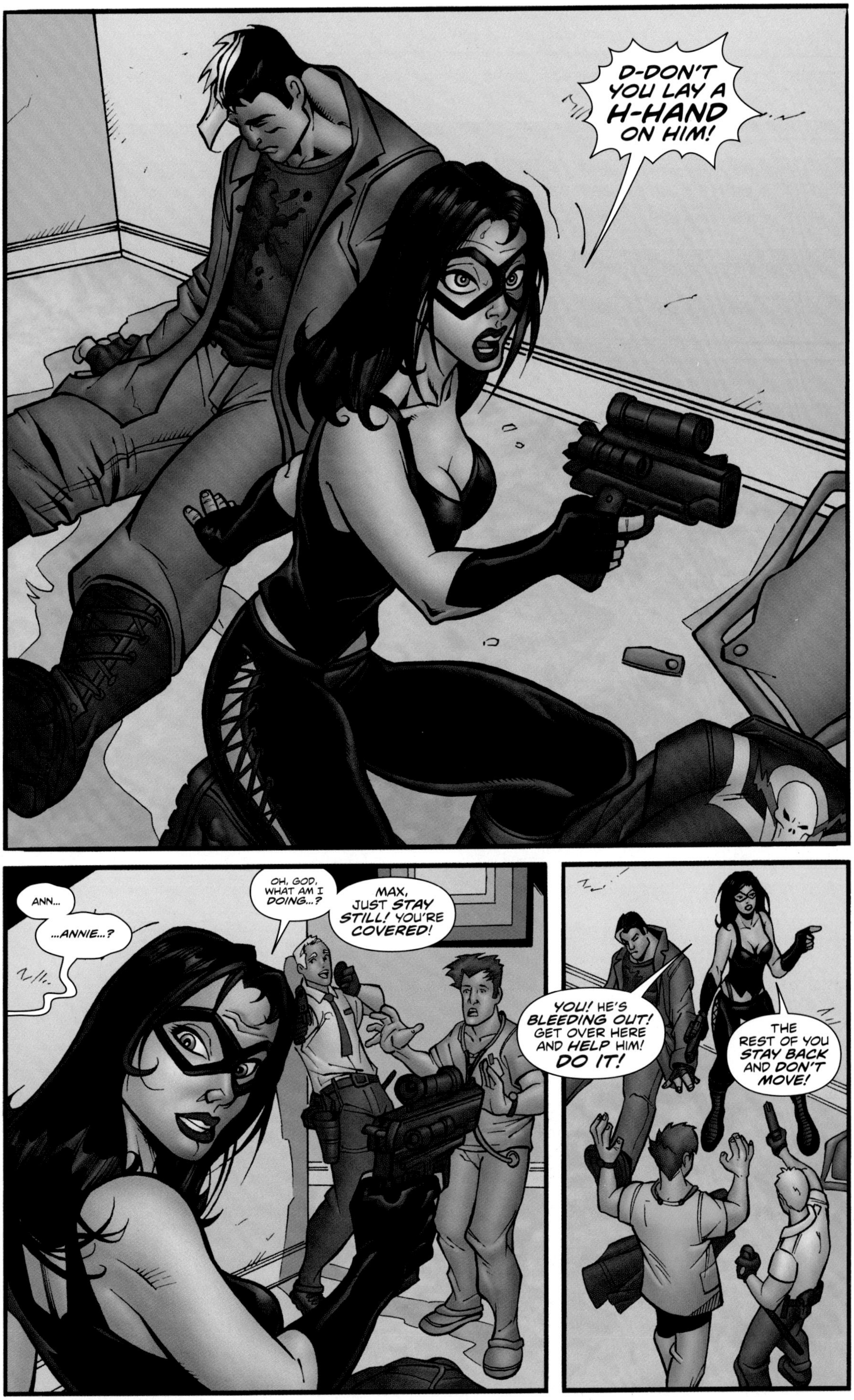
D-DON'T YOU LAY A H-HAND ON HIM!
ANN...
...ANNIE...?
OH, GOD, WHAT AM I DOING...?
MAX, JUST STAY STILL! YOU'RE COVERED!
YOU! HE'S BLEEDING OUT! GET OVER HERE AND HELP HIM! DO IT!
THE REST OF YOU STAY BACK AND DON'T MOVE!

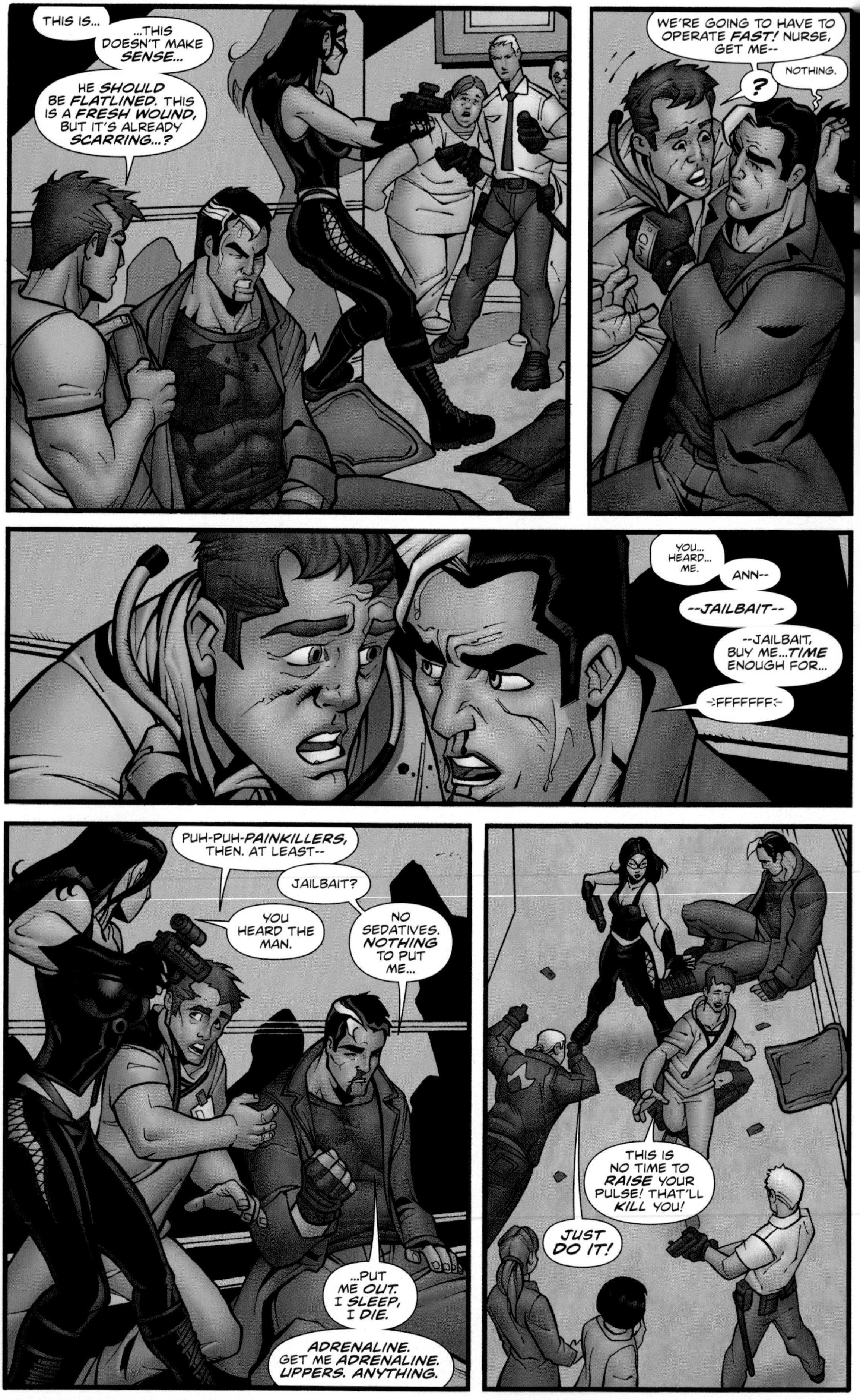
THIS IS...
...THIS DOESN'T MAKE SENSE...
HE SHOULD BE FLATLINED. THIS IS A FRESH WOUND, BUT IT'S ALREADY SCARRING...?
WE'RE GOING TO HAVE TO OPERATE FAST! NURSE, GET ME--
NOTHING.
?
YOU... HEARD... ME.
ANN--
--JAILBAIT--
--JAILBAIT, BUY ME...TIME ENOUGH FOR...
FFFFFFF
PUH-PUH-PAINKILLERS, THEN. AT LEAST--
JAILBAIT?
YOU HEARD THE MAN.
NO SEDATIVES. NOTHING TO PUT ME...
...PUT ME OUT. I SLEEP, I DIE.
ADRENALINE. GET ME ADRENALINE. UPPERS. ANYTHING.
THIS IS NO TIME TO RAISE YOUR PULSE! THAT'LL KILL YOU!
JUST DO IT!

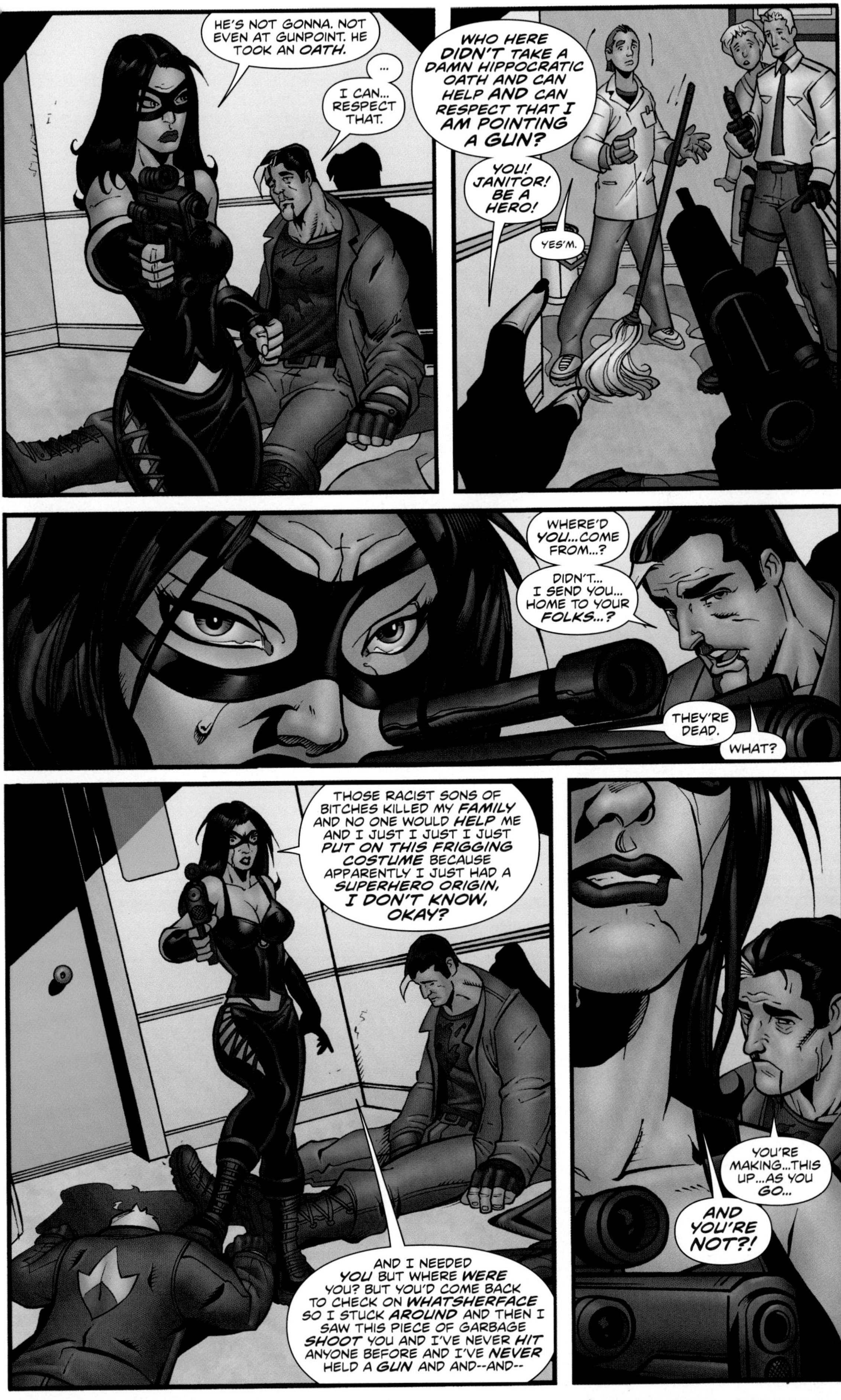
HE'S NOT GONNA. NOT EVEN AT GUNPOINT. HE TOOK AN OATH.
...
I CAN... RESPECT THAT.
WHO HERE DIDN'T TAKE A DAMN HIPPOCRATIC OATH AND CAN HELP AND CAN RESPECT THAT I AM POINTING A GUN?
YOU! JANITOR! BE A HERO!
YES'M.
WHERE'D YOU...COME FROM...?
DIDN'T... I SEND YOU... HOME TO YOUR FOLKS...?
THEY'RE DEAD.
WHAT?
THOSE RACIST SONS OF BITCHES KILLED MY FAMILY AND NO ONE WOULD HELP ME AND I JUST I JUST I JUST PUT ON THIS FRIGGING COSTUME BECAUSE APPARENTLY I JUST HAD A SUPERHERO ORIGIN, I DON'T KNOW, OKAY?
AND I NEEDED YOU BUT WHERE WERE YOU? BUT YOU'D COME BACK TO CHECK ON WHATSHERFACE SO I STUCK AROUND AND THEN I SAW THIS PIECE OF GARBAGE SHOOT YOU AND I'VE NEVER HIT ANYONE BEFORE AND I'VE NEVER HELD A GUN AND AND--AND--
YOU'RE MAKING...THIS UP...AS YOU GO...
AND YOU'RE NOT?!

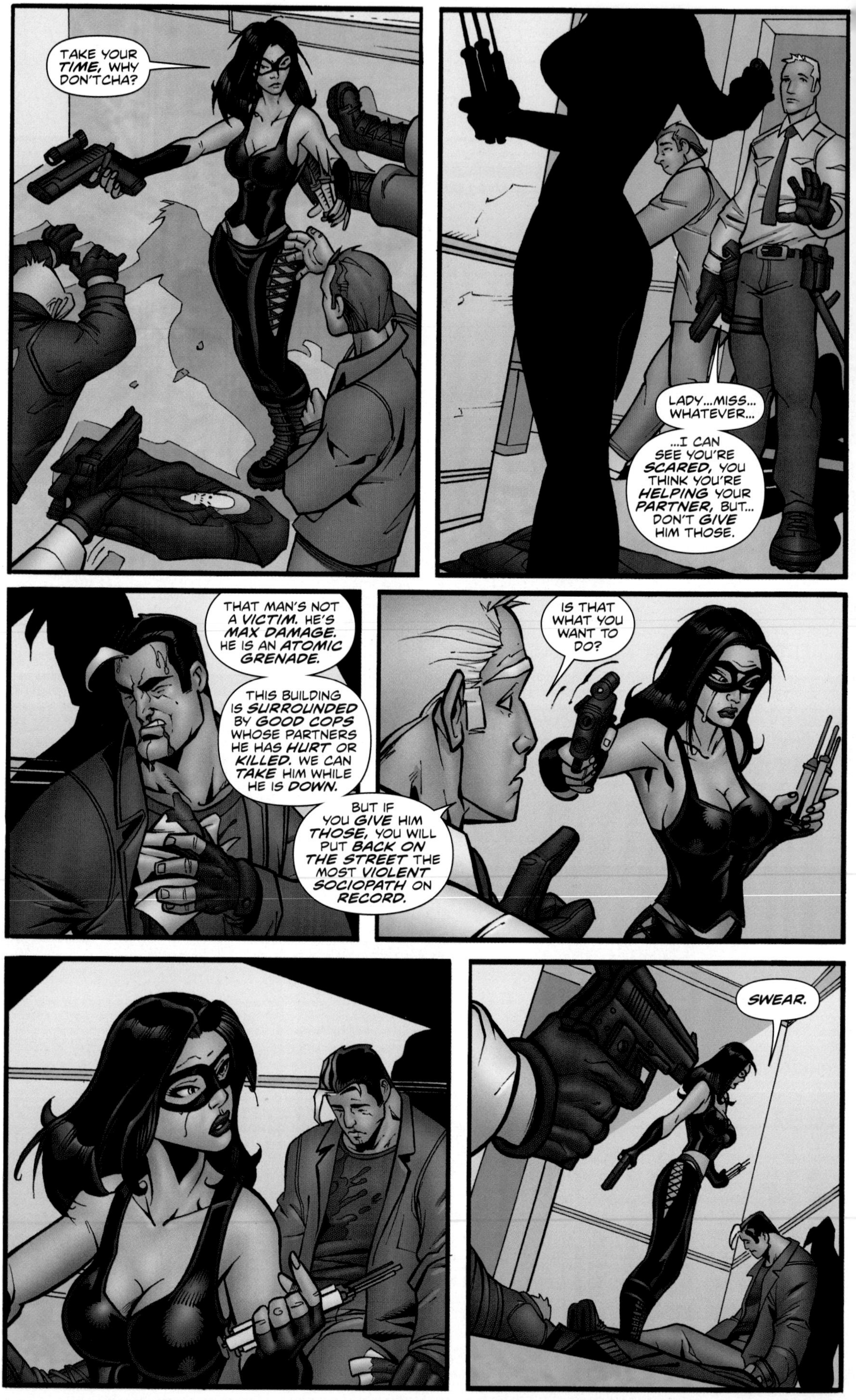

TAKE YOUR TIME, WHY DON'TCHA?
LADY...MISS... WHATEVER...
...I CAN SEE YOU'RE SCARED, YOU THINK YOU'RE HELPING YOUR PARTNER, BUT... DON'T GIVE HIM THOSE.
THAT MAN'S NOT A VICTIM. HE'S MAX DAMAGE. HE IS AN ATOMIC GRENADE.
THIS BUILDING IS SURROUNDED BY GOOD COPS WHOSE PARTNERS HE HAS HURT OR KILLED. WE CAN TAKE HIM WHILE HE IS DOWN.
BUT IF YOU GIVE HIM THOSE, YOU WILL PUT BACK ON THE STREET THE MOST VIOLENT SOCIOPATH ON RECORD.
IS THAT WHAT YOU WANT TO DO?
SWEAR.

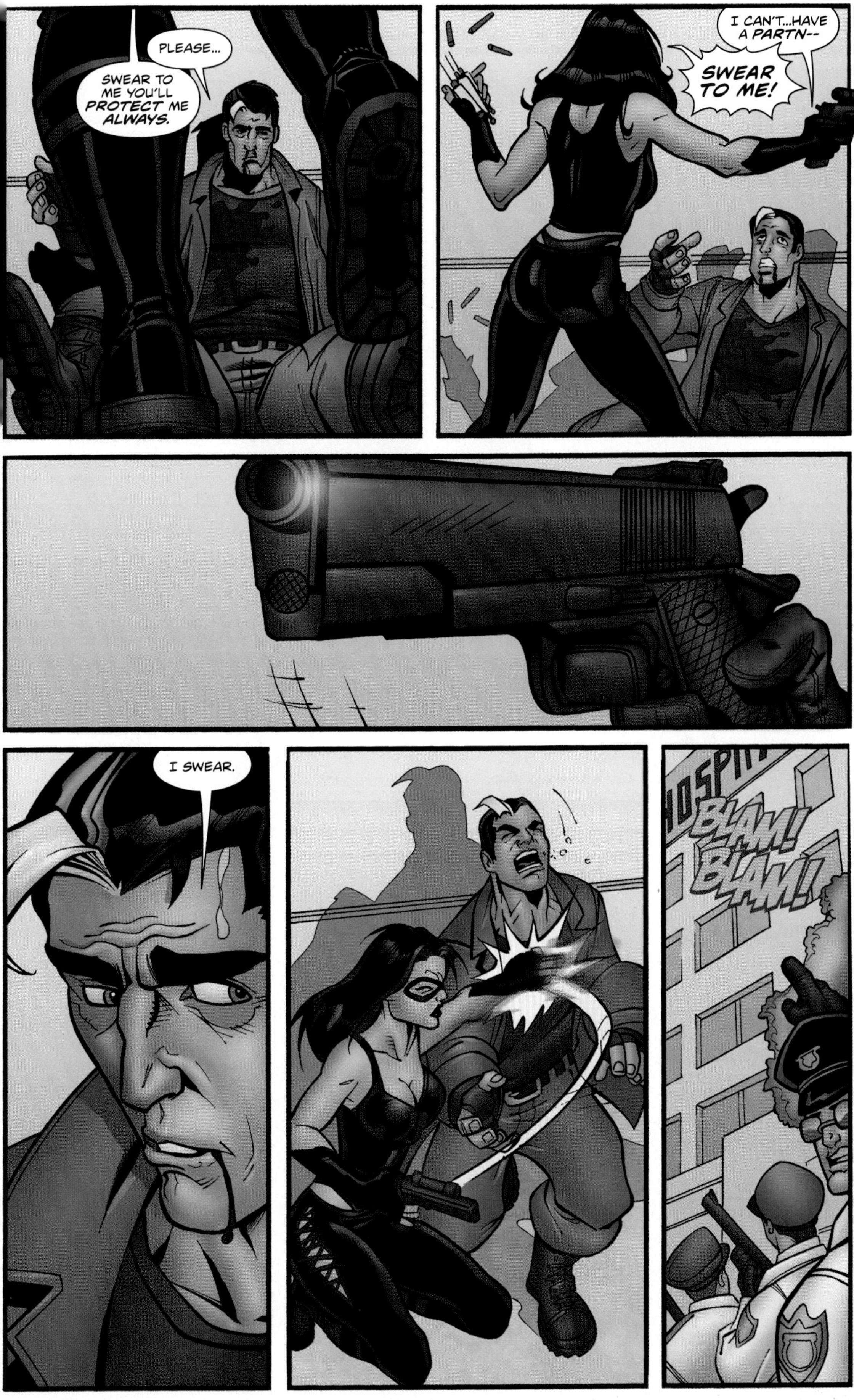
PLEASE...
SWEAR TO ME YOU'LL PROTECT ME ALWAYS.
I CAN'T...HAVE A PARTN--
SWEAR TO ME!
I SWEAR.
BLAM! BLAM!

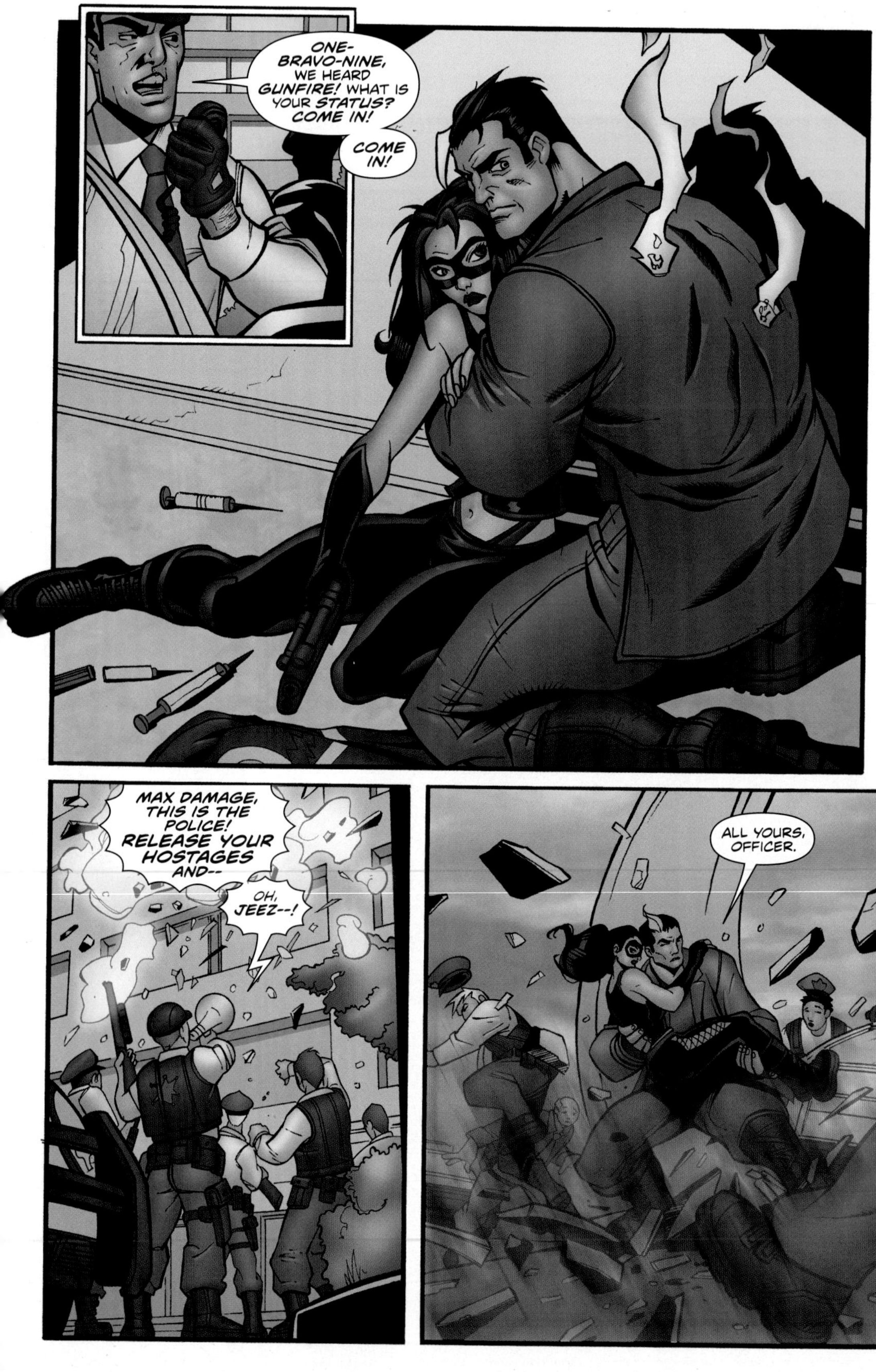
ONE-BRAVO-NINE, WE HEARD GUNFIRE! WHAT IS YOUR STATUS? COME IN!
COME IN!
MAX DAMAGE, THIS IS THE POLICE! RELEASE YOUR HOSTAGES AND--
OH, JEEZ--!
ALL YOURS, OFFICER.

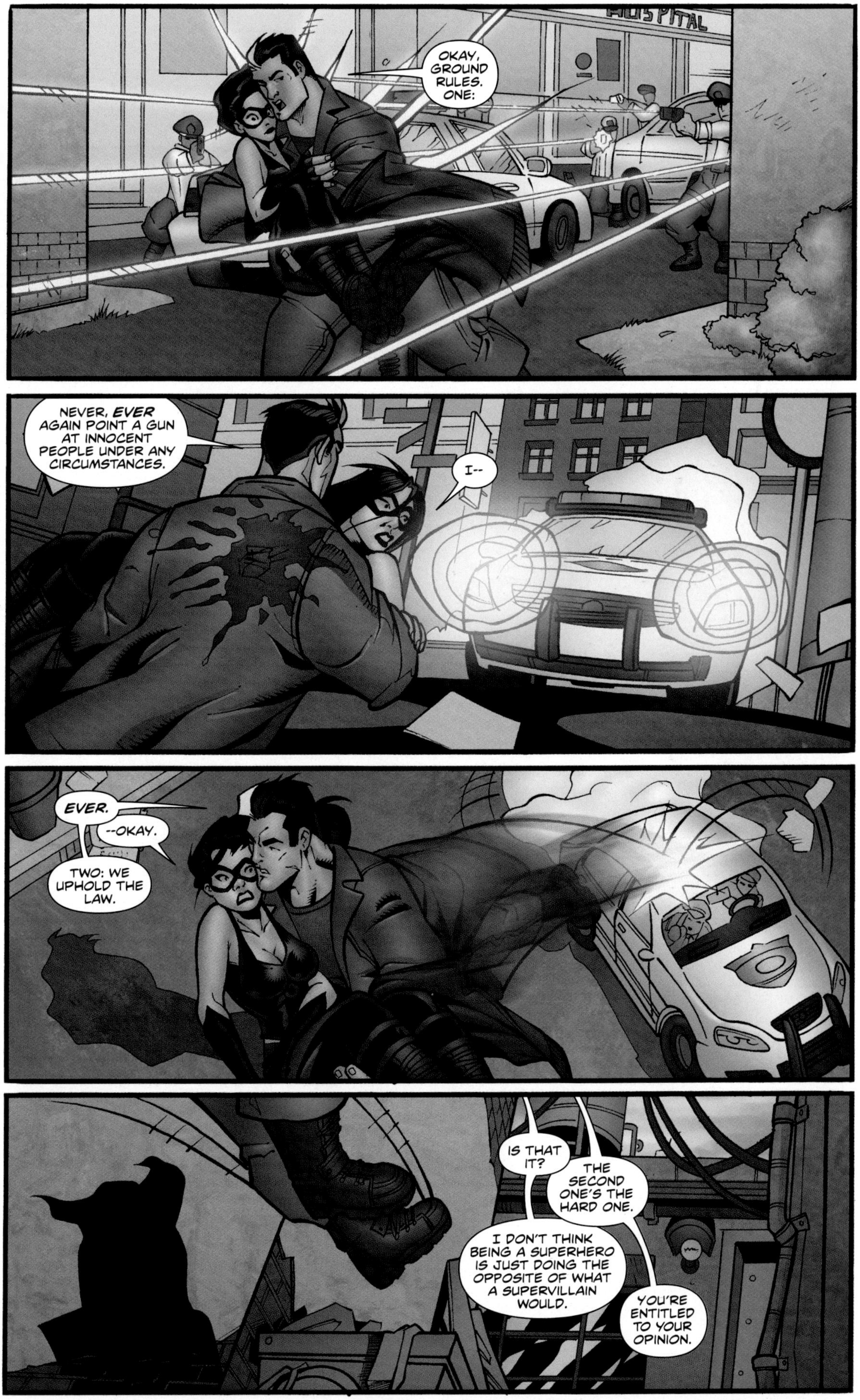
HOSPITAL
OKAY, GROUND RULES. ONE:
NEVER, EVER AGAIN POINT A GUN AT INNOCENT PEOPLE UNDER ANY CIRCUMSTANCES.
I--
EVER.
--OKAY.
TWO: WE UPHOLD THE LAW.
IS THAT IT?
THE SECOND ONE'S THE HARD ONE.
I DON'T THINK BEING A SUPERHERO IS JUST DOING THE OPPOSITE OF WHAT A SUPERVILLAIN WOULD.
YOU'RE ENTITLED TO YOUR OPINION.

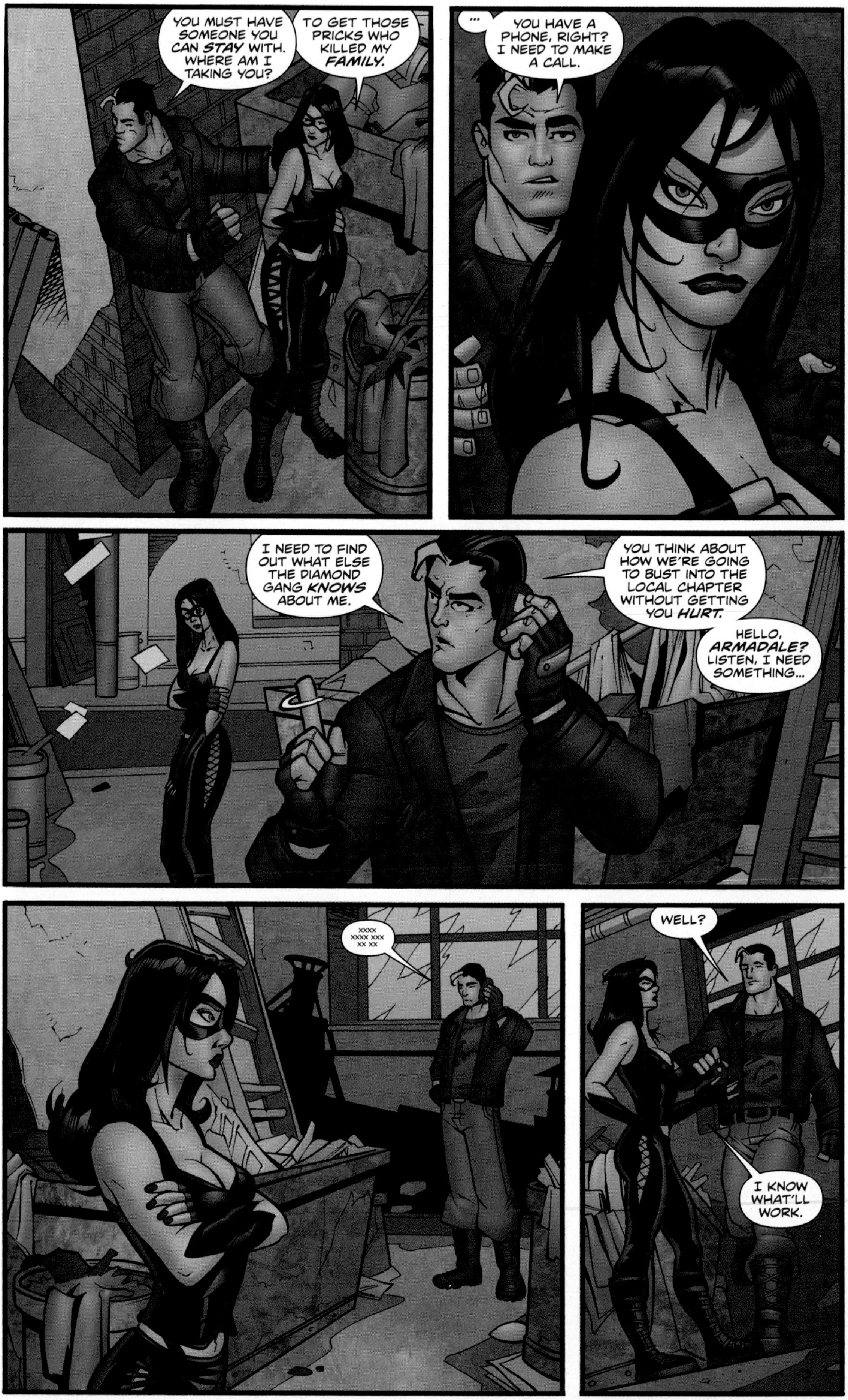
YOU MUST HAVE SOMEONE YOU CAN STAY WITH. WHERE AM I TAKING YOU?
TO GET THOSE PRICKS WHO KILLED MY FAMILY.
...
YOU HAVE A PHONE, RIGHT? I NEED TO MAKE A CALL.
I NEED TO FIND OUT WHAT ELSE THE DIAMOND GANG KNOWS ABOUT ME.
YOU THINK ABOUT HOW WE'RE GOING TO BUST INTO THE LOCAL CHAPTER WITHOUT GETTING YOU HURT.
HELLO, ARMADALE? LISTEN, I NEED SOMETHING...
XXXX XXXX XXX XX XX
WELL?
I KNOW WHAT'LL WORK.

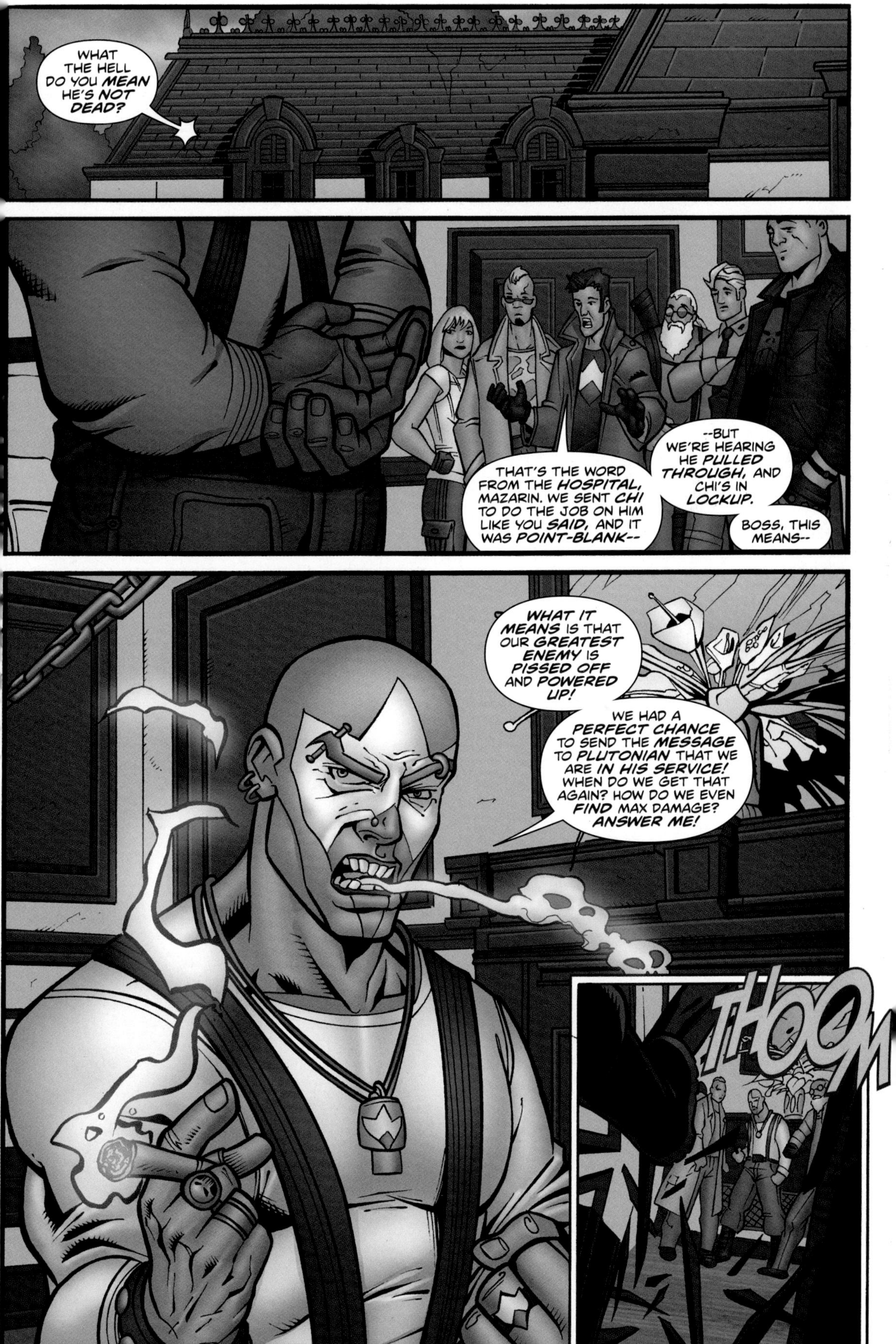
WHAT THE HELL DO YOU MEAN HE'S NOT DEAD?
THAT'S THE WORD FROM THE HOSPITAL, MAZARIN. WE SENT CHI TO DO THE JOB ON HIM LIKE YOU SAID, AND IT WAS POINT-BLANK--
--BUT WE'RE HEARING HE PULLED THROUGH, AND CHI'S IN LOCKUP.
BOSS, THIS MEANS--
WHAT IT MEANS IS THAT OUR GREATEST ENEMY IS PISSED OFF AND POWERED UP!
WE HAD A PERFECT CHANCE TO SEND THE MESSAGE TO PLUTONIAN THAT WE ARE IN HIS SERVICE! WHEN DO WE GET THAT AGAIN? HOW DO WE EVEN FIND MAX DAMAGE? ANSWER ME!
THOOM

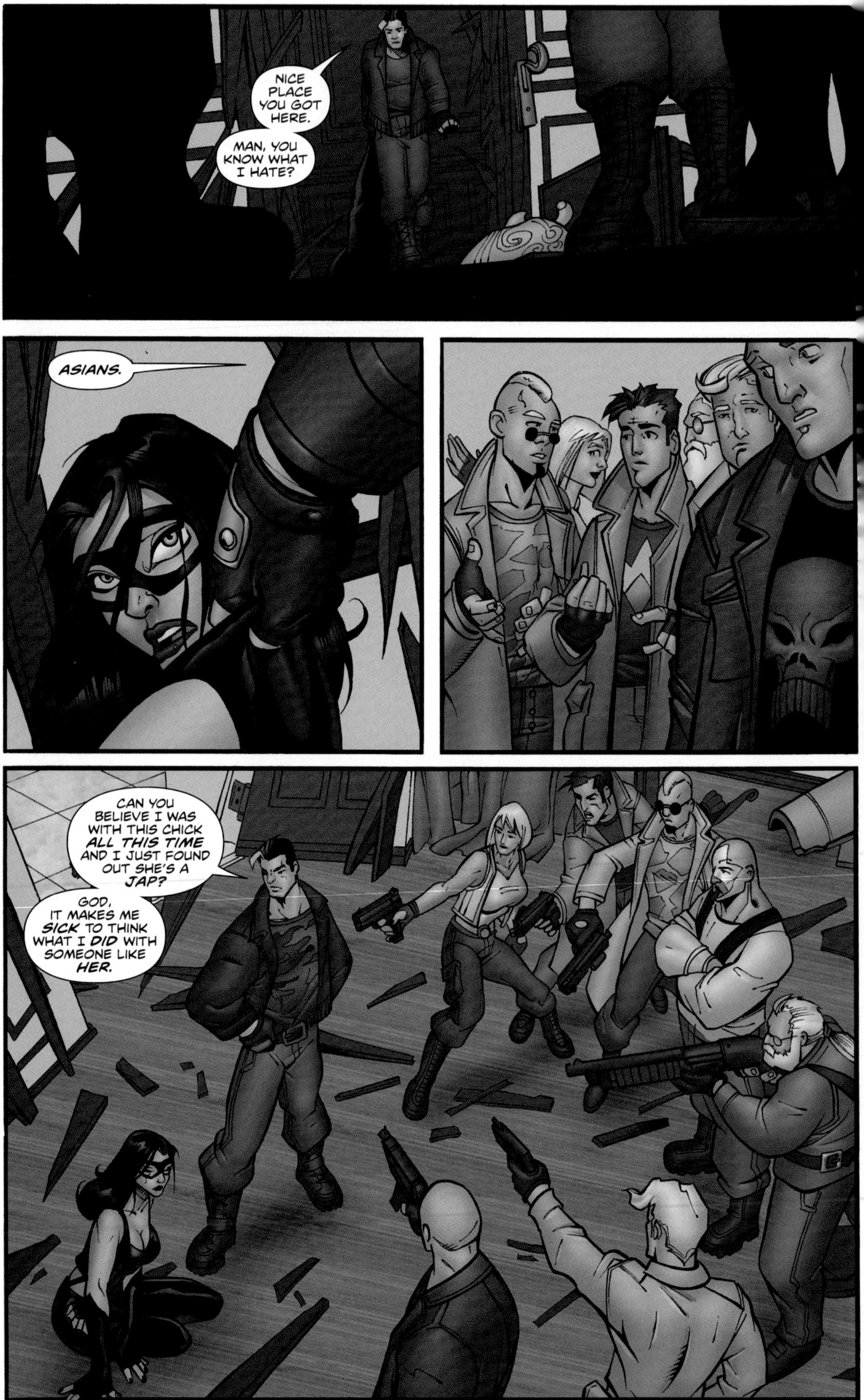
NICE PLACE YOU GOT HERE.
MAN, YOU KNOW WHAT I HATE?
ASIANS.
CAN YOU BELIEVE I WAS WITH THIS CHICK ALL THIS TIME AND I JUST FOUND OUT SHE'S A JAP?
GOD, IT MAKES ME SICK TO THINK WHAT I DID WITH SOMEONE LIKE HER.

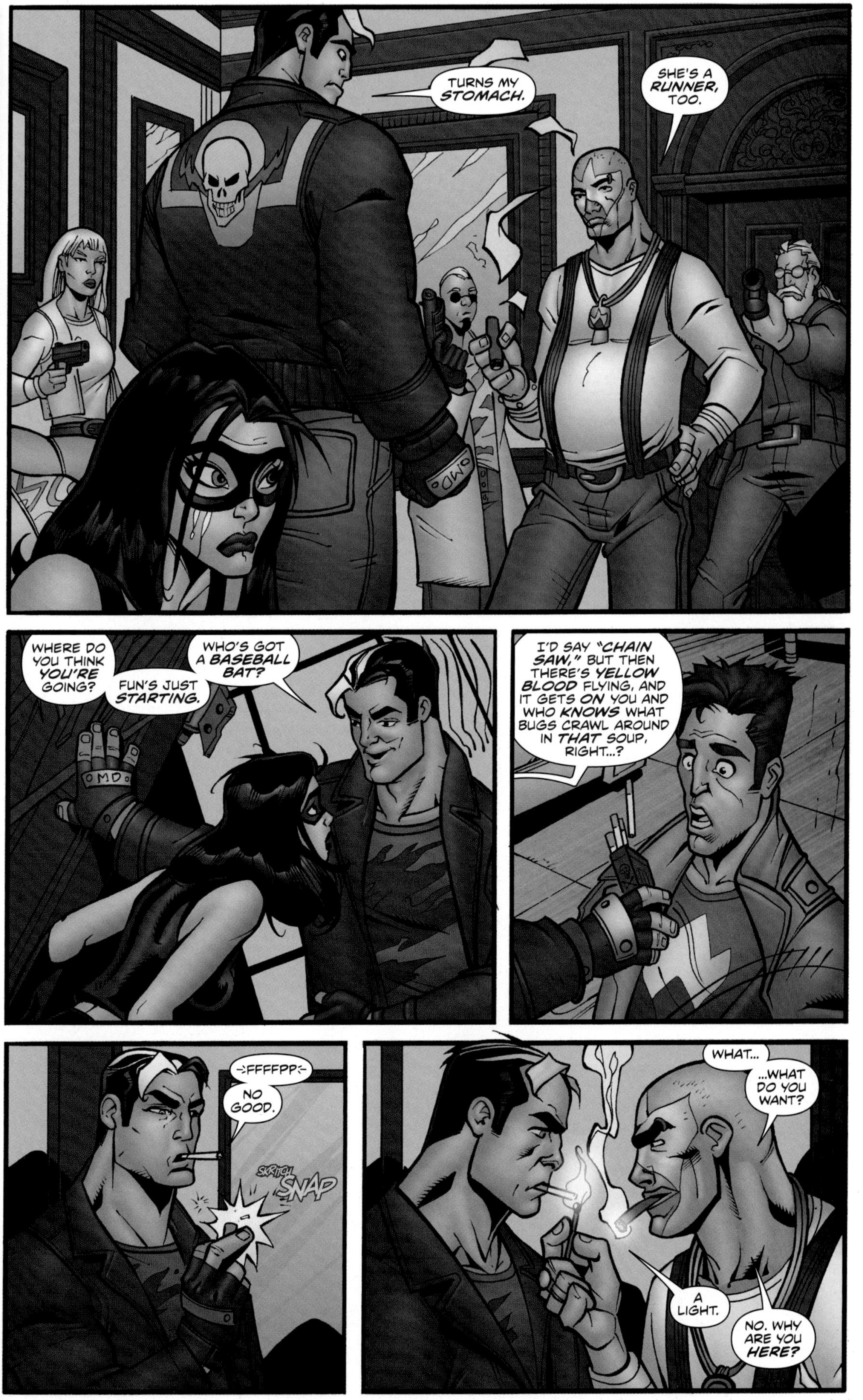
TURNS MY STOMACH.
SHE'S A RUNNER, TOO.
WHERE DO YOU THINK YOU'RE GOING?
FUN'S JUST STARTING.
WHO'S GOT A BASEBALL BAT?
I'D SAY "CHAIN SAW," BUT THEN THERE'S YELLOW BLOOD FLYING, AND IT GETS ON YOU AND WHO KNOWS WHAT BUGS CRAWL AROUND IN THAT SOUP, RIGHT...?
-FFFFPP-
NO GOOD.
SKRITCH SNAP
WHAT...
...WHAT DO YOU WANT?
A LIGHT.
NO. WHY ARE YOU HERE?

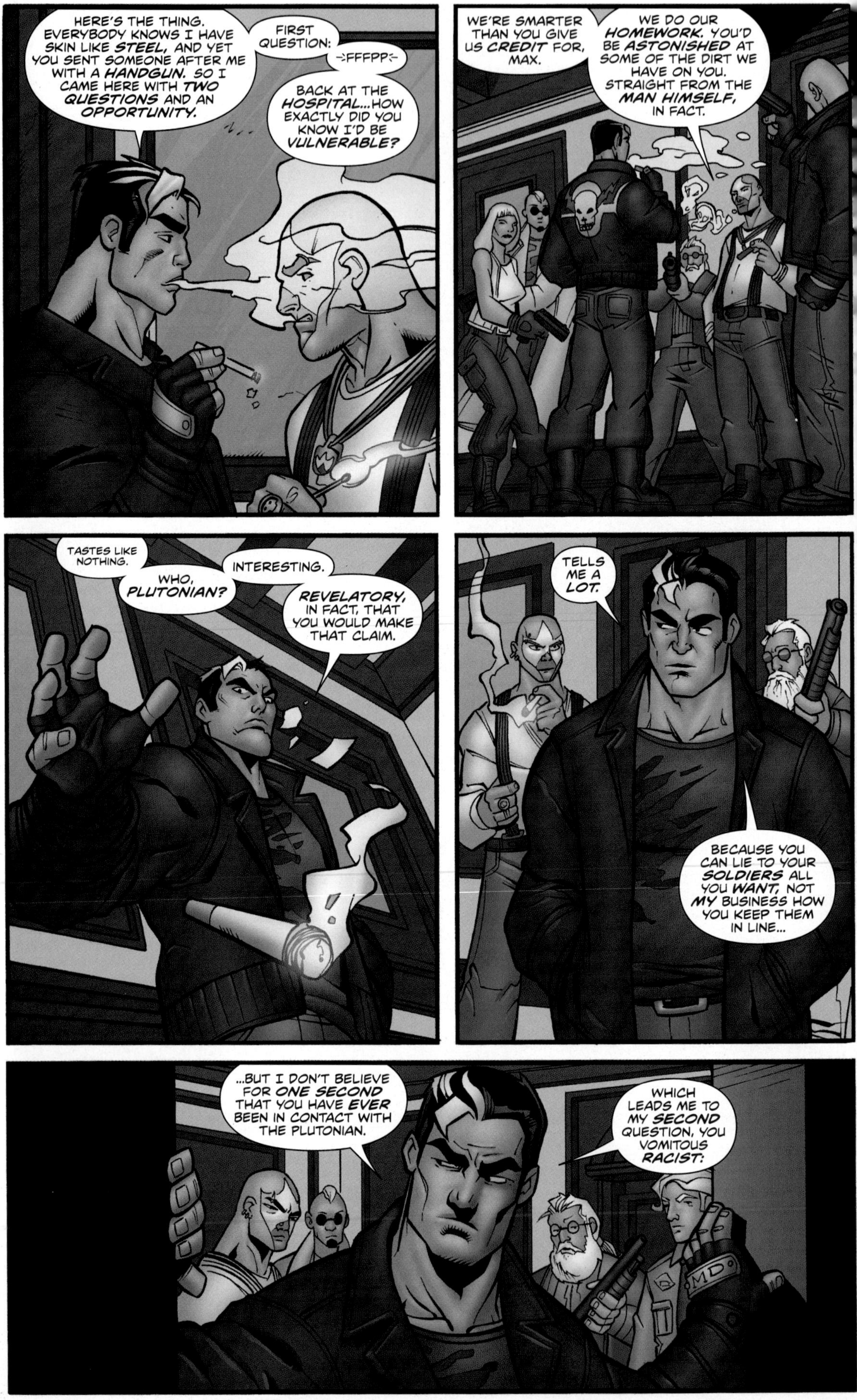
HERE'S THE THING. EVERYBODY KNOWS I HAVE SKIN LIKE STEEL, AND YET YOU SENT SOMEONE AFTER ME WITH A HANDGUN. SO I CAME HERE WITH TWO QUESTIONS AND AN OPPORTUNITY.
FIRST QUESTION:
FFFPP
BACK AT THE HOSPITAL...HOW EXACTLY DID YOU KNOW I'D BE VULNERABLE?
WE'RE SMARTER THAN YOU GIVE US CREDIT FOR, MAX.
WE DO OUR HOMEWORK. YOU'D BE ASTONISHED AT SOME OF THE DIRT WE HAVE ON YOU. STRAIGHT FROM THE MAN HIMSELF, IN FACT.
TASTES LIKE NOTHING.
WHO, PLUTONIAN?
INTERESTING.
REVELATORY, IN FACT, THAT YOU WOULD MAKE THAT CLAIM.
TELLS ME A LOT.
BECAUSE YOU CAN LIE TO YOUR SOLDIERS ALL YOU WANT, NOT MY BUSINESS HOW YOU KEEP THEM IN LINE...
...BUT I DON'T BELIEVE FOR ONE SECOND THAT YOU HAVE EVER BEEN IN CONTACT WITH THE PLUTONIAN.
WHICH LEADS ME TO MY SECOND QUESTION, YOU VOMITOUS RACIST:

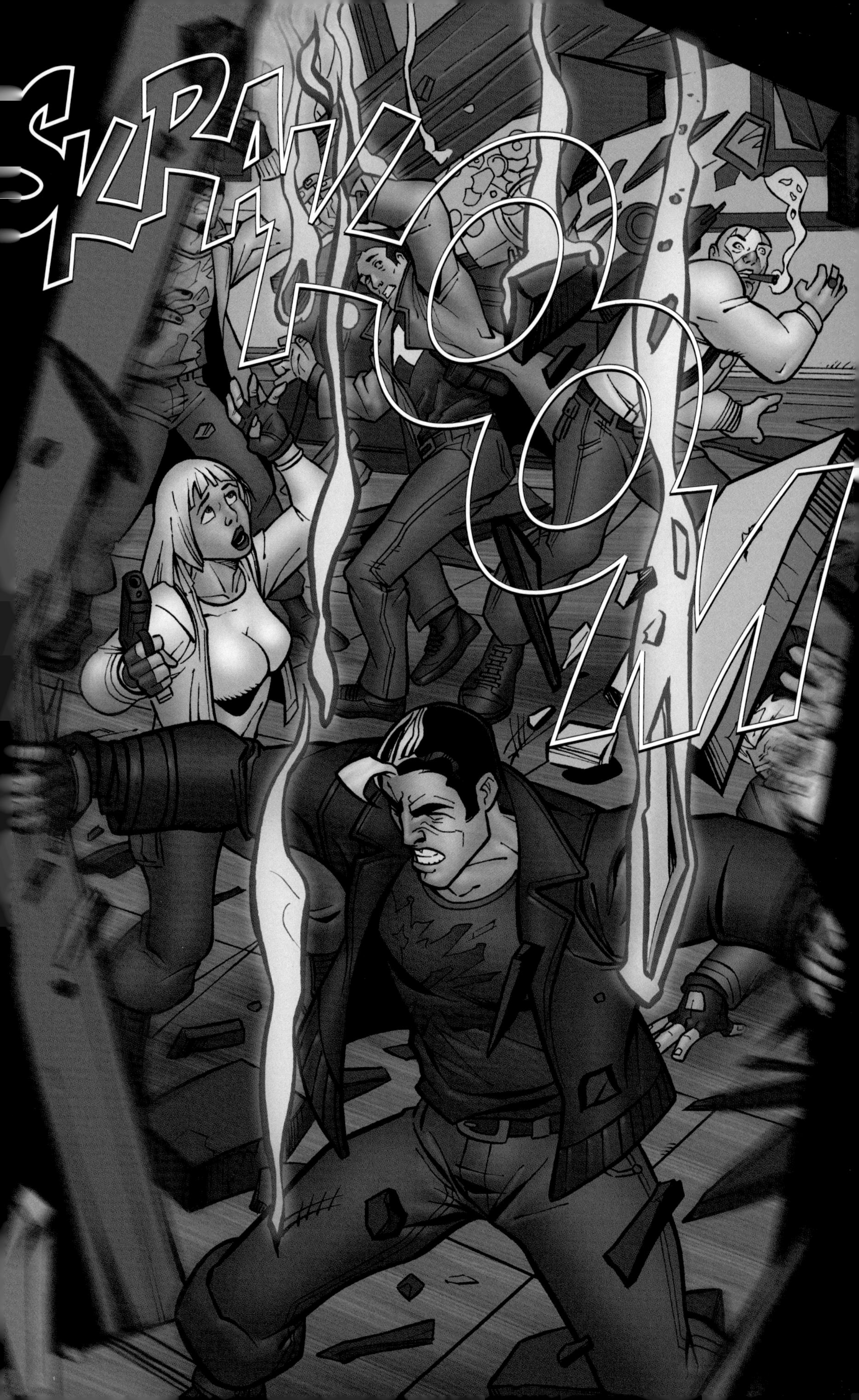
SKRAKLOOM

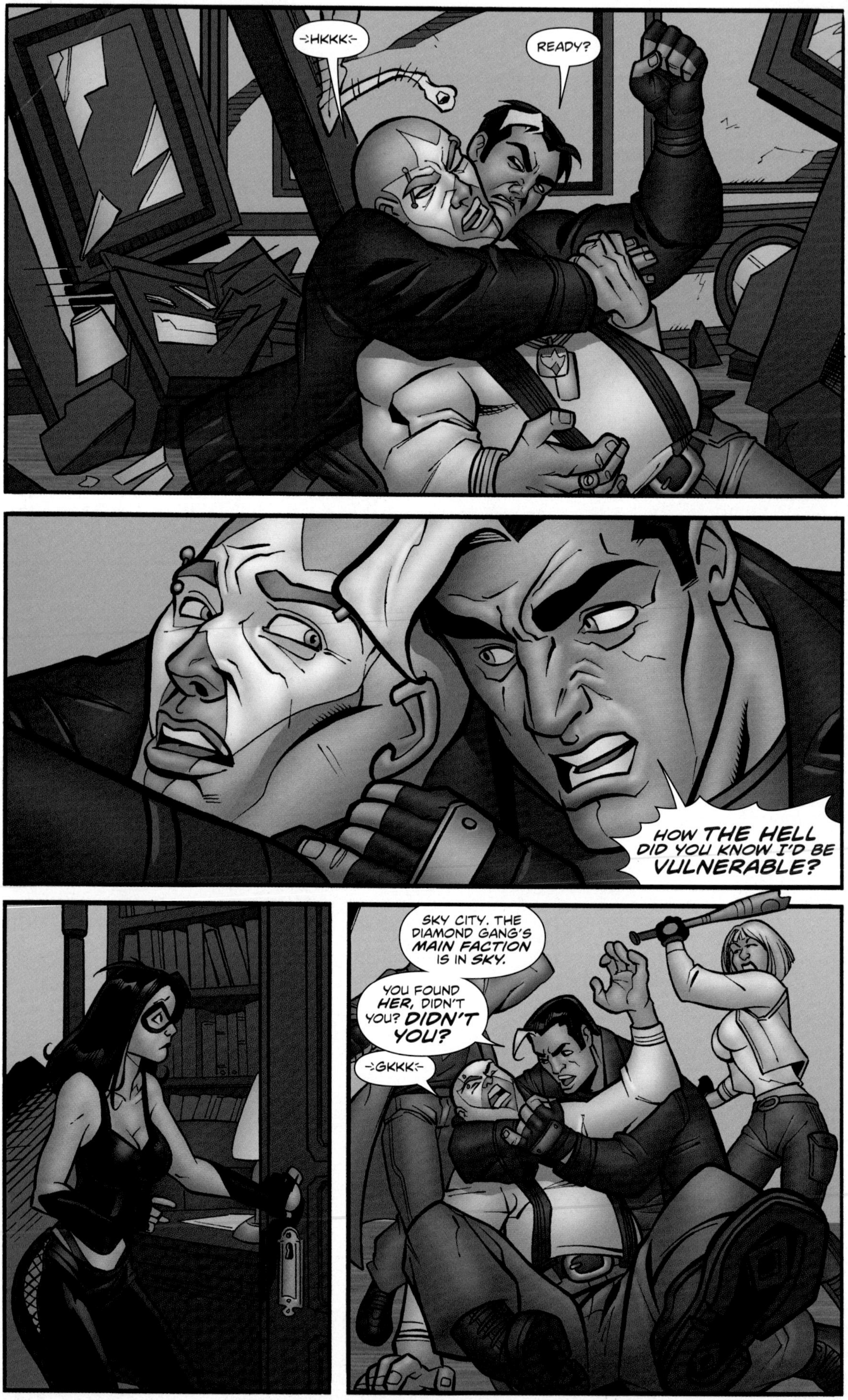
-HKKK-
READY?
HOW THE HELL DID YOU KNOW I'D BE VULNERABLE?
SKY CITY. THE DIAMOND GANG'S MAIN FACTION IS IN SKY.
YOU FOUND HER, DIDN'T YOU? DIDN'T YOU?
-GKKK-

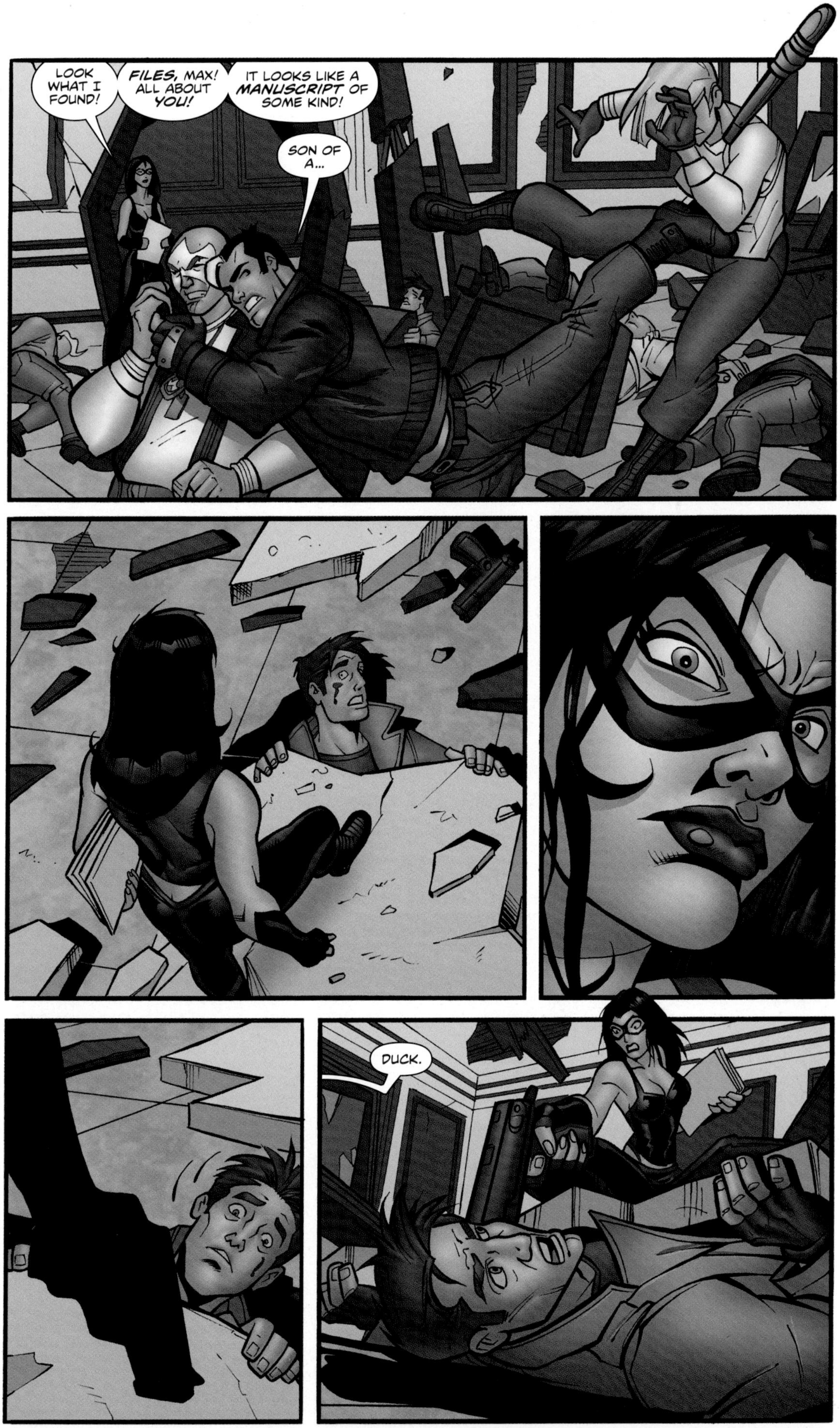
LOOK WHAT I FOUND!
FILES, MAX! ALL ABOUT YOU!
IT LOOKS LIKE A MANUSCRIPT OF SOME KIND!
SON OF A...
DUCK.

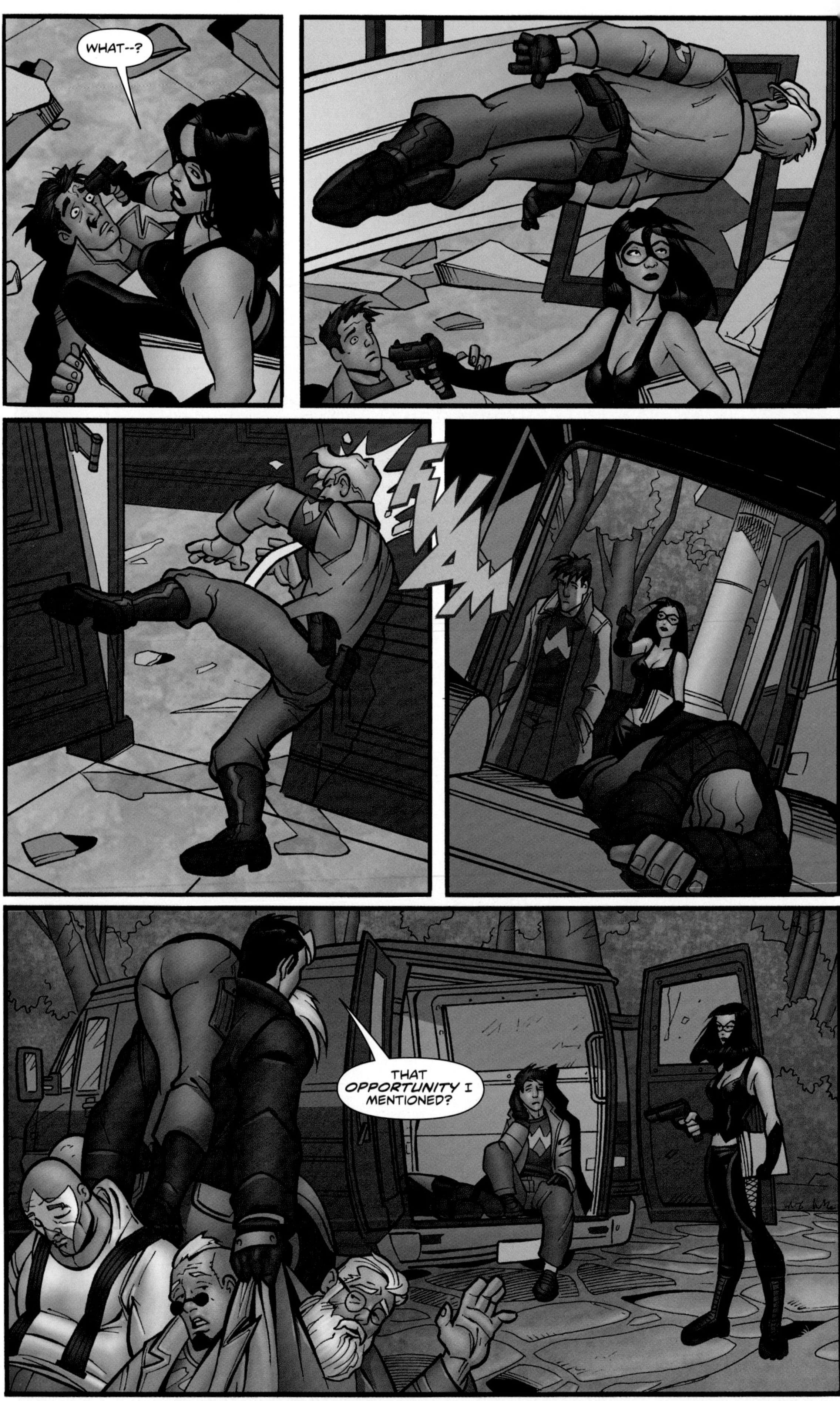
WHAT--?
FWAM
THAT OPPORTUNITY I MENTIONED?

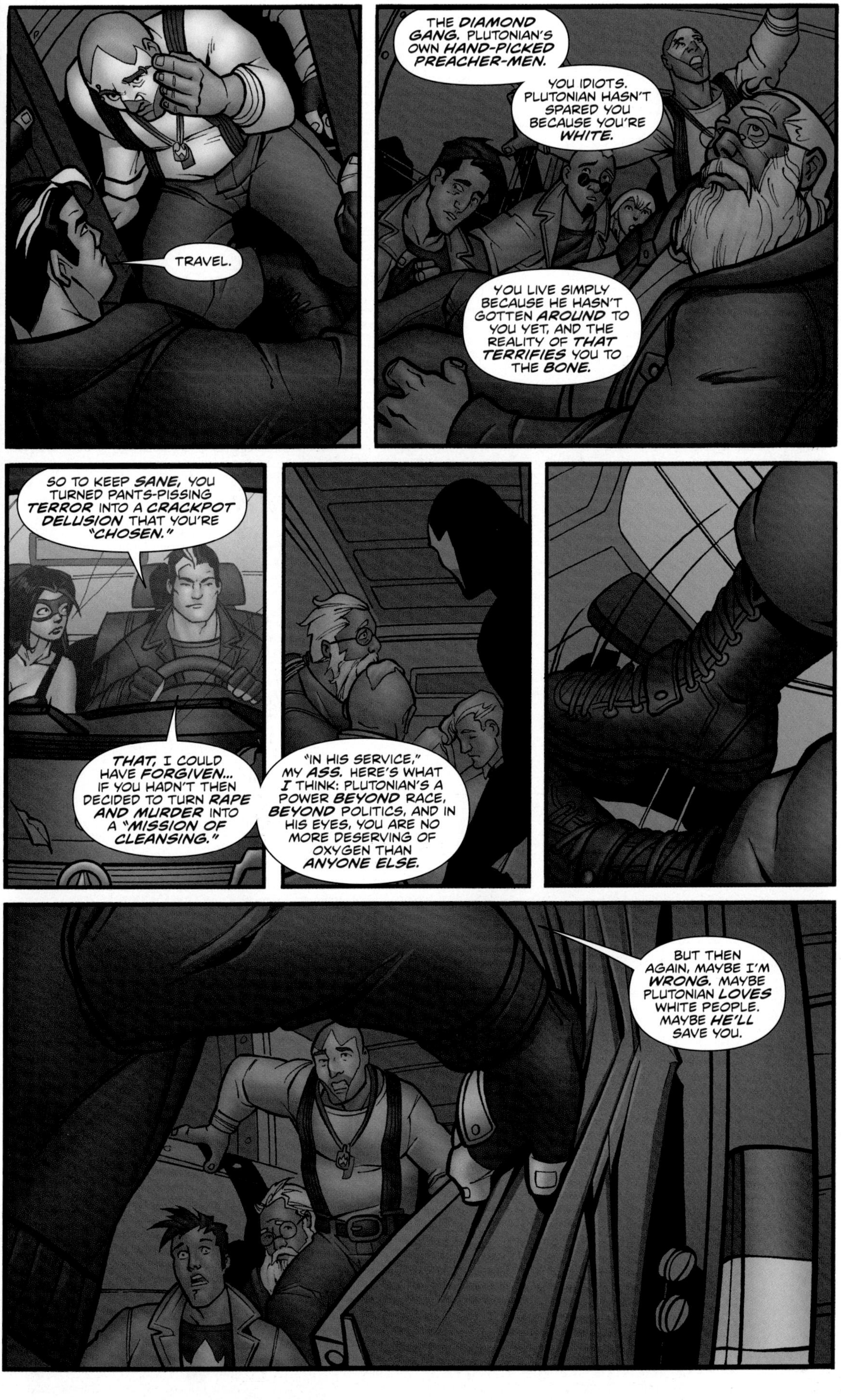
TRAVEL.
THE DIAMOND GANG. PLUTONIAN'S OWN HAND-PICKED PREACHER-MEN.
YOU IDIOTS. PLUTONIAN HASN'T SPARED YOU BECAUSE YOU'RE WHITE.
YOU LIVE SIMPLY BECAUSE HE HASN'T GOTTEN AROUND TO YOU YET, AND THE REALITY OF THAT TERRIFIES YOU TO THE BONE.
SO TO KEEP SANE, YOU TURNED PANTS-PISSING TERROR INTO A CRACKPOT DELUSION THAT YOU'RE "CHOSEN."
THAT, I COULD HAVE FORGIVEN... IF YOU HADN'T THEN DECIDED TO TURN RAPE AND MURDER INTO A "MISSION OF CLEANSING."
"IN HIS SERVICE," MY ASS. HERE'S WHAT I THINK: PLUTONIAN'S A POWER BEYOND RACE, BEYOND POLITICS, AND IN HIS EYES, YOU ARE NO MORE DESERVING OF OXYGEN THAN ANYONE ELSE.
BUT THEN AGAIN, MAYBE I'M WRONG. MAYBE PLUTONIAN LOVES WHITE PEOPLE. MAYBE HE'LL SAVE YOU.

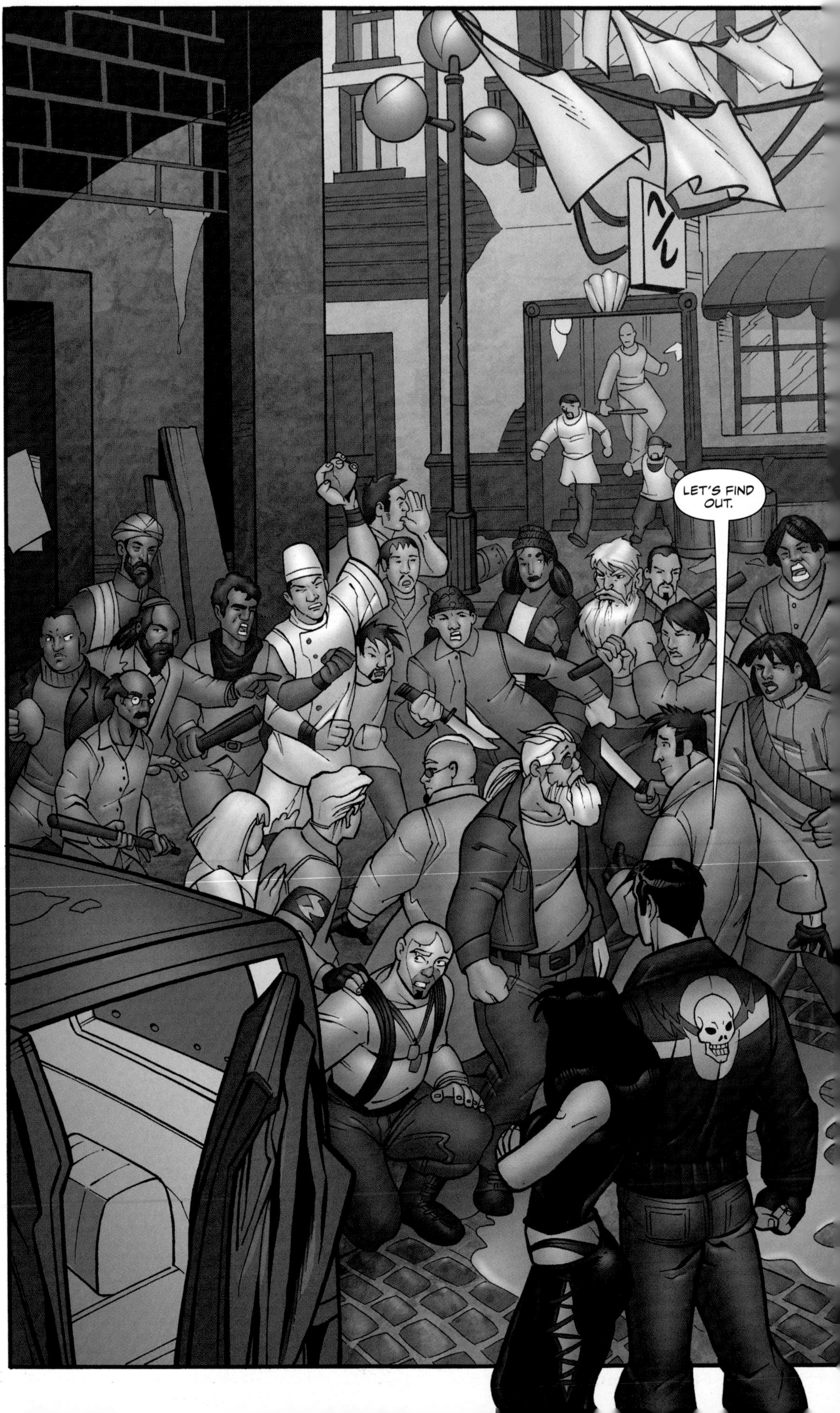
LET'S FIND OUT.

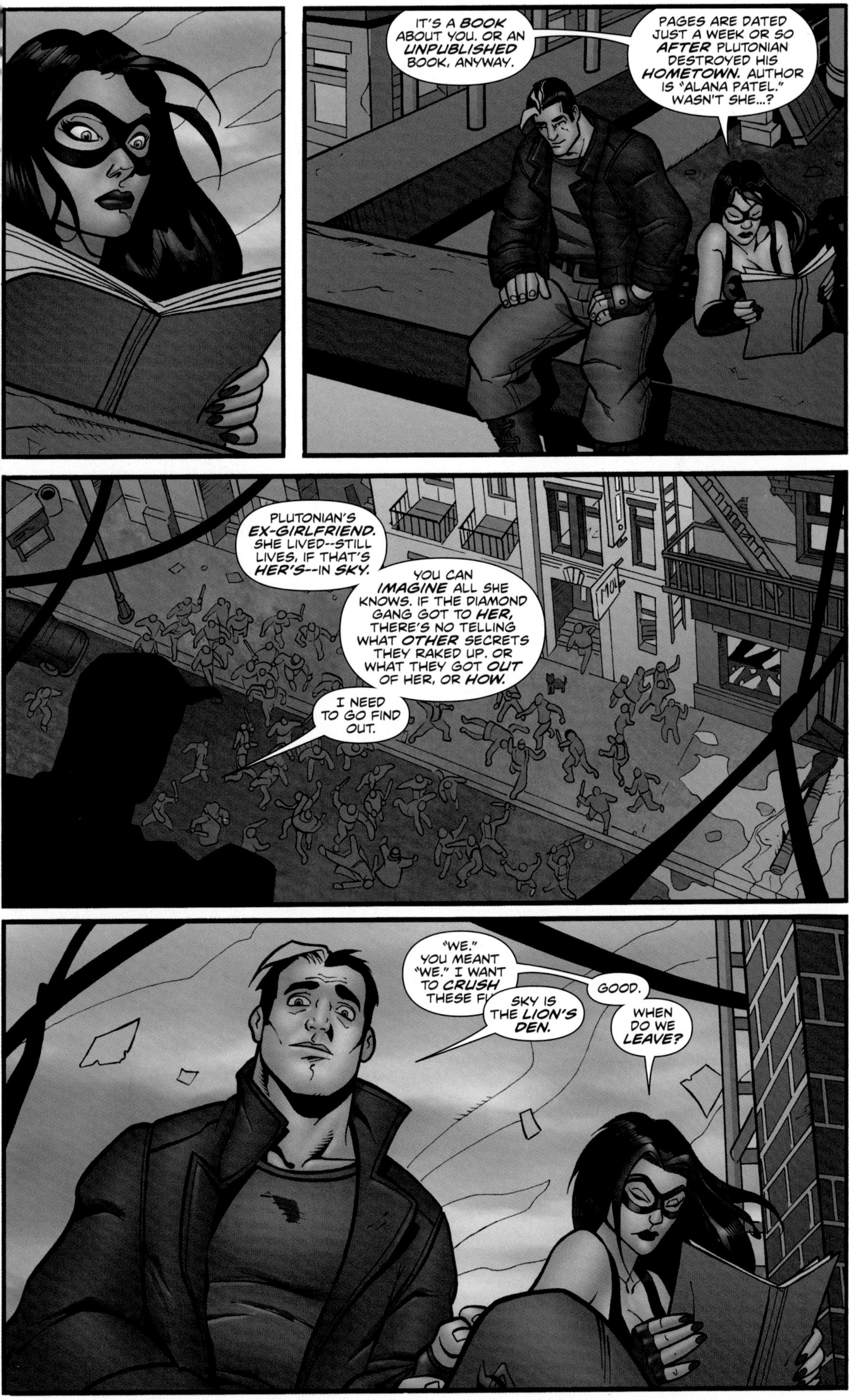
IT'S A BOOK ABOUT YOU. OR AN UNPUBLISHED BOOK, ANYWAY.
PAGES ARE DATED JUST A WEEK OR SO AFTER PLUTONIAN DESTROYED HIS HOMETOWN. AUTHOR IS "ALANA PATEL." WASN'T SHE...?
PLUTONIAN'S EX-GIRLFRIEND. SHE LIVED--STILL LIVES, IF THAT'S HER'S--IN SKY.
YOU CAN IMAGINE ALL SHE KNOWS. IF THE DIAMOND GANG GOT TO HER, THERE'S NO TELLING WHAT OTHER SECRETS THEY RAKED UP. OR WHAT THEY GOT OUT OF HER, OR HOW.
I NEED TO GO FIND OUT.
"WE." YOU MEANT "WE." I WANT TO CRUSH THESE F
SKY IS THE LION'S DEN.
GOOD.
WHEN DO WE LEAVE?

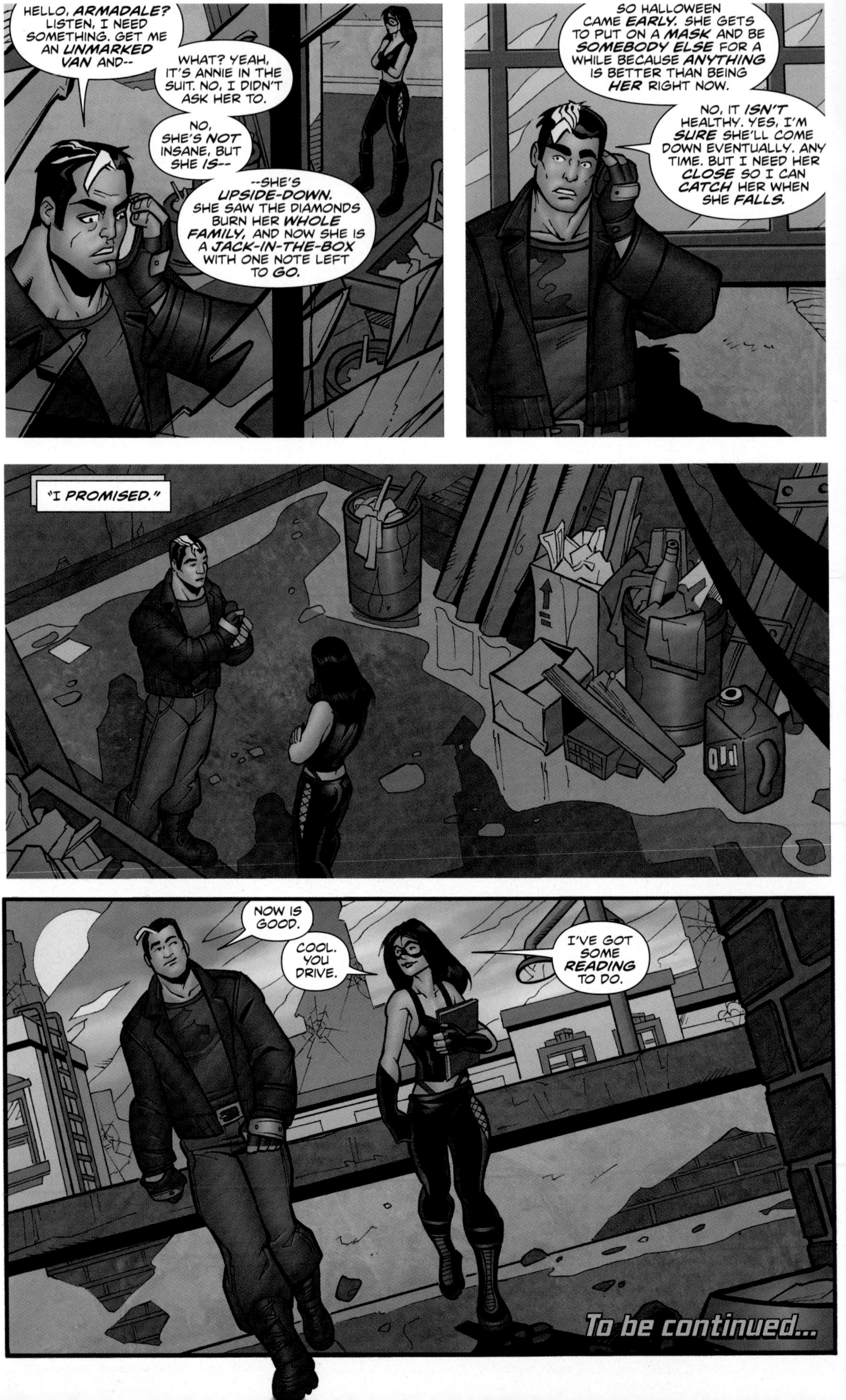
HELLO, ARMADALE? LISTEN, I NEED SOMETHING. GET ME AN UNMARKED VAN AND--
WHAT? YEAH, IT'S ANNIE IN THE SUIT. NO, I DIDN'T ASK HER TO.
NO, SHE'S NOT INSANE, BUT SHE IS--
--SHE'S UPSIDE-DOWN. SHE SAW THE DIAMONDS BURN HER WHOLE FAMILY, AND NOW SHE IS A JACK-IN-THE-BOX WITH ONE NOTE LEFT TO GO.
SO HALLOWEEN CAME EARLY. SHE GETS TO PUT ON A MASK AND BE SOMEBODY ELSE FOR A WHILE BECAUSE ANYTHING IS BETTER THAN BEING HER RIGHT NOW.
NO, IT ISN'T HEALTHY. YES, I'M SURE SHE'LL COME DOWN EVENTUALLY. ANY TIME. BUT I NEED HER CLOSE SO I CAN CATCH HER WHEN SHE FALLS.
"I PROMISED."
NOW IS GOOD.
COOL. YOU DRIVE.
I'VE GOT SOME READING TO DO.
To be continued...

COVER GALLERY

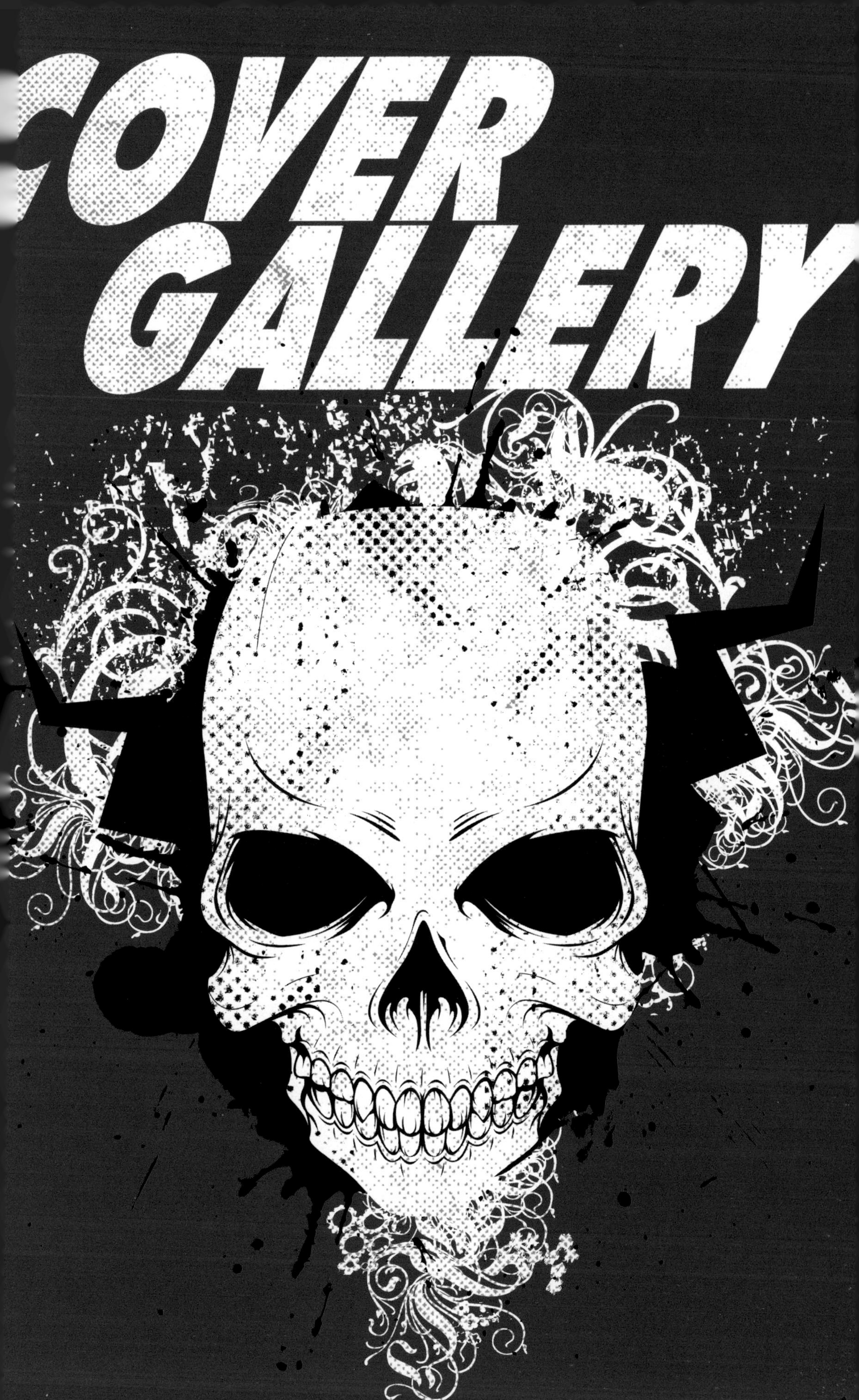

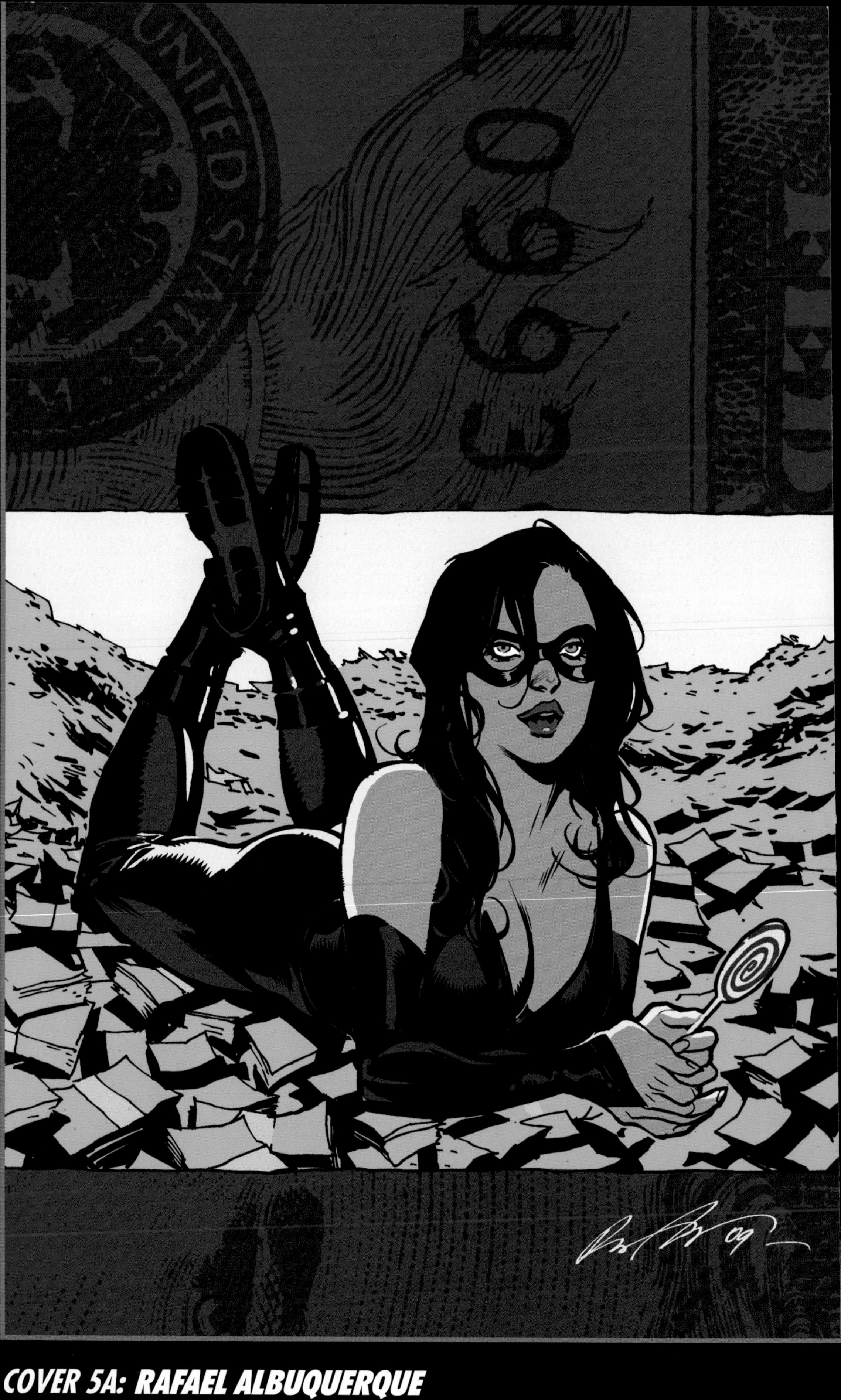

COVER 5A: RAFAEL ALBUQUERQUE

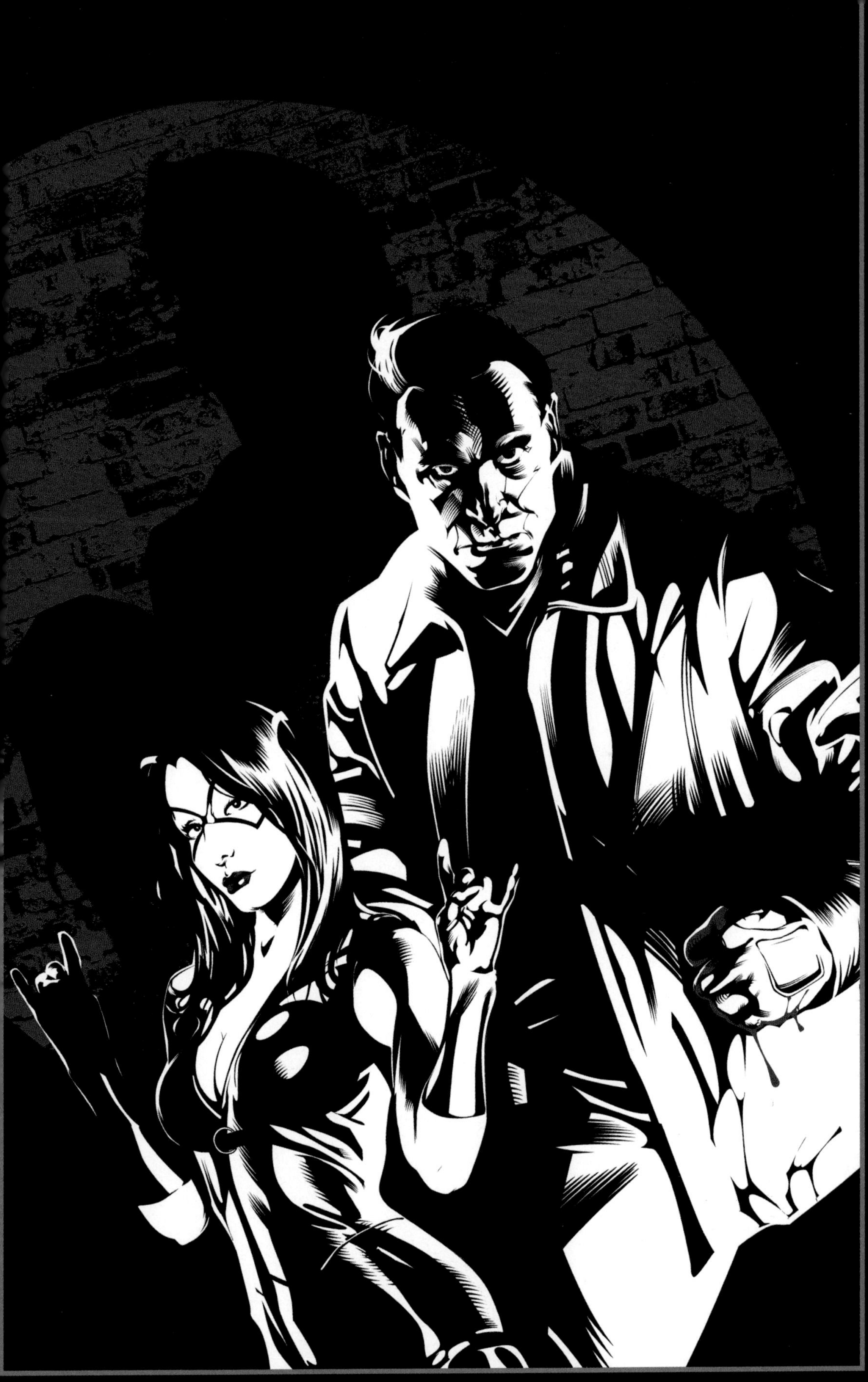

COVER 5B: DENNIS CALERO

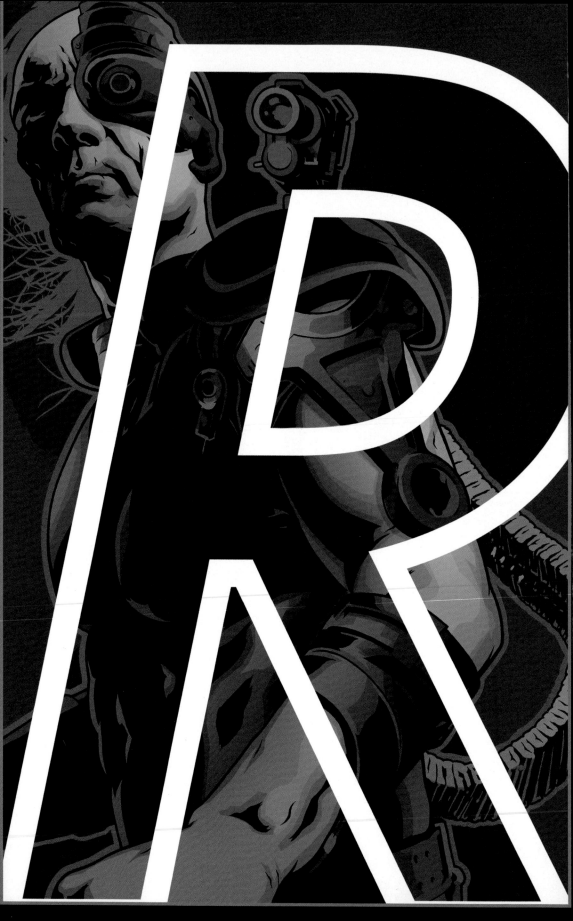

COVER 5C: **JEFFREY SPOKES**

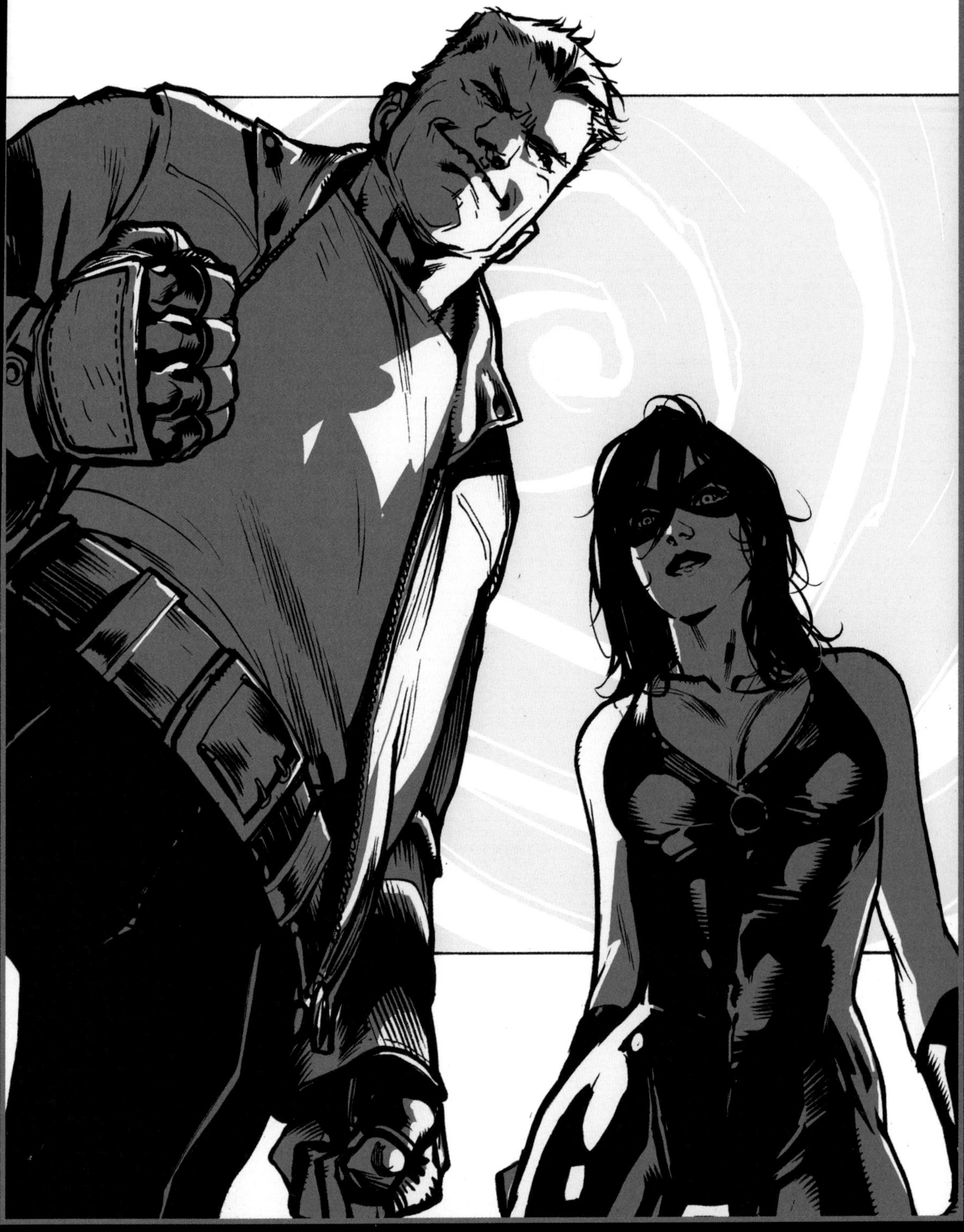

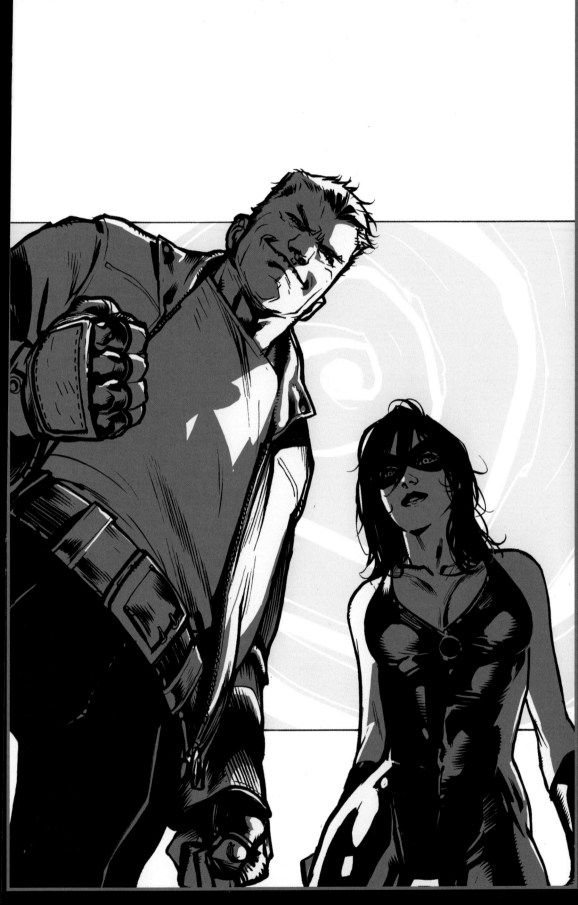

COVER 6A: **RAFAEL ALBUQUERQUE**

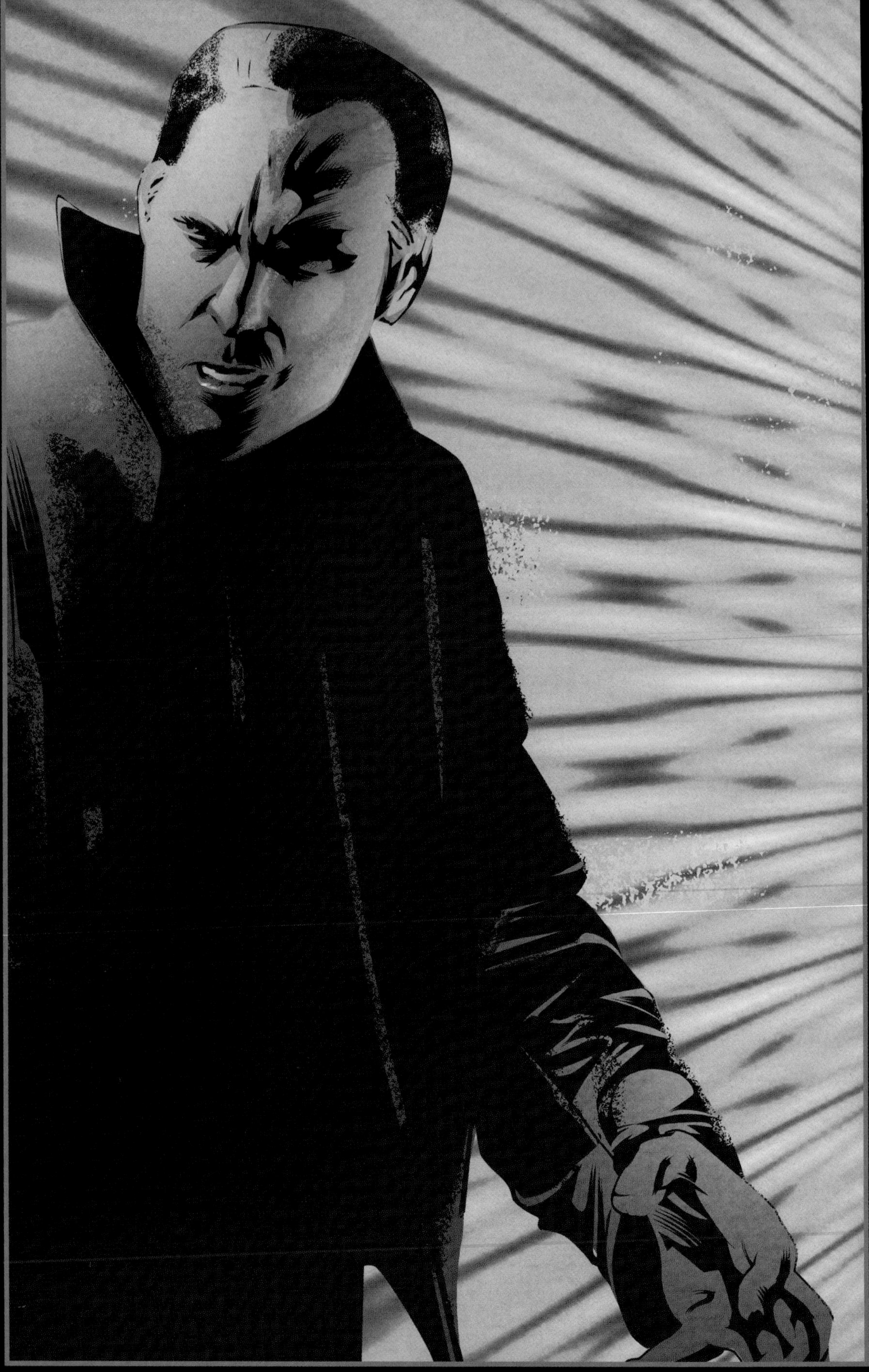

COVER 6B: DENNIS CALERO

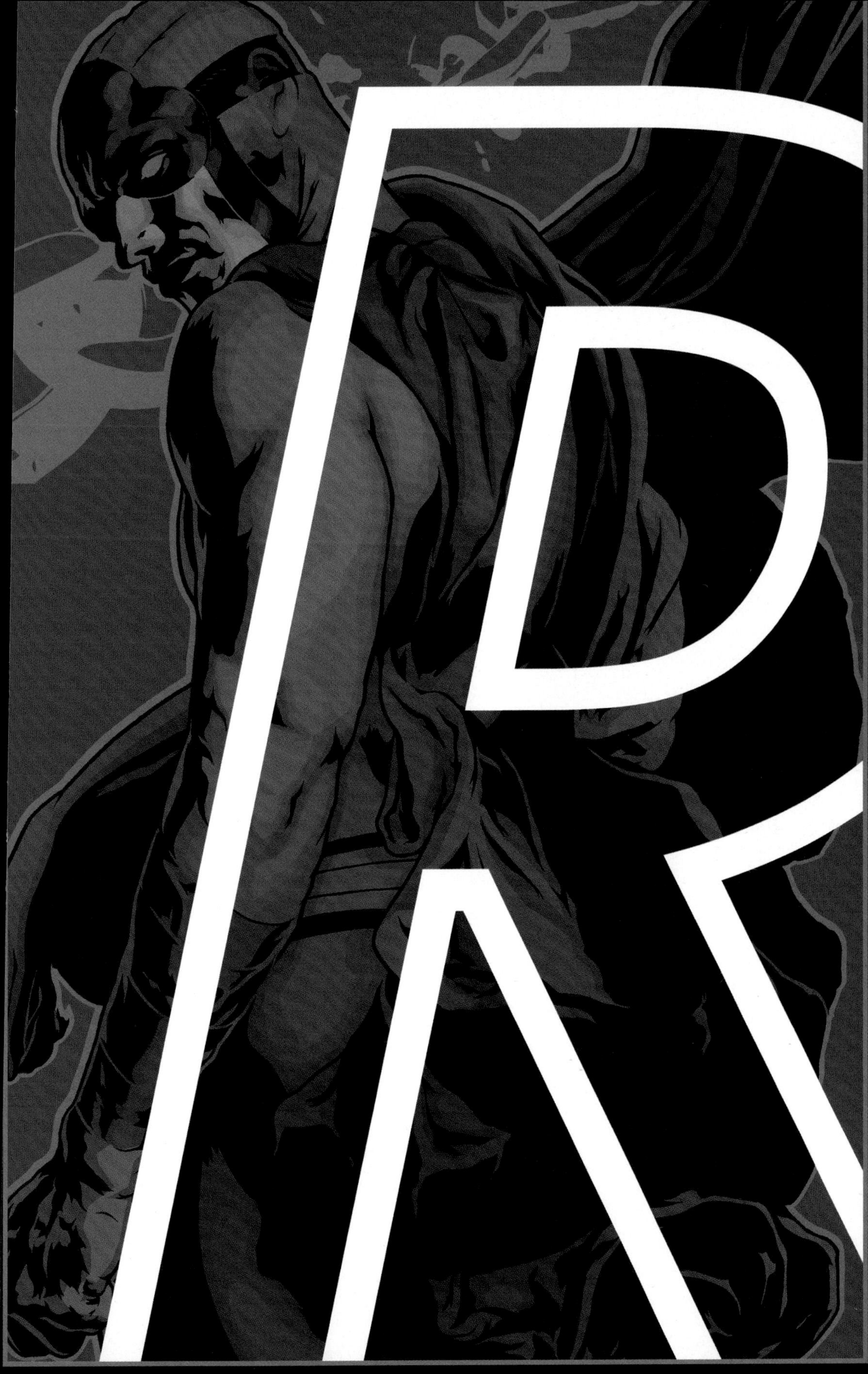

COVER 6C: JEFFREY SPOKES

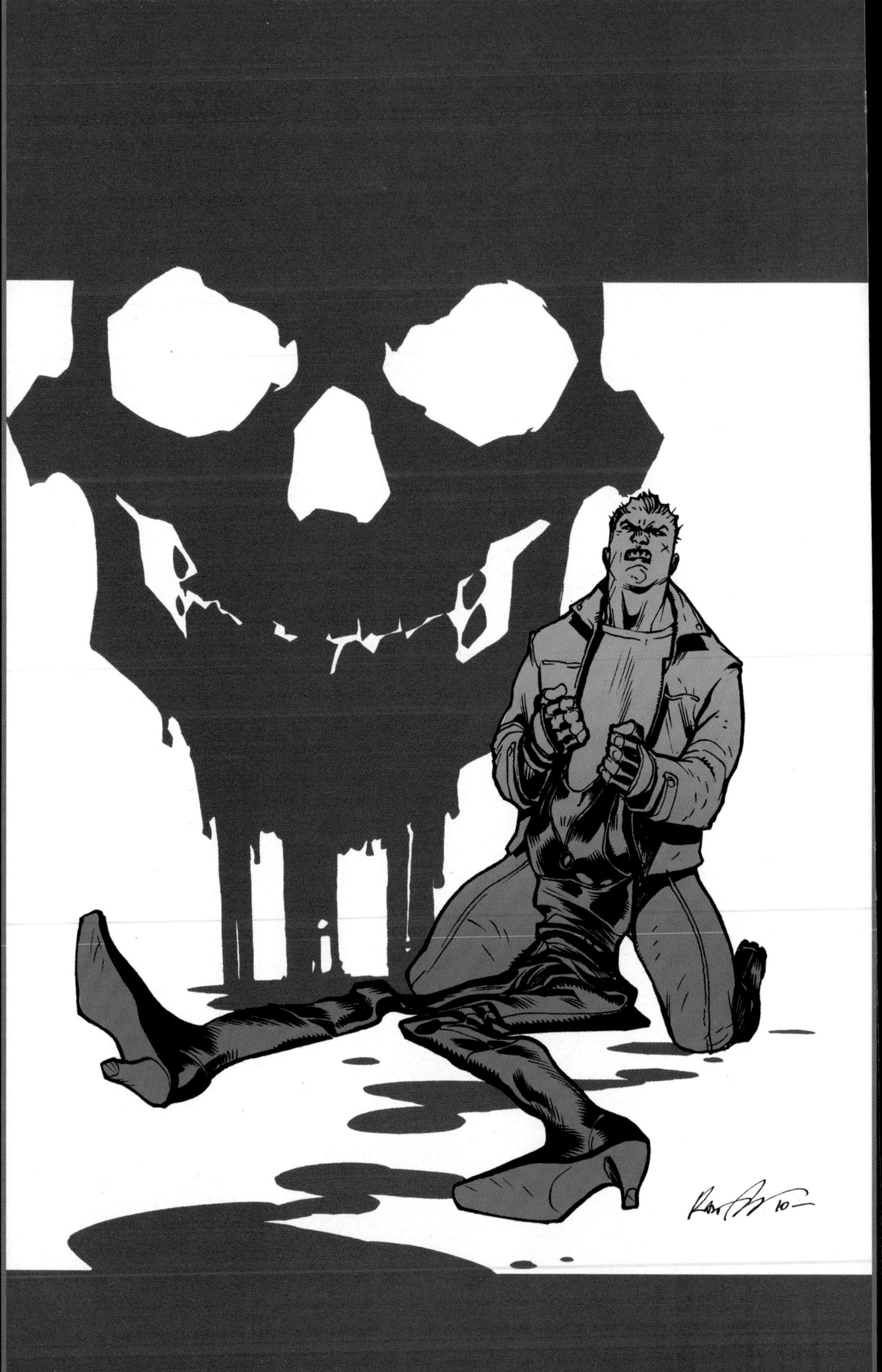

COVER 7A: RAFAEL ALBUQUERQUE

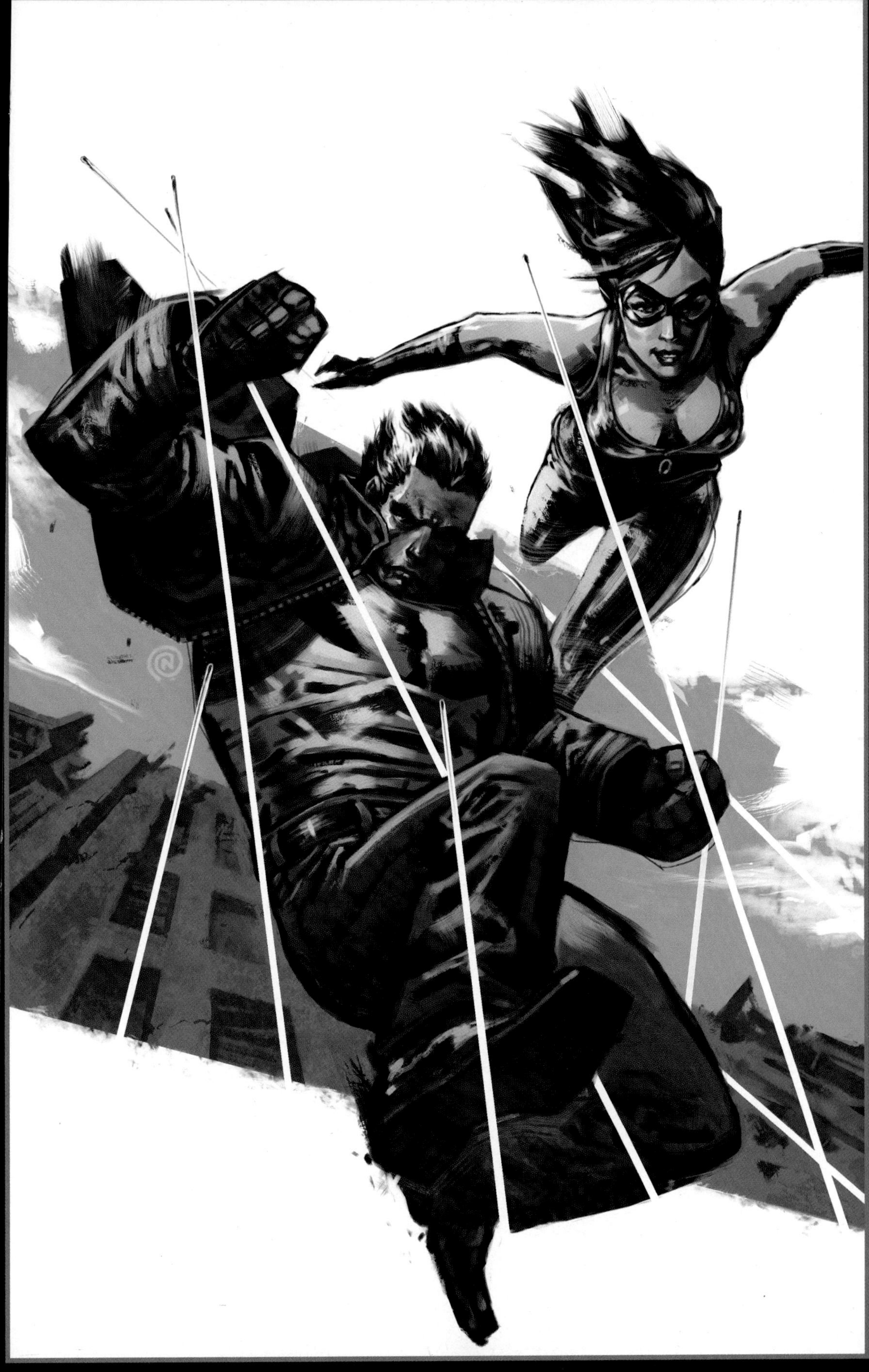

COVER 7B: CHRISTIAN NAUCK

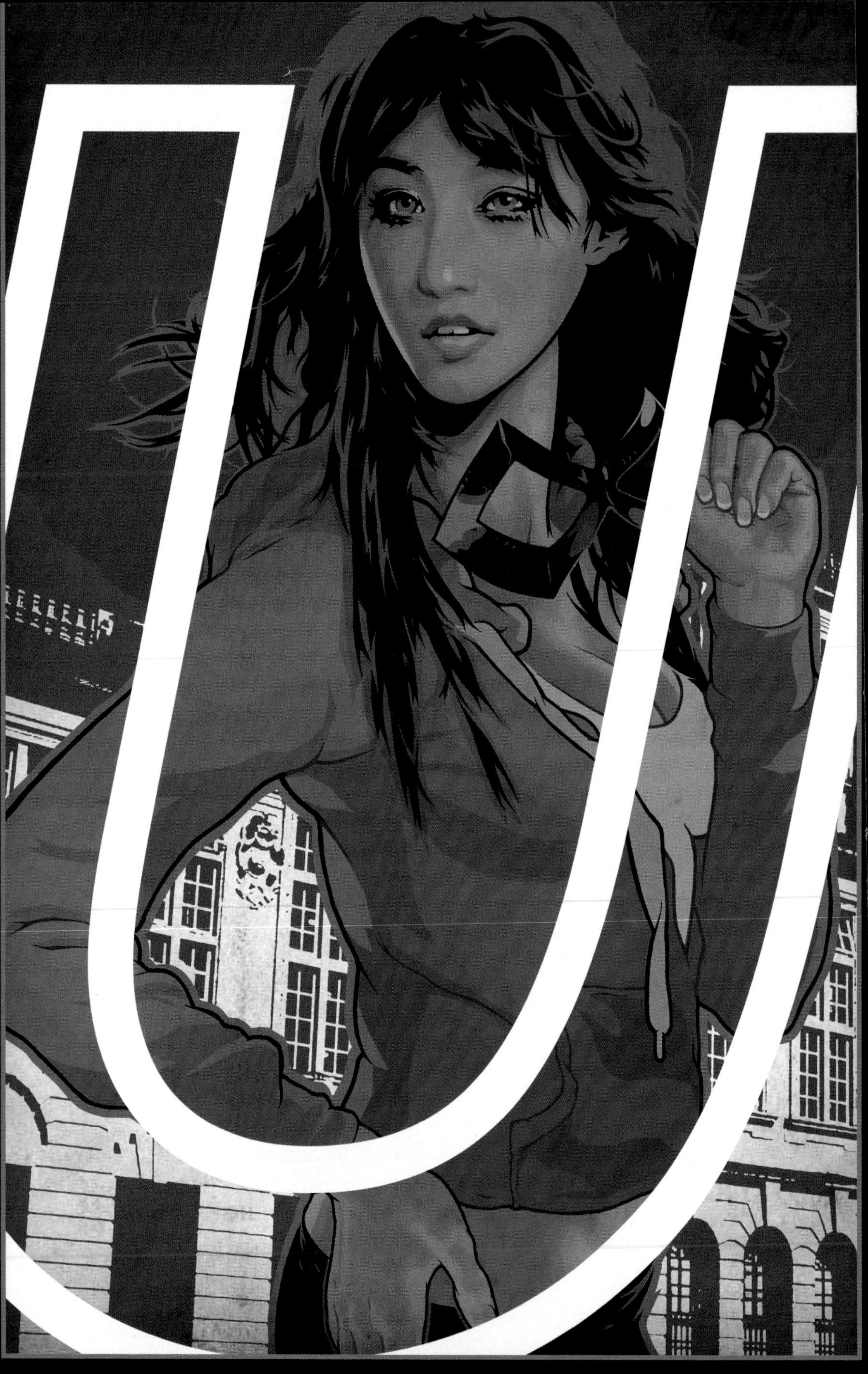

COVER 7C: JEFFREY SPOKES

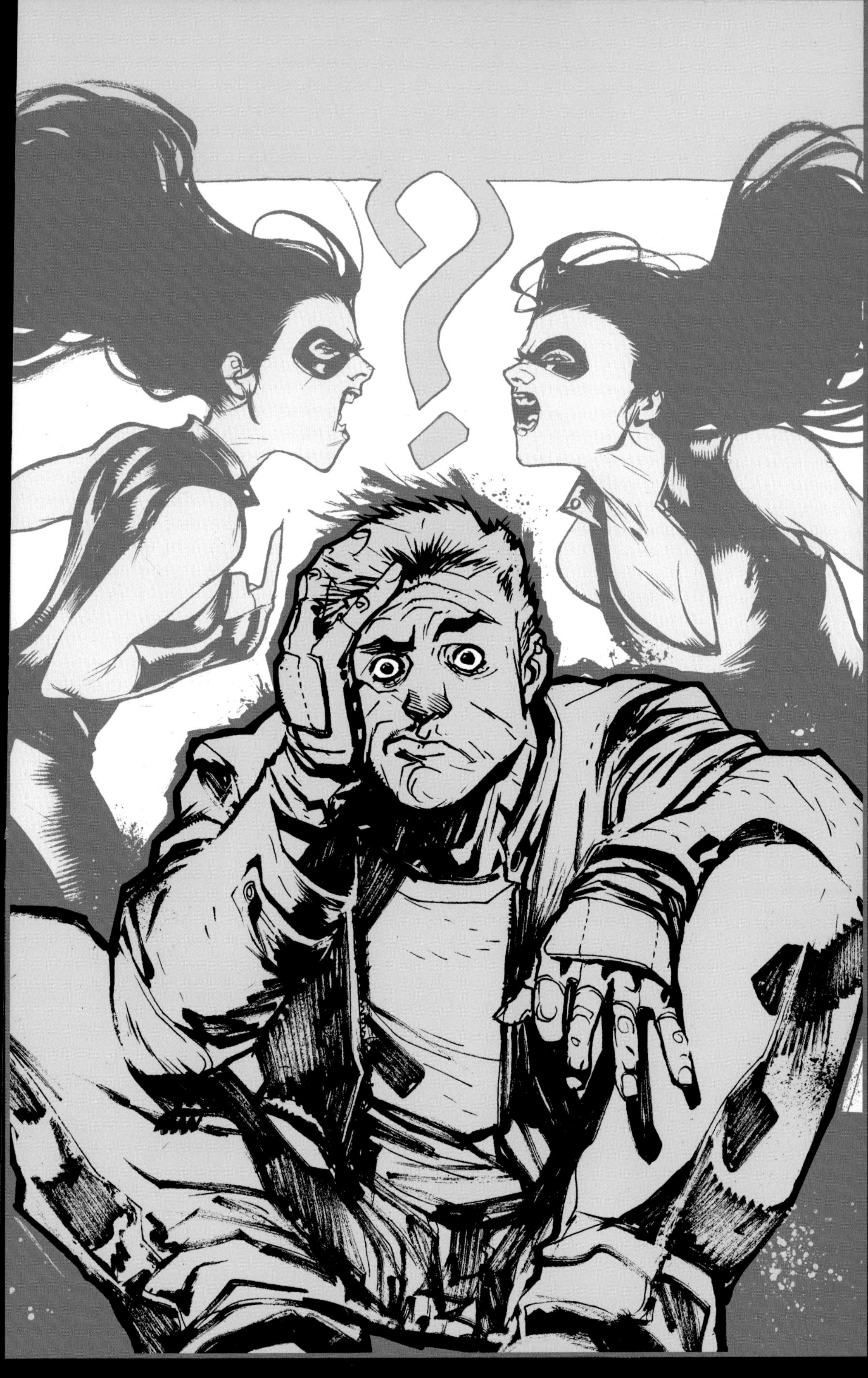

COVER 8A: RAFAEL ALBUQUERQUE

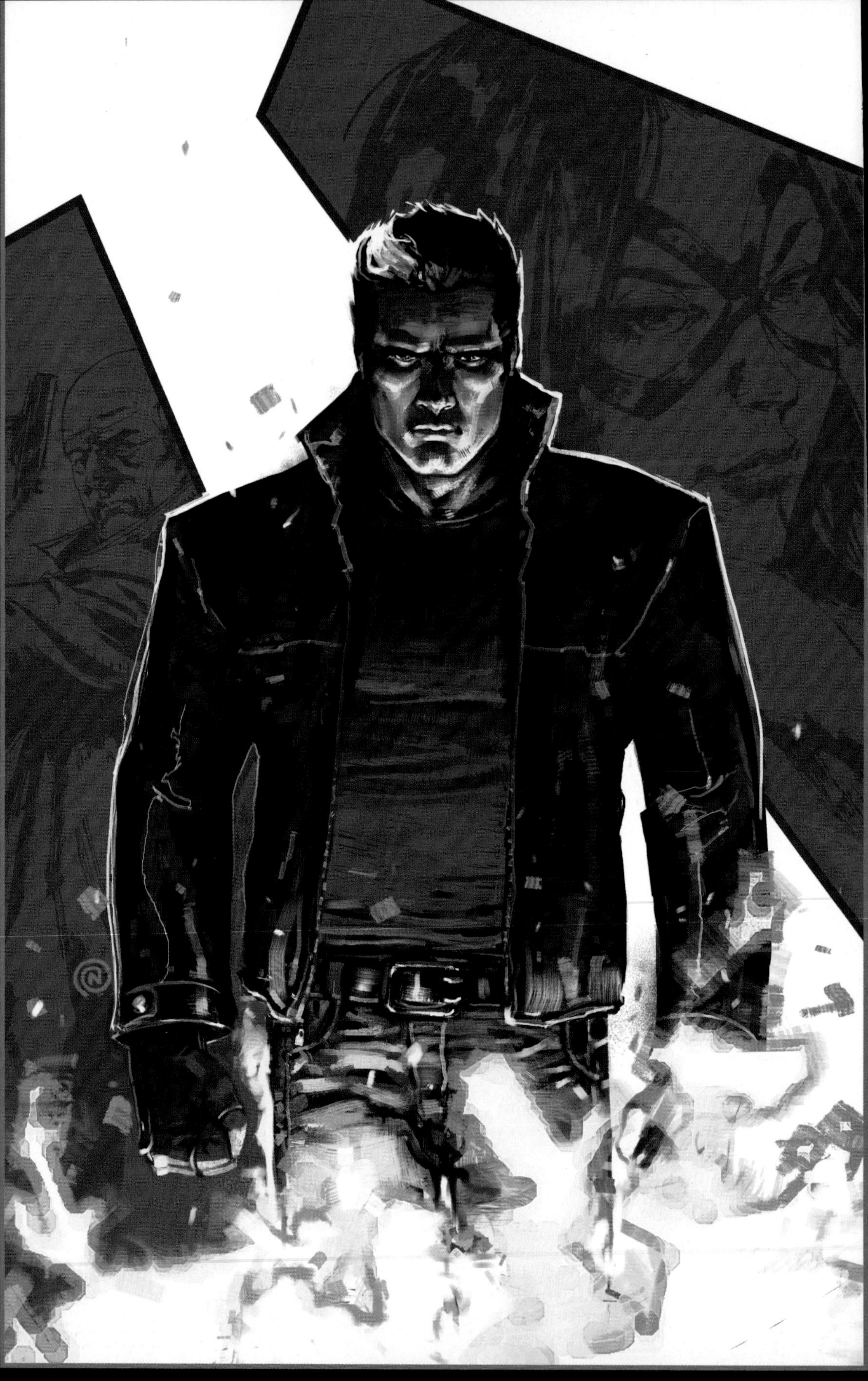

COVER 8B: CHRISTIAN NAUCK

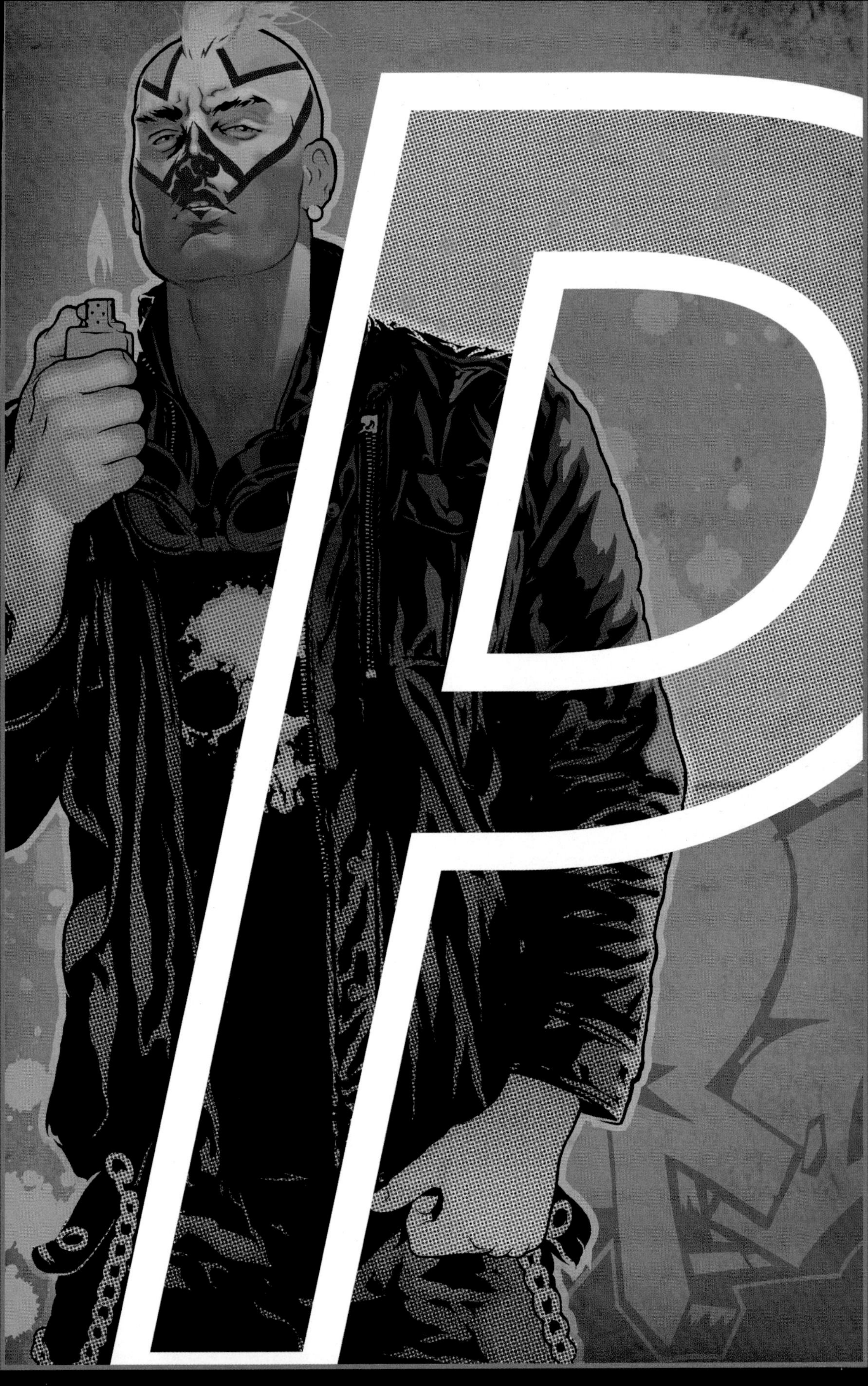

COVER 8C: JEFFREY SPOKES

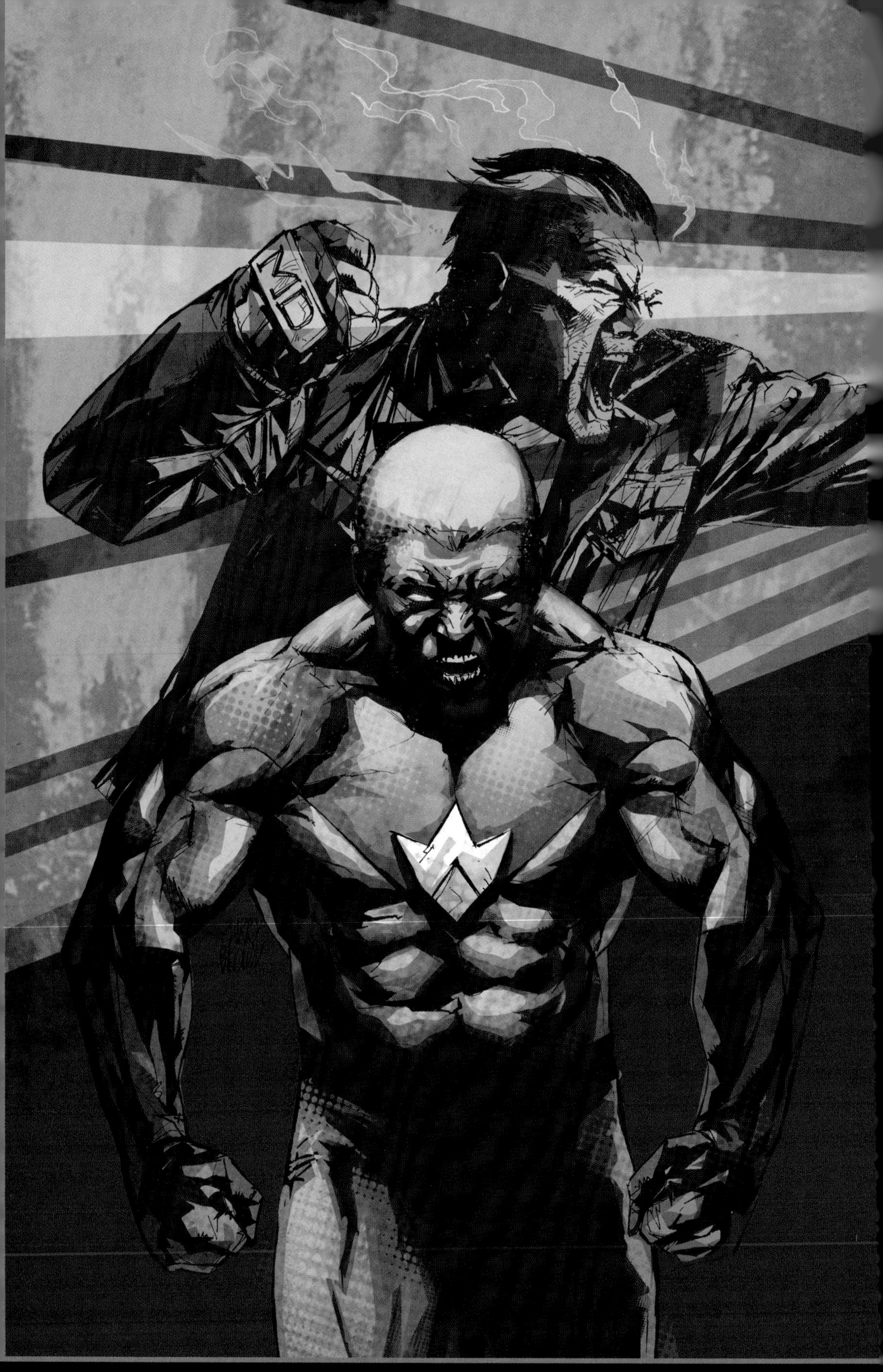
MD

SAN DIEGO COMIC-CON EXCLUSIVE: GARRY BROWN

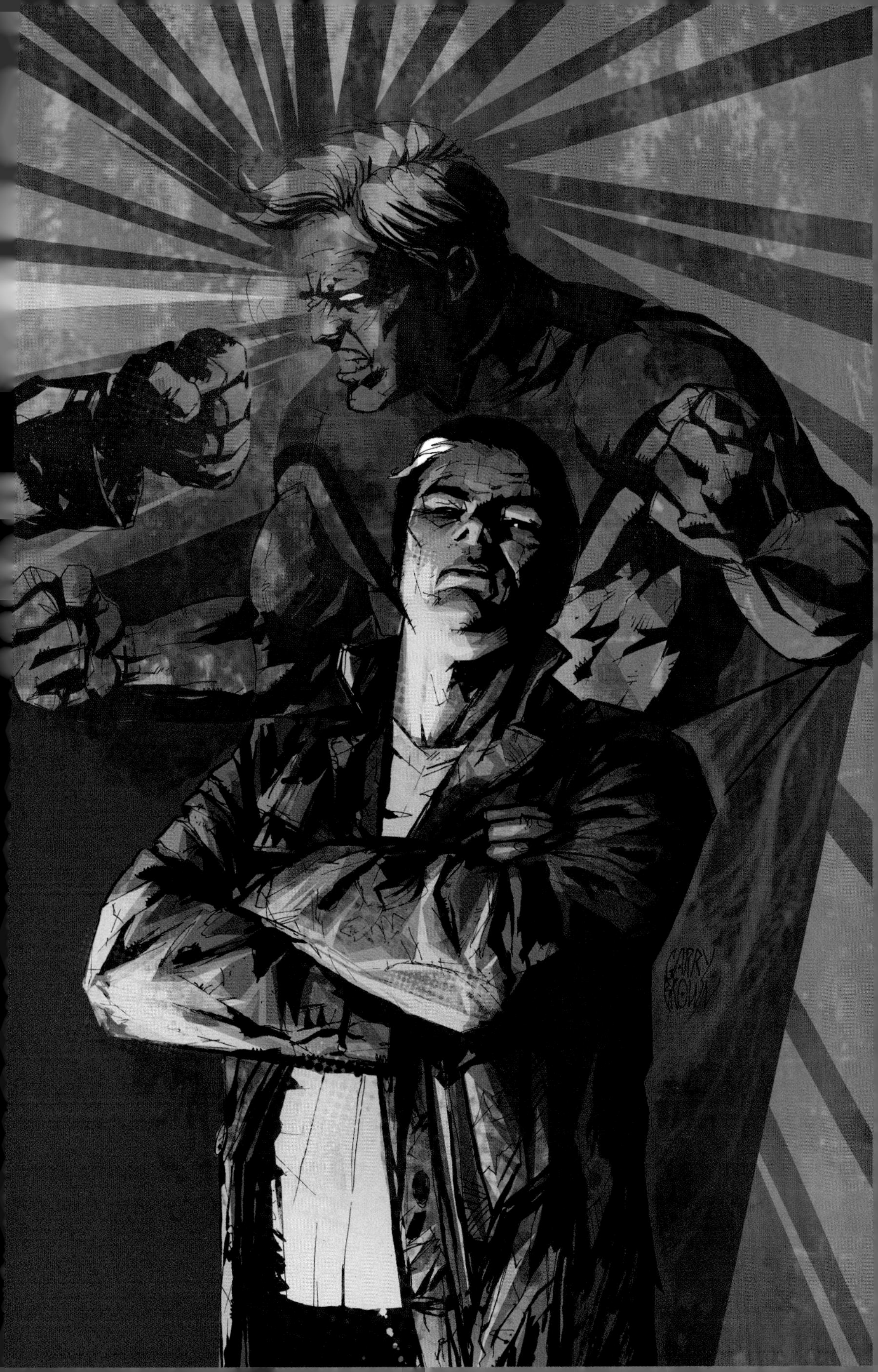
GARRY BROWN

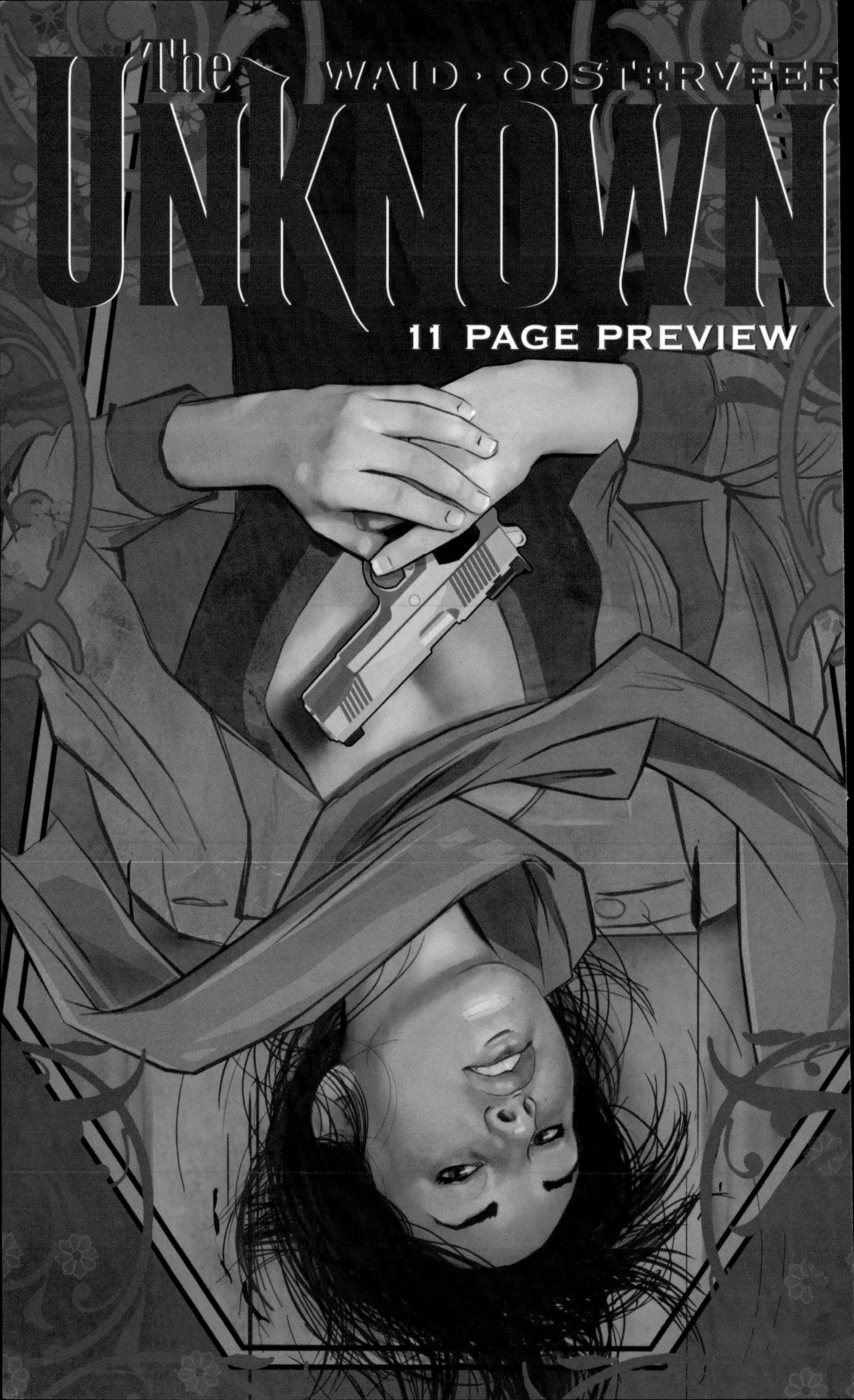

The UNKNOWN
WAID · OOSTERVEER
11 PAGE PREVIEW

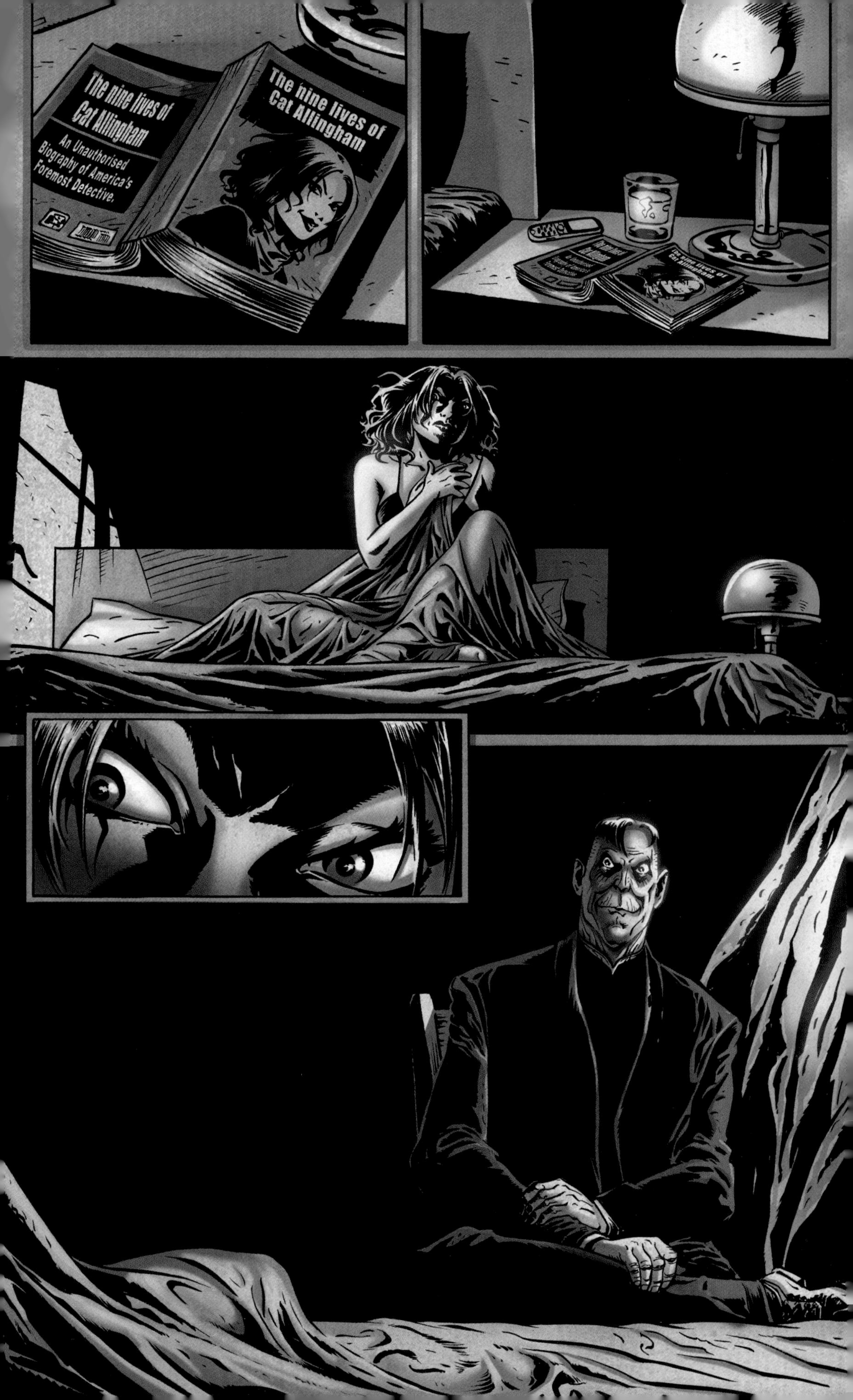
The nine lives of Cat Allingham
An Unauthorised Biography of America's Foremost Detective.
The nine lives of Cat Allingham

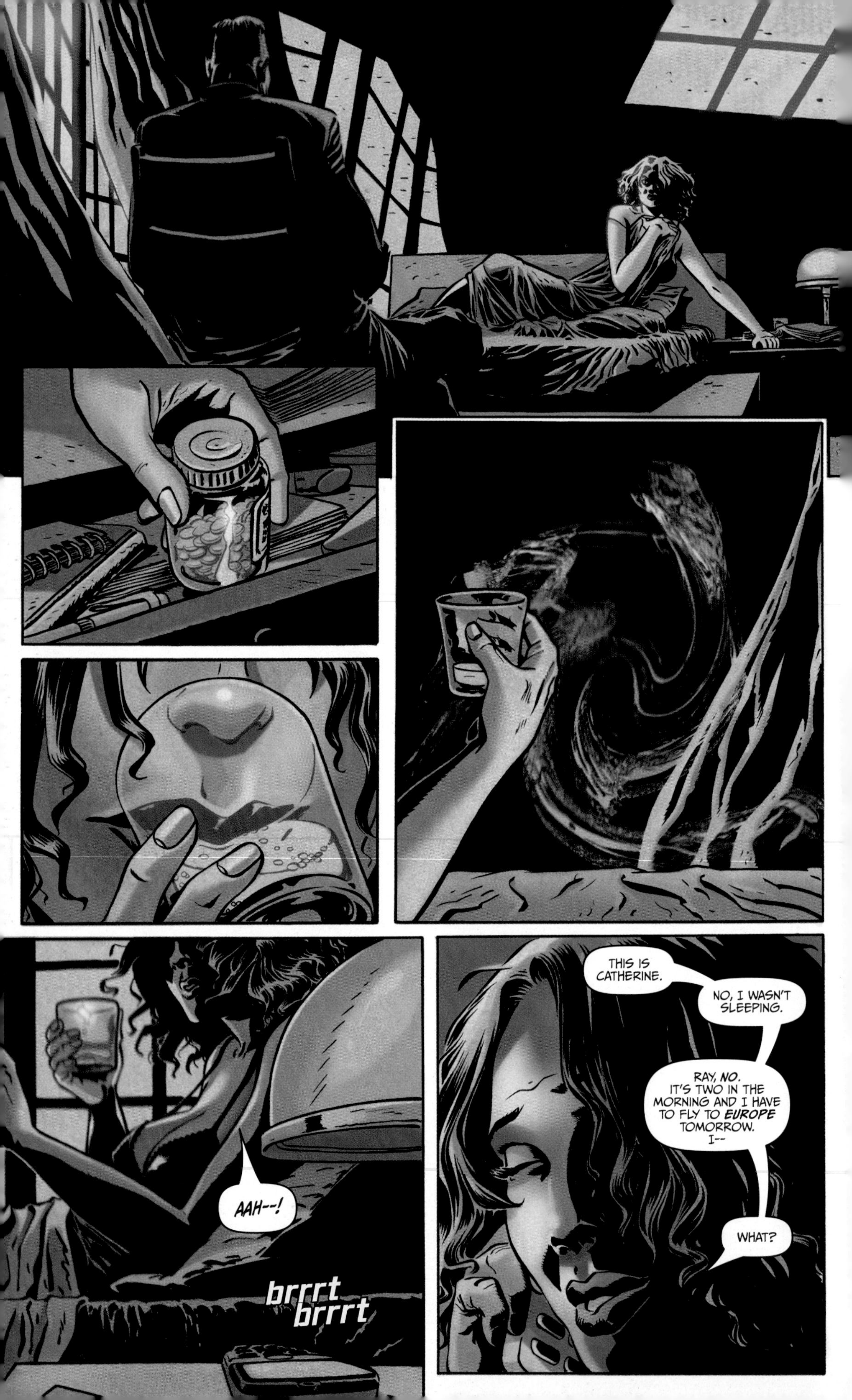
AAH--!
brrrt
brrrt
THIS IS CATHERINE.
NO, I WASN'T SLEEPING.
RAY, *NO.* IT'S TWO IN THE MORNING AND I HAVE TO FLY TO *EUROPE* TOMORROW. I--
WHAT?

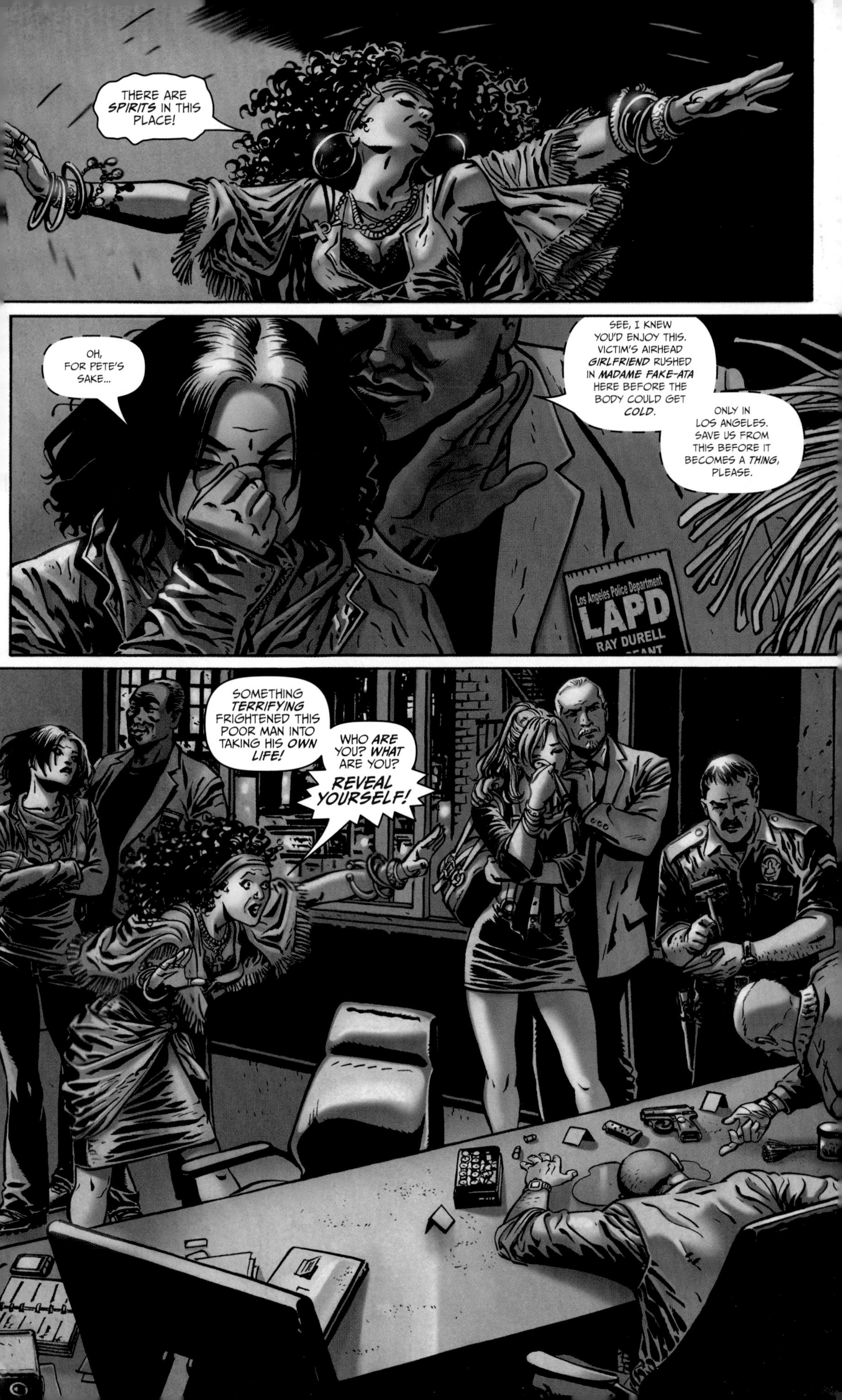
THERE ARE SPIRITS IN THIS PLACE!
OH, FOR PETE'S SAKE...
SEE, I KNEW YOU'D ENJOY THIS. VICTIM'S AIRHEAD GIRLFRIEND RUSHED IN MADAME FAKE-ATA HERE BEFORE THE BODY COULD GET COLD.
ONLY IN LOS ANGELES. SAVE US FROM THIS BEFORE IT BECOMES A THING, PLEASE.
Los Angeles Police Department
LAPD
RAY DURELL
SOMETHING TERRIFYING FRIGHTENED THIS POOR MAN INTO TAKING HIS OWN LIFE!
WHO ARE YOU? WHAT ARE YOU?
REVEAL YOURSELF!

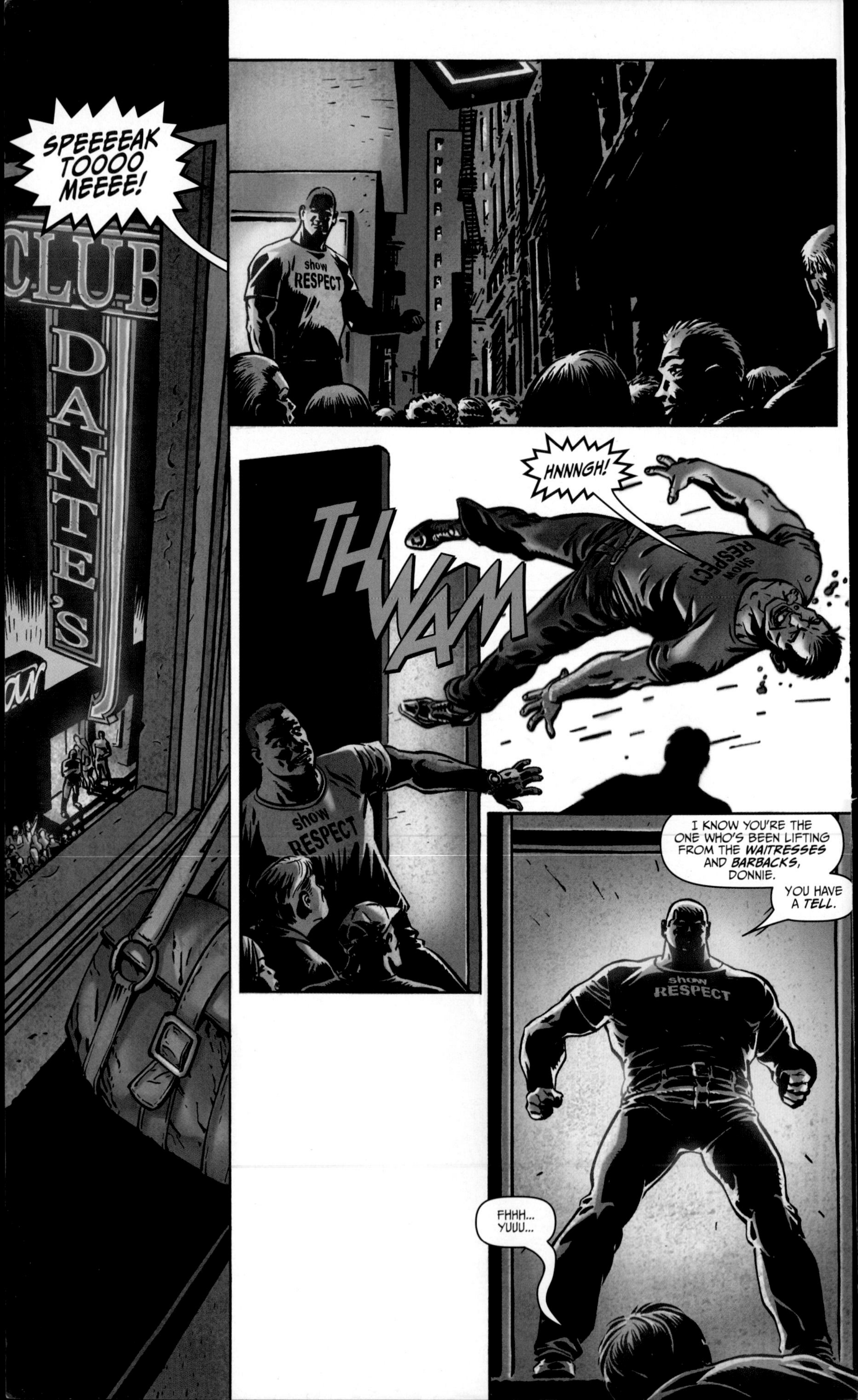
SPEEEEAK TOOOO MEEEE!
CLUB DANTE'S
show RESPECT
HNNNGH!
THWAM
show RESPECT
show RESPECT
I KNOW YOU'RE THE ONE WHO'S BEEN LIFTING FROM THE WAITRESSES AND BARBACKS, DONNIE.
YOU HAVE A TELL.
show RESPECT
FHHH... YUUU...

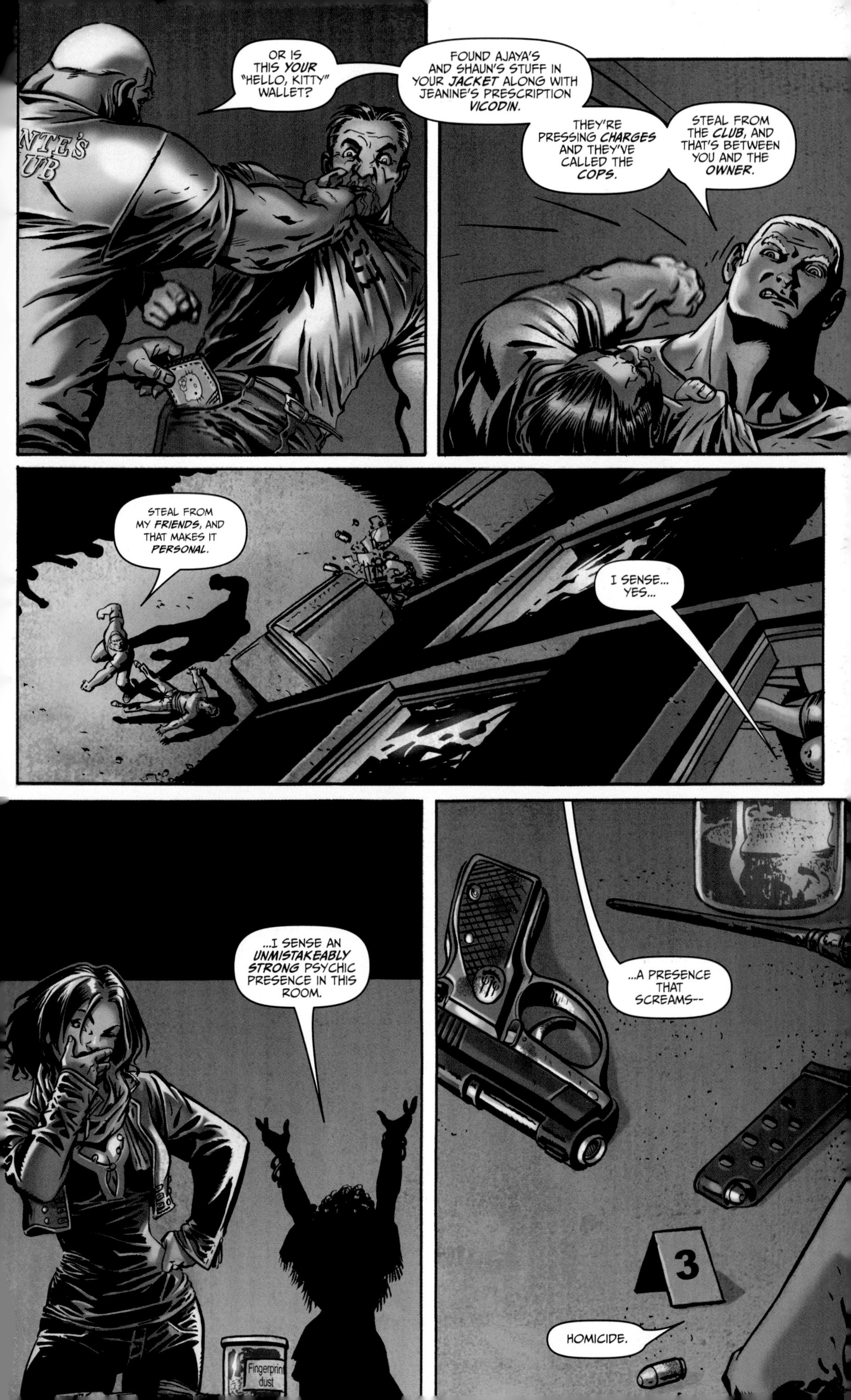
OR IS THIS *YOUR* "HELLO, KITTY" WALLET?
FOUND AJAYA'S AND SHAUN'S STUFF IN YOUR *JACKET* ALONG WITH JEANINE'S PRESCRIPTION *VICODIN*.
THEY'RE PRESSING *CHARGES* AND THEY'VE CALLED THE *COPS*.
STEAL FROM THE *CLUB*, AND THAT'S BETWEEN YOU AND THE *OWNER*.
STEAL FROM MY *FRIENDS*, AND THAT MAKES IT *PERSONAL*.
I SENSE... YES...
...I SENSE AN *UNMISTAKEABLY STRONG* PSYCHIC PRESENCE IN THIS ROOM.
Fingerprint dust
...A PRESENCE THAT SCREAMS--
3
HOMICIDE.

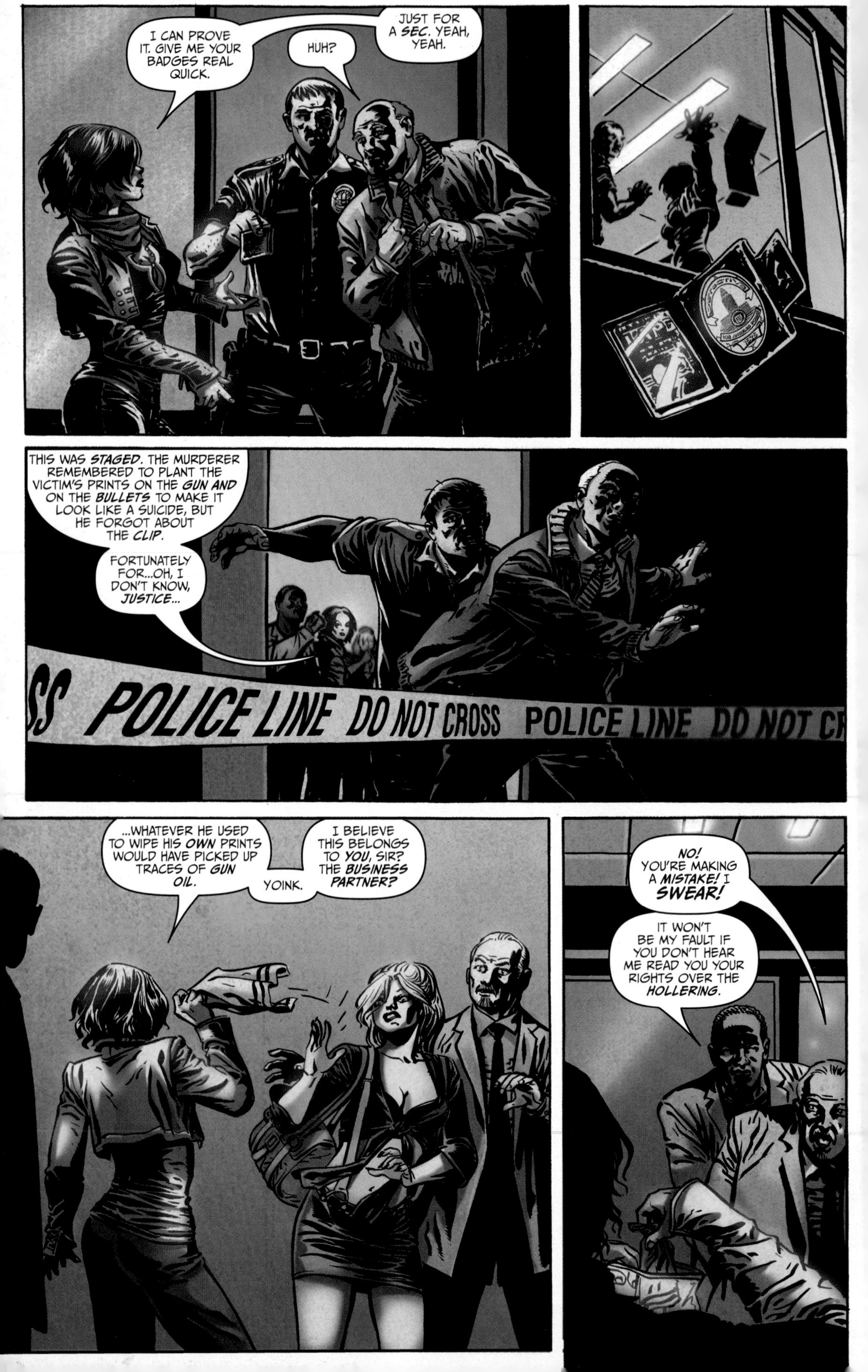
I CAN PROVE IT. GIVE ME YOUR BADGES REAL QUICK.
HUH?
JUST FOR A SEC. YEAH, YEAH.
THIS WAS STAGED. THE MURDERER REMEMBERED TO PLANT THE VICTIM'S PRINTS ON THE GUN AND ON THE BULLETS TO MAKE IT LOOK LIKE A SUICIDE, BUT HE FORGOT ABOUT THE CLIP.
FORTUNATELY FOR...OH, I DON'T KNOW, JUSTICE...
POLICE LINE DO NOT CROSS POLICE LINE
...WHATEVER HE USED TO WIPE HIS OWN PRINTS WOULD HAVE PICKED UP TRACES OF GUN OIL.
YOINK.
I BELIEVE THIS BELONGS TO YOU, SIR? THE BUSINESS PARTNER?
NO! YOU'RE MAKING A MISTAKE! I SWEAR!
IT WON'T BE MY FAULT IF YOU DON'T HEAR ME READ YOU YOUR RIGHTS OVER THE HOLLERING.

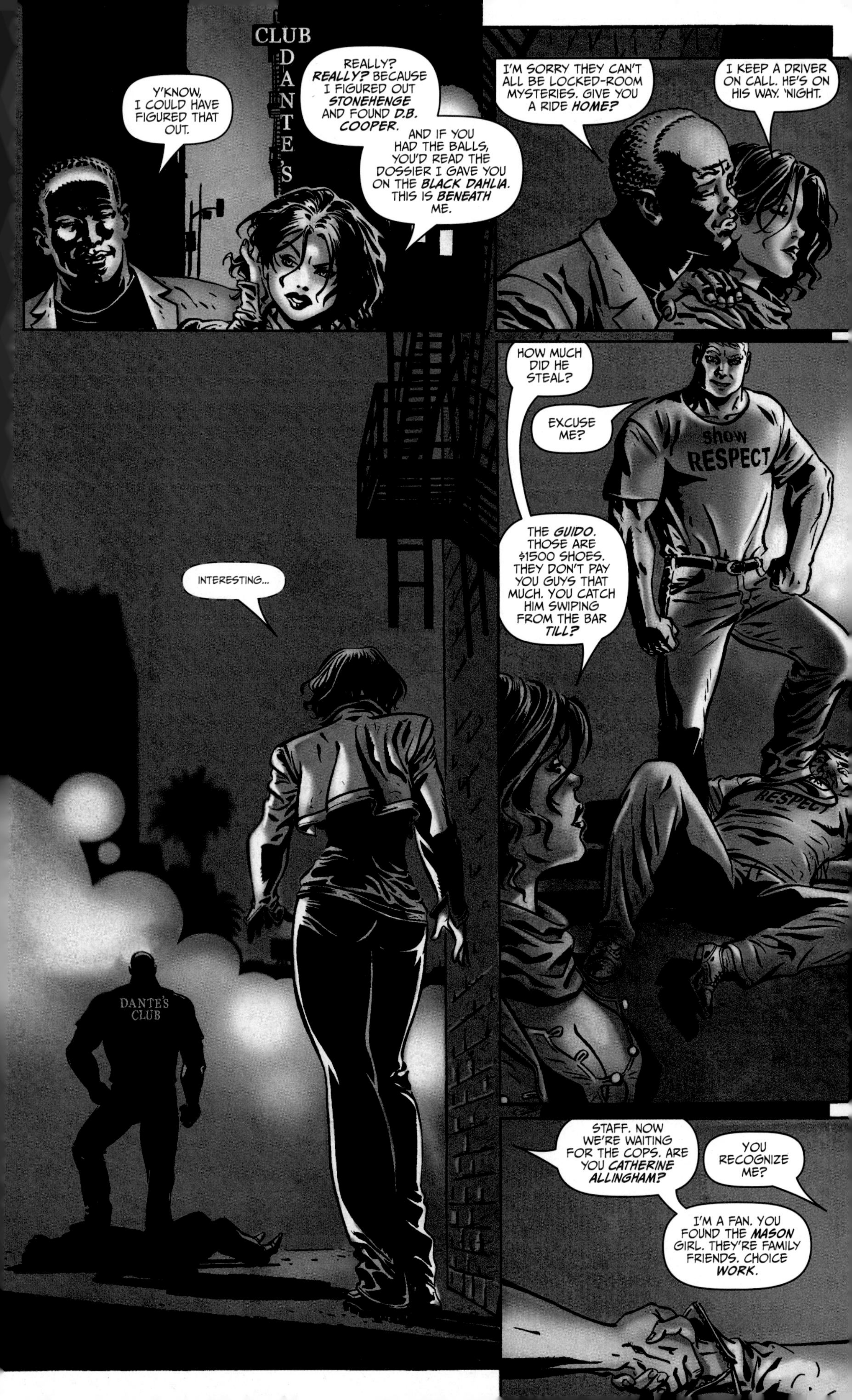
CLUB DANTE'S
Y'KNOW, I COULD HAVE FIGURED THAT OUT.
REALLY? REALLY? BECAUSE I FIGURED OUT STONEHENGE AND FOUND D.B. COOPER.
AND IF YOU HAD THE BALLS, YOU'D READ THE DOSSIER I GAVE YOU ON THE BLACK DAHLIA. THIS IS BENEATH ME.
I'M SORRY THEY CAN'T ALL BE LOCKED-ROOM MYSTERIES. GIVE YOU A RIDE HOME?
I KEEP A DRIVER ON CALL. HE'S ON HIS WAY. 'NIGHT.
INTERESTING...
DANTE'S CLUB
HOW MUCH DID HE STEAL?
EXCUSE ME?
show RESPECT
THE GUIDO. THOSE ARE $1500 SHOES. THEY DON'T PAY YOU GUYS THAT MUCH. YOU CATCH HIM SWIPING FROM THE BAR TILL?
RESPECT
STAFF. NOW WE'RE WAITING FOR THE COPS. ARE YOU CATHERINE ALLINGHAM?
YOU RECOGNIZE ME?
I'M A FAN. YOU FOUND THE MASON GIRL. THEY'RE FAMILY FRIENDS. CHOICE WORK.

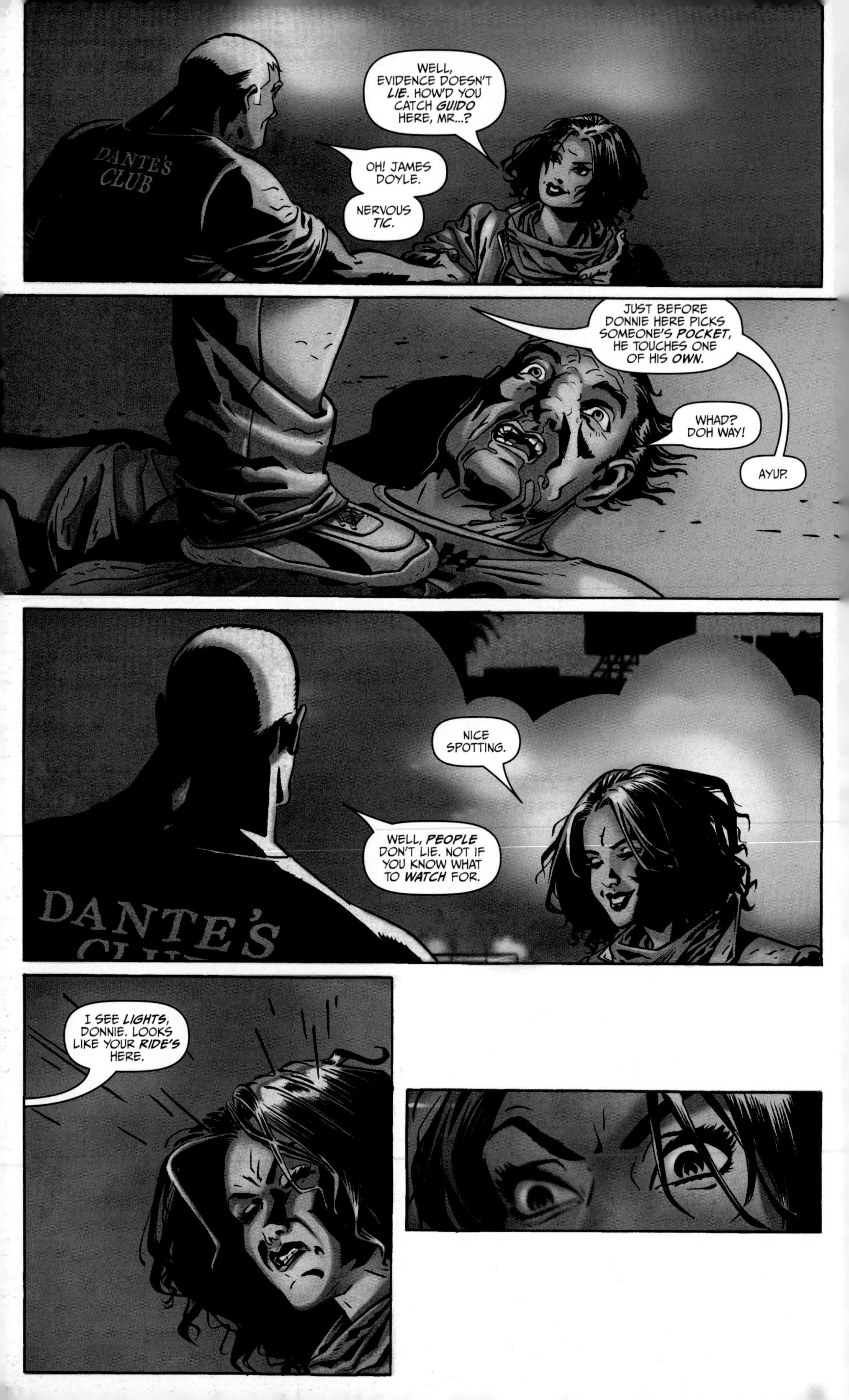
WELL, EVIDENCE DOESN'T LIE. HOW'D YOU CATCH GUIDO HERE, MR...?
OH! JAMES DOYLE.
NERVOUS TIC.
DANTE'S CLUB
JUST BEFORE DONNIE HERE PICKS SOMEONE'S POCKET, HE TOUCHES ONE OF HIS OWN.
WHAD? DOH WAY!
AYUP.
NICE SPOTTING.
WELL, PEOPLE DON'T LIE. NOT IF YOU KNOW WHAT TO WATCH FOR.
DANTE'S
I SEE LIGHTS, DONNIE. LOOKS LIKE YOUR RIDE'S HERE.

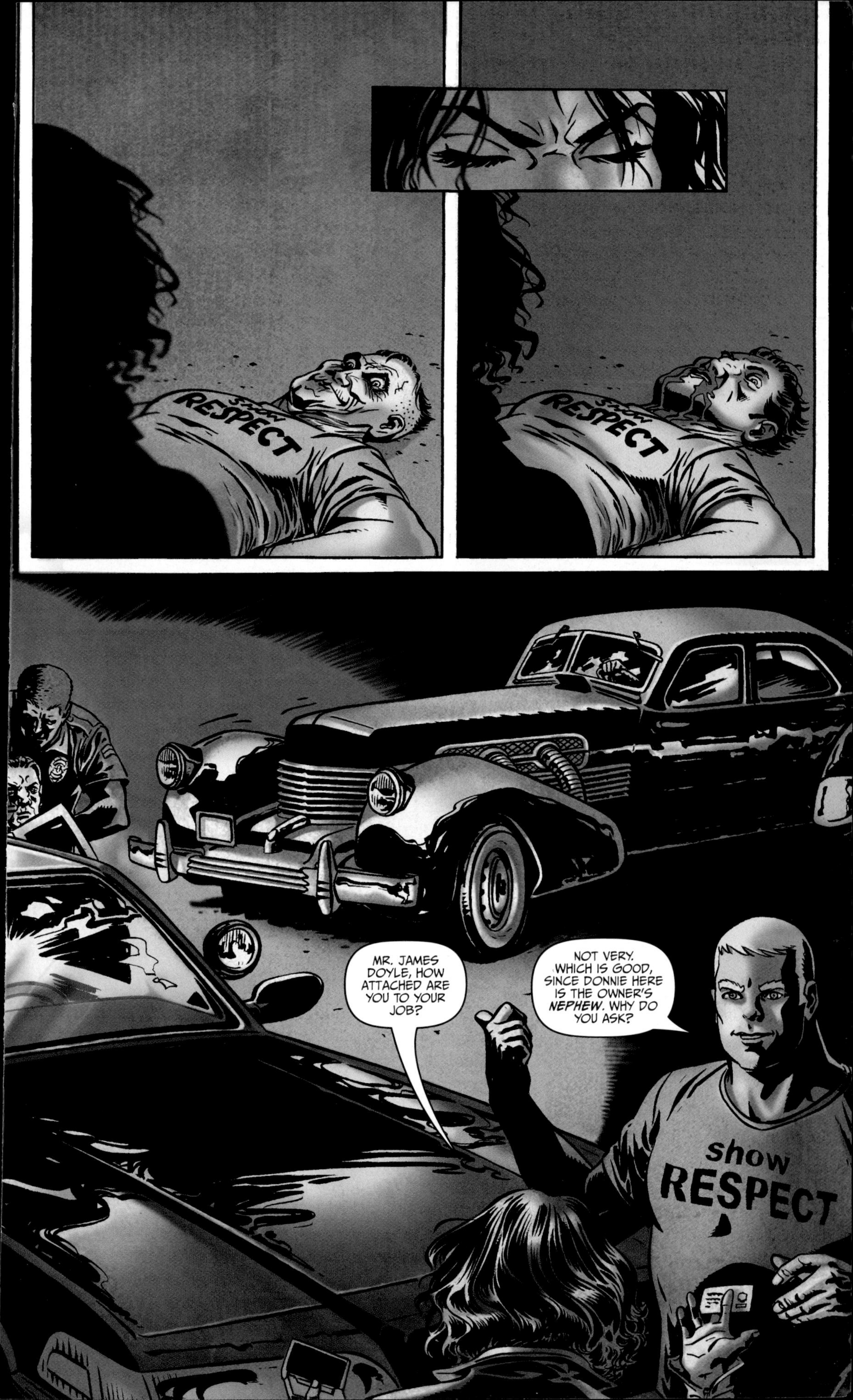
show
RESPECT
show
RESPECT
MR. JAMES DOYLE, HOW ATTACHED ARE YOU TO YOUR JOB?
NOT VERY. WHICH IS GOOD, SINCE DONNIE HERE IS THE OWNER'S NEPHEW. WHY DO YOU ASK?
show
RESPECT

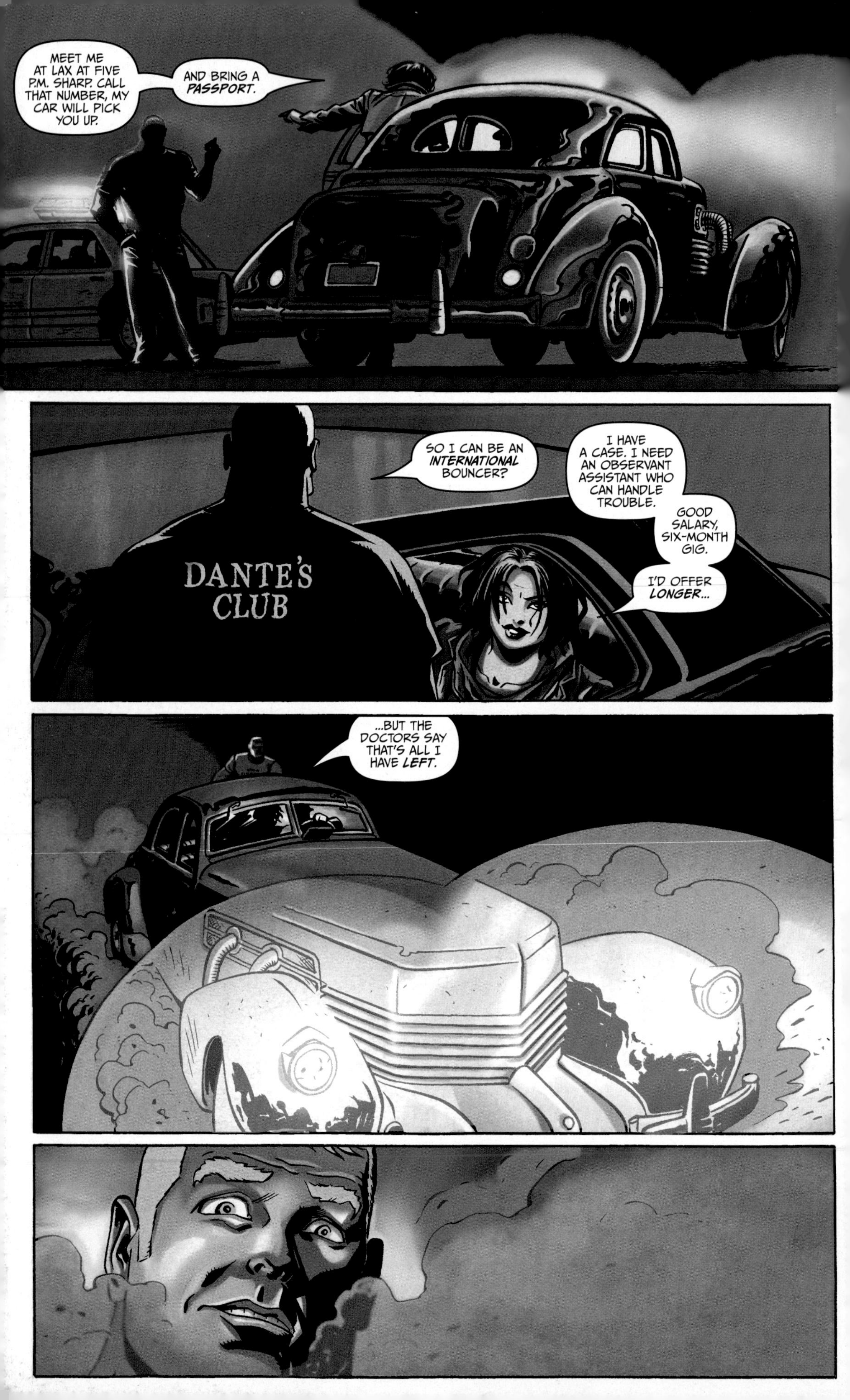
MEET ME AT LAX AT FIVE P.M. SHARP. CALL THAT NUMBER, MY CAR WILL PICK YOU UP.
AND BRING A PASSPORT.
DANTE'S CLUB
SO I CAN BE AN INTERNATIONAL BOUNCER?
I HAVE A CASE. I NEED AN OBSERVANT ASSISTANT WHO CAN HANDLE TROUBLE.
GOOD SALARY, SIX-MONTH GIG.
I'D OFFER LONGER...
...BUT THE DOCTORS SAY THAT'S ALL I HAVE LEFT.

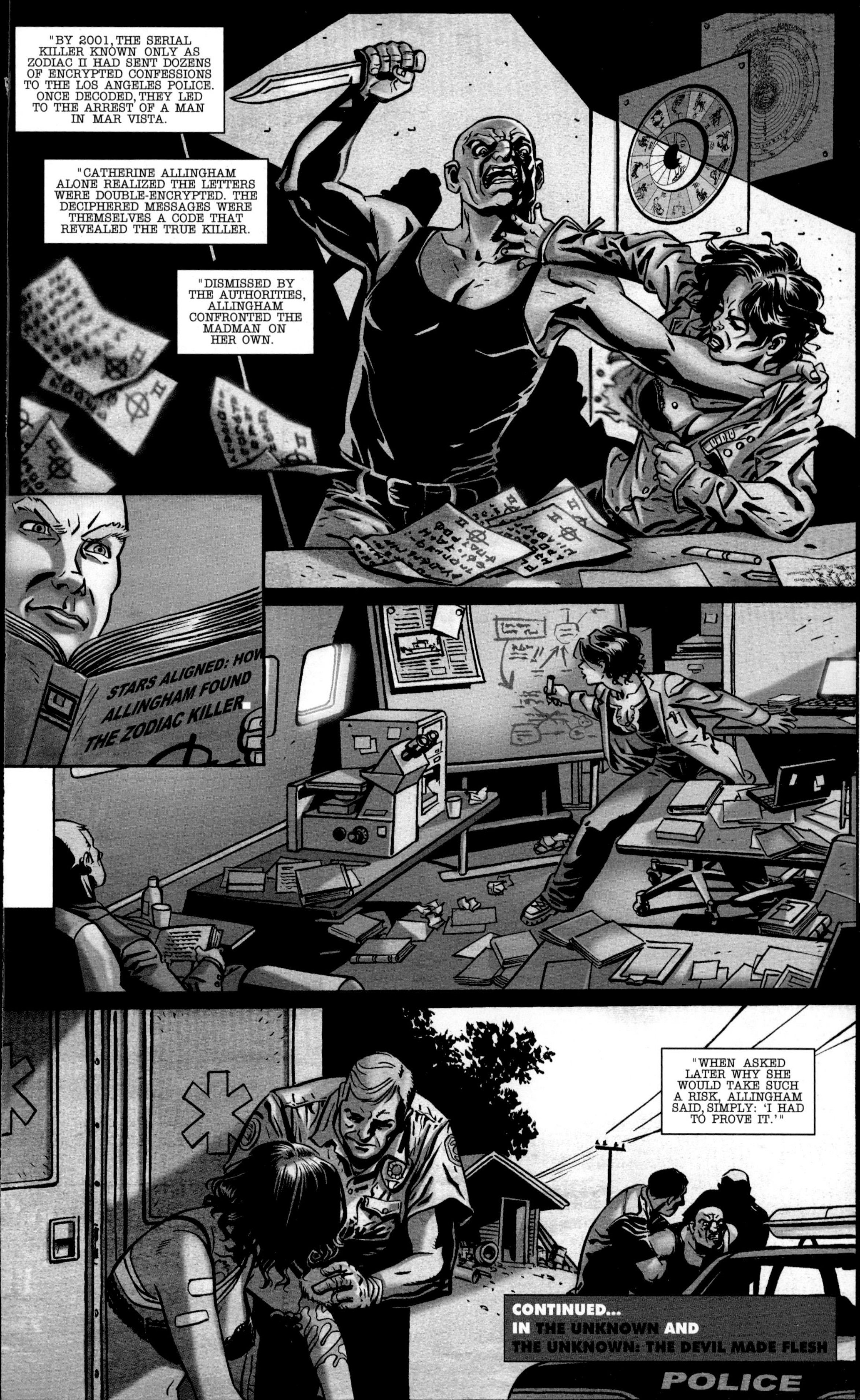
"BY 2001, THE SERIAL KILLER KNOWN ONLY AS ZODIAC II HAD SENT DOZENS OF ENCRYPTED CONFESSIONS TO THE LOS ANGELES POLICE. ONCE DECODED, THEY LED TO THE ARREST OF A MAN IN MAR VISTA.
"CATHERINE ALLINGHAM ALONE REALIZED THE LETTERS WERE DOUBLE-ENCRYPTED. THE DECIPHERED MESSAGES WERE THEMSELVES A CODE THAT REVEALED THE TRUE KILLER.
"DISMISSED BY THE AUTHORITIES, ALLINGHAM CONFRONTED THE MADMAN ON HER OWN.
STARS ALIGNED: HOW ALLINGHAM FOUND THE ZODIAC KILLER
"WHEN ASKED LATER WHY SHE WOULD TAKE SUCH A RISK, ALLINGHAM SAID, SIMPLY: 'I HAD TO PROVE IT.'"
CONTINUED...
IN THE UNKNOWN AND
THE UNKNOWN: THE DEVIL MADE FLESH
POLICE

MD

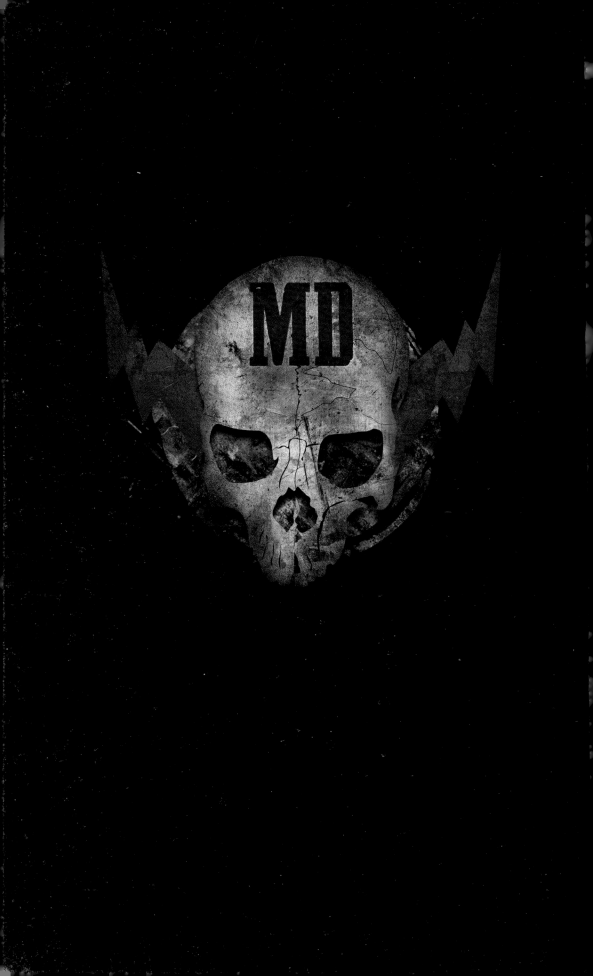